r

SACRED PLACES, PILGRIM PATHS

SACRED PLACES, PILGRIM PATHS

An Anthology of Pilgrimage

Martin Robinson

Marshall Pickering
An Imprint of HarperCollins*Publishers*

HarperCollins*Publishers*
77–85 Fulham Palace Road, London W6 8JB

First published in Great Britain
in 1997 by HarperCollins*Publishers*

3 5 7 9 10 8 6 4 2

Copyright in this compilation and in the Introduction © Martin Robinson 1997

Martin Robinson asserts the moral right to be
identified as the compiler of this work

A catalogue record for this book is
available from the British Library

ISBN 0 551 03051 8

Printed and bound in Great Britain by
Caledonian International Book Manufacturing Ltd, Glasgow

CONTENTS

INTRODUCTION

The word 'pilgrim' often conjures up a strongly medieval image in the minds of modern Western people. Yet in truth, pilgrimage existed long before the medieval period. It traces its ancestry through the Christian ages, into the history of the people of Israel. There is every indication that pilgrimage took place long before Abraham ever left his home in Ur of the Chaldeans (Genesis 11:31).

Although precise figures are almost impossible to obtain, pilgrimage has undergone a remarkable resurgence in recent years. In many parts of the world, pilgrimage has never lost its appeal, but in Europe the ancient pilgrimage routes to Rome and to Santiago de Compostela, as well as to other traditional destinations, have gradually attracted a new upsurge of visitors keen to experience the attractions of pilgrimage. Not all those who embark on pilgrimage are devout believers. Some are simply curious, others are not even certain what they seek but travel hopefully.

What is it that attracts such large numbers to engage in an activity that has no obvious immediate purpose? The particular stimulus for any one pilgrimage may vary greatly from one individual to another. For one it might be the realization of a long-held dream, for others the death of a loved one. Some may have in mind the fulfilment of a pledge or promise. Some might undertake the journey in gratitude for an answered prayer. Others are spurred by a wish to review the direction of their life.

Just as the very fact of our existence seems to prompt questions as to who we are, where we come from and where we are going to, so the act of pilgrimage echoes questions that come to us from that deeper journey of the heart. What is the reason for my being? It is no coincidence that many who go on pilgrimage are at a critical stage of life – the transition from teenage years to adulthood, a mid-life point or at the start of retirement. Pilgrimage uses travel to a particular place as a means of exploring these deeper questions.

The Holy

Pilgrimage is not just travel to any place but to a place which in itself is seen to have a profound significance. It is a journey to a holy place. But what is the 'holy' in such a context? The experience of many pilgrims might be one of disappointment with the place itself. The pressing crowds, the rather tawdry religious artefacts on sale, the commercial exploitation of the pilgrim seem to many to detract from any sense of the holy. And yet, despite these more obvious external dimensions which surround great centres of pilgrimage, a deeper fascination with many of these holy places remains.

Pilgrimage sites are associated with holy people, with saints, sometimes in the sense of the presence of relics, or with the miraculous, for example, the location of visions or healing events. Acts of healing are often sought and sometimes reported by pilgrims. The holy place is seen as a physical location where the membrane between this world and a reality beyond is especially thin, where a transcendent reality impinges on the immanent. The hopeful traveller seeks to meet with the holy as a means of bringing meaning to this life.

Simply arriving at the place of the holy, however, does not in itself describe pilgrimage. Although the destination is not without significance, the act of travelling is also part of the experience. For the Christian pilgrim, pilgrimage acts as a symbol for the Christian life. The whole people of God are sometimes described as a pilgrim people travelling to a destination that is beyond this world. The Christian life also comprises an individual pilgrimage. That life has a beginning, often but not always the point of conversion. There are significant moments or places along the way, vantage points from which the journey can be surveyed. Its end is both to be with Christ and to be changed to be more like him. The pilgrim is often seeking to make progress in their broader Christian life by undertaking one journey. They are attempting to understand and advance their Christian life by symbolizing the whole Christian pilgrimage in a single drama.

Within the broader canvas of the Christian pilgrimage, the events surrounding Christ's journey to Calvary hold a particular symbolic force. The gospel of Luke portrays the whole ministry of Jesus as a single journey from Galilee to Jerusalem. The events which take place within Jerusalem, from the triumphant entry to the crucifixion, replay in dramatic form the whole ministry of Christ to that moment. The meaning of his earlier journey is finally made clear in the much shorter journey from the upper room to Calvary. Thus, to some extent, all Christian pilgrimage is also an identification with Christ in his final journey to the cross.

The Heavenly City

For this reason, Jerusalem has a particular significance for the Christian pilgrim. Jerusalem is above all the Holy City, the centre of the Holy Land. In a spiritual sense Jerusalem is the Heavenly City and so a place of special intersection between the divine and the earthly. For the Christian, a visit to Jerusalem provides the opportunity to re-enact the events of the life of Christ, but it also allows the Christian to be as close as possible to the last place on earth where the physical presence of Christ was laid. The tomb of Christ has always been a place of especial fascination and devotion for Christians.

Although, unlike in Judaism, there is no special instruction for Christians to visit Jerusalem, since Christianity depends so heavily not on abstract ideas but on concrete events, the place where the most important of those events took place has naturally attracted the curiosity of those whose lives have been influenced by those events. But devotion stimulated by those sites is more than mere curiosity. It is almost as if the greater the distance in time between the events and the individual worshipper, the greater is the mystical import which surrounds the experience of visiting those same places. For the devout, contact with physical places is a means of making connection with the unseen events commemorated in those same locations, of obtaining benefit and perhaps even personal holiness and renewal. Faith is strengthened for the journey still to come.

The Origins of Christian Pilgrimage

There are some records of Christians visiting the Holy Land in the first few centuries of the Christian era. In these first visits, curiosity rather than devotion seems to have predominated. The first recorded Christian pilgrim to Jerusalem was Melito of Sardis, who visited the city in around AD 170. His motive was to see the places spoken of in Scripture so that he could in some measure confirm these gospel accounts for himself. The Christian writer Jerome expressed the view that a visit to the Holy Land would enable pilgrims to understand Scripture better. But these rather scholarly interests became very secondary following the action of Constantine to both excavate sites of particular interest to Christians and then to mark out these same places by the building of a series of magnificent churches.

The state recognition of Christianity which followed Constantine's accession as emperor utterly transformed the status of the sites important to Christians. It is reported that the emperor's mother, Helena, visited Jerusalem for an extended stay after her son took power. Her reports of what she found drove Constantine to action. Particular excitement surrounded the rediscovery of the site of the burial place of Jesus, as well as remnants of the sacred cross. According to the accounts of the day, the Christian community which had remained in Jerusalem had remembered where Jesus' tomb was located. The city had expanded so that it was now within the city walls and it had become concealed under heaps of rubble and the construction of a city street. Once the Christians were in the ascendancy, it became possible to excavate the site. Constantine then ordered the building of a beautiful church – the Church of the Holy Sepulchre.

It was clear that, in the view of the Christians at least, the covering of this site had been no mere accident but rather the deliberate action of pagan worshippers who had wished the site to remain hidden. For the Christian community, the recovery of ancient Christian sites represented something of a power struggle between themselves and the pagans under whose domination they had lived for so long. The recovery of these sites therefore represented more than mere historical interest, it was a stimulus to devotional fervour. The sites became important foci for worship. The liturgical life of the Christian community could now be fully integrated with these sites of special devotional interest.

We can speculate that for Constantine the renewed interest in Jerusalem as a focus for worship became also a means of emphasizing the unity that the Christian faith could bring to the empire itself. Thus Constantine was not simply helping the local Christian community in Jerusalem, he was also assisting the faith throughout the empire in providing a focus for unity and devotion. The implication was that pilgrimage to Jerusalem was not merely possible but highly desirable. The very fact that those so close to the emperor had visited Jerusalem indicated that this should be a priority for all those who wished to exercise their own devotion in a tangible way.

The increase in pilgrimage to Jerusalem can certainly be dated from this point on. But this growth in travel to the Holy Land was not an isolated phenomenon – an early version of tourism. It was accompanied by the growth of what has been called *desert spirituality*. The new position of Christianity in society produced vast numbers of converts to the faith. So many, in fact, that the line between being a good citizen and becoming a Christian was blurred. Inevitably, for many devout Christians, there came a feeling that the faith was becoming too worldly. Partly in reaction to this development, increasing numbers of individual hermits and monastic communities retreated to the desert to escape the world but also to pray for the world. The centre for this new movement was in Egypt. It did not take long for these

Egyptian centres to spill over into the more remote areas within Palestine and close to Jerusalem itself. Some of the communities undertook to meet the physical and spiritual needs of those who came on pilgrimage to the Holy Land. A number of important connections between monasticism and pilgrimage have remained ever since.

The Monastic Connection

Many of those who chose to go on pilgrimage were themselves monks or nuns. One of the earliest and best-known pilgrims was the Spanish nun Egeria. She travelled to Palestine towards the end of the fourth century and kept a very full account of her visit. Egeria was already well known to Spanish Christians before she made her visit to Palestine. Her fame and the extent to which the accounts of her experiences were circulated help to form a pattern or expectation of one aspect of the monastic life.

This should not suggest that the more mature in faith were under an illusion that a visit to Jerusalem would induce holiness when none existed before. Thus pilgrimage was seen as an aid to those who were already devout rather than a means of inducing devotion amongst those for whom faith was peripheral. Who more than the communities of the religious could be better candidates to benefit from pilgrimage? The fact that so many wished to leave their monasteries and convents to travel on pilgrimage led eventually to some medieval monarchs insisting that monks and nuns must have the proper permission of their superiors before wandering through Europe.

That permission was sometimes refused. Such a refusal was not necessarily related to the suitability or otherwise of the individual pilgrim but to a growing realization, especially in the Middle Ages, that the spiritual journey within was actually more important than a physical pilgrimage. Indeed, only to the extent that the physical acted as an aid to the spiritual could pilgrimage be seen as helpful to the religious man or woman. But the fact that the relationship between the spiritual life and pilgrimage was known, noted and consciously developed was important. The concept of the monastic life as a superior alternative to pilgrimage developed during the Middle Ages to the point where some orders, for example the Cistercians, did not permit any monk to go on pilgrimage to Jerusalem. They could rather imitate Christ within the walls of the monastery, taking up their cross on the road to Calvary daily, and travel to Jerusalem in an interior or spiritual sense.

A more practical relationship lay in the provision for pilgrims which convents and monasteries often provided. The charitable actions of such communities in the Holy Land itself were echoed across the pilgrim routes of Europe. Indeed some communities were specifically founded for the purpose of caring for the needs of pilgrims. The hospices and other such lodgings for pilgrims, found at regular intervals along the great pilgrim routes of Europe, bear testimony to this form of ministry.

Pilgrimage Extended

The inspiration of the desert spread to an unusual group of missionaries operating on the outer fringes of Western Europe. This new group of ascetics were also monks and interpreted the pilgrimage theme in some new and imaginative ways. The Celtic saints saw pilgrimage, spirituality and mission as intrinsically connected. The great Irish saints employed the imagery of Hebrews, which describes the founders of Judaism as 'strangers and pilgrims on the earth' (Hebrews 11:13), to construct the idea of pilgrimage as an exile. Unlike other forms of pilgrimage, there was no fixed destination on earth. Some of the Celtic ascetics delighted in leaving their homeland by setting sail in their coracles and allowing the wind of the spirit to take them where it would. The place where they landed would become their new, albeit temporary mission field.

Clearly not all the Celtic missions were of this type. Many, such as Cuthbert of Lindisfarne, were much more intentional in terms of their destination, they were specifically sent to a given area or kingdom. But even in these cases, constant travelling within the area in which they were working was central to their ministry. Others did not have to come to them, they were inclined to journey in the process of sowing the seed of the gospel message. Used in this sense, pilgrimage was absence from home. But this was an absence with a purpose. It was to travel for Christ, the *peregrinatio pro Christo*, to take the message of the cross to shores and lands which had never heard the gospel proclaimed. The journey was a real journey and not just a spiritual metaphor but one never expected to arrive. The destination was heaven itself, there was no earthly end point for pilgrimage of this type.

To the modern mind, it might seem as though the metaphor of pilgrimage is being stretched to breaking point with this Celtic interpretation. But from a pre-modern perspective it is a usage that is highly consistent with the actual experience of pilgrimage. Even though pilgrims normally set out for particular destinations, the journey was sometimes so hazardous and so long that there could never be any certainty of return. Some pilgrims who set out for Jerusalem with an eschatological motive, hoping to be present in Jerusalem when

Jesus returned, remained in the Holy Land, hoping to finish their life living, praying and working in the vicinity of Jerusalem. So the Celtic exile or *peregrinatio* was not entirely different from the wider experience of pilgrimage.

The idea of the *peregrinatio* was later developed by those who became perpetual wanderers. For these pilgrims, the destination was unimportant compared with the journey within. The wandering might be from one holy place to another, but the primary intention was not to preach the gospel so much as to attend to the interior spiritual life. The goal was to imitate Christ, and the wandering was really an aid to this end. This tradition has been particularly strong in Russia, fostered partly by the mysticism of the Orthodox tradition.

Pilgrimage as Penance

It follows from what has been said already that there has traditionally been a strong penitential dimension to pilgrimage. The connection with the imitation of Christ, with sacrifice and exile, with the development of the spiritual life and so with a contemplation of the inner life all point towards pilgrimage as a penance, even if that penance is not related to a particular act of wrongdoing. Certainly this dimension was greatly developed at the height of the popularity of pilgrimage during the medieval period. Indulgences were sometimes attached to pilgrimage, and, inevitably, excesses became attached to this development. Sometimes these excesses came in the form of the flagellants who visited acts of physical suffering upon themselves. In extreme cases these individuals might wander naked as part of their penitential offering. Such strange pilgrims would hardly be well received today! Another kind of abuse took the form of professional pilgrims who would be paid by the wealthy to perform a pilgrimage on their behalf. Many of the so-called 'palmers', so named because of the symbolic palm which they brought back from Jerusalem, were in fact professional pilgrims.

This penitential dimension was sometimes extended in the form of a judicial pilgrimage. Criminals, sometimes even murderers, could pay for their crimes by engaging in a pilgrimage. Such judicial punishments took many forms, but one example would be to send the offender on pilgrimage to Rome. The penitent would be required to return with a signed certificate to prove that he had accomplished the task. Clearly this enforced exile was a long way from the enthusiastic and heroic act of the devout individual seeking to imitate Christ.

The medieval crusade is another related use of the concept of the pilgrimage. Indeed, the first crusade was described by the Pope who promoted it as a 'holy pilgrimage'. Despite the very great reserve of modern Christians concerning the mix of war and pilgrimage, there is no doubting the devotional fervour of at least some of the participants in the crusades. The romantic attraction of Jerusalem mixed with the desire to earn a penitential reward goes some way to explaining the medieval view of crusading as a form of pilgrimage.

Pilgrimage Far and Wide

The capture of Jerusalem by Muslim rulers served to diminish its ancient attraction as a pilgrimage centre. Prior to the crusades, while it was strictly possible for Christian pilgrims to travel to the Holy Land, the difficulty and the cost were greatly increased by Muslim occupation. The loss of Jerusalem at the end of the crusader period, and the subsequent difficulties for Christians in visiting the Holy Land at all, served to enhance the attraction of other pilgrimage centres.

Other centres had been in existence for many years in some parts of Europe. The Celtic saints, in particular, had tended to Christianize many older pagan holy places. These were frequently associated with sites which emphasized natural features as compared with relics or visions. For example, holy wells and high places were often given a new Christian significance. Other sites throughout Europe were maintained as centres of pilgrimage, but in most cases these were rather local in their importance.

Rome had of course long been an important centre of Christian pilgrimage. Its ancient association with St Peter and St Paul as well as its growing importance as a centre of Christendom guaranteed its position of popularity with pilgrims. But this ancient site was almost rivalled in importance during the medieval period by a new centre which had lacked any significance before the beginning of the ninth century. Santiago de Compostela emerged as a destination for pilgrims all over Europe during the medieval period and since then it has been eclipsed in importance only by Rome and Jerusalem. Arguably, in recent years, within Europe, Lourdes has been its closest rival for Roman Catholics, at least, in terms of the number of visitors.

The remarkable emergence of Santiago was made possible by the conjunction of a number of events. The supposedly miraculous discovery of the relics of St James the Apostle began the process. The tradition which suggests that St James preached the gospel in Spain gives St James (St Iago) a special significance to the Spanish. This, even apart from his close earthly link with Jesus, ensured that any site which claimed to be the location for his relics would inspire devotional

attention. The addition of visions and miracles (hence Compostela –
'field of stars'), added to the impact of this discovery. It was clearly not
unimportant that the Spanish kings were then in conflict with the
forces of Islam in the shape of the Moors. Santiago acted as a national
rallying point for the Spanish nation at a critical time in its history. The
romance and drama of this event, coupled with the loss of Jerusalem to
other Muslims, helped to establish the popularity of Santiago.

Holy Places and Holy Days

Holy places had added importance on holy days. Thus, in the case of
Santiago de Compostela, many pilgrims ensured that they arrived on
the feast of St James, 25 July. The rich ceremonies surrounding the
holy day attracted vast numbers of worshippers and pilgrims alike.
Today, the resurgence of pilgrimage echoes this practice. A visit to
Santiago de Compostela on the feast day of St James sees many who
are local worshippers, deliberate pilgrims and holiday-makers all
mixed together.

Many have remarked on the relationship between holidays or
tourism and pilgrimage. Some have even wanted to make the case that
modern tourism is the secular equivalent of pilgrimage. Clearly, the
origin of the word holiday, derived as it is from holy day, together
with medieval sources such as Chaucer's *Canterbury Tales*, encourages
such an association. This ancient connection is further reinforced by
the fact that many modern pilgrims use the tools of tourism to reach
their destination.

However, such a case does not really take account of the clear differences between the pilgrim and the tourist. The pilgrim seeks to be
changed by the experience of pilgrimage. Even when modern pilgrims
utilize the convenience of mass transportation rather than walking, the
journey is as important as the arrival. It could be argued that tourists
do not seek to be changed by their holiday. For the tourist, except in
unusual cases, the journey is almost always not part of the experience
but merely an inconvenience to be overcome. Tourists tend to change
the landscape that they visit rather than be changed by their destination. The growing popularity of pilgrimage in Europe recovers when
possible the experience of the journey as well as the arrival. The ranks
of devout pilgrims are currently being swelled by the presence of those
who would not call themselves believers. For some of these, the journey is all important and the arrival almost incidental, if not disap-
pointing.

Pilgrimage as Metaphor

I have already commented on the fact that for many Christians, pilgrimage acts as a metaphor for the whole Christian journey. But it is also true that pilgrimage is in turn used as a metaphor within Christian experience. Some describe themselves as pilgrims in relation to a particular quest, journey or difficult experience within their Christian life. So, some who have been missionaries refer to their whole missionary experience as a pilgrimage. Others use the term to describe their ecumenical journey or their work for peace or reconciliation. Even though this is a minority use of the word 'pilgrim', it occurs often enough in Christian literature for this usage to be included within these pages.

The material selected for the anthology covers a wide range of sources. Although pilgrimage is an important theme in many religions, especially within Islam, this anthology has deliberately chosen to concentrate on pilgrimage within the Christian tradition, partly if not entirely because no single anthology could really do justice to the quantity of material represented by every religious tradition. I want to thank my researcher, Joseph Gelfer, for his help in the location and selection of extracts from the diversity of sources available.

The material in the anthology is arranged in sections which as far as possible echo the stages in the pilgrimage experience itself. There has been a deliberate decision to include more descriptive historical pieces than purely devotional material, in the hope that these sources will themselves serve to tell something of the story of pilgrimage. Each section has its own brief introduction, but for the most part the intention is to allow the sources themselves to tell the story of pilgrimage.

The mass involvement in pilgrimage helped to shape the culture of Europe. Perhaps it is no coincidence, at a time when Western culture is undergoing a further period of considerable change, that pilgrimage should re-emerge to allow thoughtful men and women to travel with hope into a new millennium.

Martin Robinson

Chapter One

THE POINT OF PILGRIMAGE

The particular reasons which drive an individual towards an act of pilgrimage are inevitably deeply personal, and in many cases beyond the exercise of logic alone. Even though the physical dangers are not as great as they once were, the psychological and spiritual ferment remains. Those who are close to the pilgrim may well ask why they have undertaken such an action. The act of pilgrimage disturbs the lives of those who surround the pilgrim.

Despite the diversity of motivation, certain themes clearly emerge. The very historicity of the sites seems to exert its own natural attraction. Pilgrims travel in search of forgiveness for sins committed and so search for cleansing. A few travel as a form of punishment inflicting hardship on themselves as they go. Others journey in the hope of physical healing and inner spiritual healing. But above all, pilgrims travel in search of God and so hope to find themselves.

How strange it is that so many are drawn to leave home to find themselves. Yet the familiar sometimes obscures the eternal, not because it is not present but because it simply cannot be recognized without the experience of a broader canvas. Those who travel have understood the essential paradox that we cannot truly find the 'I' within until we have found the 'Thou' without.

Every year his parents went to Jerusalem for the Feast of the Passover. When he was twelve years old, he went up to the Feast, according to the custom. After the Feast was over, while his parents were returning home, the boy Jesus stayed behind in Jerusalem, but they were unaware of it. Thinking he was in their company, they travelled on for a day. Then they began looking for him among their relatives and friends. When they did not find him, they went back to Jerusalem to look for him. After three days they found him in the temple courts, sitting among the teachers, listening to them and asking them questions. Everyone who heard him was amazed at his understanding and his answers. When his parents saw him, they were astonished. His mother said to him, 'Son, why have you treated us like this? Your father and I have been anxiously searching for you.'

'Why were you searching for me?' he asked. 'Didn't you know I had to be in my Father's house?' But they did not understand what he was saying to them.

Then he went down to Nazareth with them and was obedient to them. But his mother treasured all these things in her heart. And Jesus grew in wisdom and stature, and in favour with God and men.

Luke 3:41–52

The custom of sacred pilgrimages was affirmed in ancient Israelite legislation concerning the religious feasts. The three hag (pilgrim) festivals, the Feast of Passover, the Hebrew Feast of Pentecost, and the Feast of Booths (Tabernacles), were times when the Israelites were commanded to appear before the Lord (Exodus 23:14–17; Deuteronomy 16:16), a practice parallel to the Arabic hajj.

Israelite religious pilgrimages continued during and after the exile (Psalm 42). Josephus speaks of the large gatherings at Jerusalem to celebrate the feasts of Yahweh. Evidence for them in the New Testament is found in Luke 2:41–42; John 2:13; 5:1; 7:2–10; 12:20; and Acts 2:1–11.

'Pilgrimages', New Catholic Encyclopedia (1967)

Jesus is the Pilgrim par excellence. Already in the infancy narratives, the gospels endeavour to demonstrate this. In Luke (1–2), we find Jesus constantly travelling to and fro, between Nazareth in Galilee, Judaea with Bethlehem the city of David, and Jerusalem with its Temple. In Matthew, the holy family recapitulates the whole journey of its ancestors' descent into Egypt (2:14) and the return to the land of Israel (2:20).

The very structure of the gospels is dictated by the notion of pilgrimage. The Synoptists see Jesus' public life unfolding in two stages: first, an itinerant ministry in the villages and rural areas of Galilee, then a long ascent (particularly developed in Luke) to the Holy City, 'since it would not be right for a prophet to die outside Jerusalem' (Luke 13:33). John, in his own inimitable way, looks at the situation from a higher vantage point: Jesus is a pilgrim because he is not of this world (John 8:23); he has come from heaven, that is to say from God ('He who sent me', 'the Father'), in order to give life to the world (John 6:33; 8:42). John sums up, perhaps unknowingly, the two stages of the Synoptic gospels in a short and remarkably profound phrase uttered by Jesus just before his death: 'I came from the Father and have come into the world, and now I leave the world to go to the' Father' (John 16:23).

A pilgrim with no fixed abode in this world, Jesus is far more than a 'new Abraham' or a 'new Moses'. These typologies, though present in the gospel portrait of Jesus, do not yield the key to his identity. At a first level, Jesus is certainly the man who answers God's call and sets out to follow in his footsteps. But he fulfils this mission in a unique way, because he is primarily the one who comes into the world to call men: like the *Shekhinah*, he comes to chart God's path in the heart of our history. In the context of the story of Abraham, we may liken him first to the pilgrim-God who speaks, and only then to the human being who hears the divine Word and conforms his existence to it.

Brother John of Taizé, 'Pilgrimage Seen through the Bible',
Lumen Vitae 39 (1984): 388–9

Our earliest known pilgrim journey to the Holy Land, that of Melito of Sardis, had been an essentially biblical quest, to establish an accurate canon of the Old Testament – to this end Melito had sought the authority of the land 'where these things were preached and done'. In this he was pointing the way to the fundamental impetus which was to underlie the concentration of pilgrims at the holy places – and to drive Egeria on to the summit of Sinai. Whatever the varied experiences of the journey which brought them there, we can be certain that it was the same basic desiderum, rooted in the Bible, which impelled them all towards Palestine. Whether it was the solid literalism of those who expected to see every line of the Scriptures brought to reality before their eyes, or the sober and learned interest of a biblical scholar such as Origen, it was always the Bible which inspired their enterprise, and indeed shaped their whole conception of the Holy Land.

Edward Hunt, *Holy Land Pilgrimage in the Later Roman Empire* (1982), p. 81

Jerome's influence was spread through a variety of channels into the western parts of Christendom. His Bible commentaries added an assured and concrete note to the general knowledge of the Holy Land, its places, peoples, and customs, which he did not always view in a kindly light. Jerome had, in fact, serious reservations about the growing practice of pilgrimage. The question of the spiritual value of such visits had been raised somewhat earlier by Gregory of Nyssa, who had been to Jerusalem and reported on the Holy City in his Letter on Pilgrimage:

If God's grace were more plentiful in the vicinity of Jerusalem than it is elsewhere, then the people who lived there would not make sin so much their custom. But in fact there is no sort of shameful practices in which they do not indulge, and cheating, adultery, theft, idolatry, poisoning, quarrels, and murder are everyday occurrences...What proof is there, then, in a place where things like that occur, of the abundance of God's grace?

Jerome did not disagree with this late fourth-century characterization of Jerusalem, and he warned one prospective pilgrim, Paulinus of Nola, that he should expect 'a crowded city with the whole variety of people you find in such centres, prostitutes, actors, and clowns...' But on balance he approved of pilgrimage to the Holy Land, and in fact his letters on the subject must have persuaded others to follow in the footsteps of the blessed Paula, and even, like Jerome himself, to settle permanently in the Holy Land as monks. By the fifth century, Christian ascetics, many of them from Egypt, were swiftly converting the Judaean wilderness region stretching east and south of Jerusalem and Bethlehem into a new centre of Christian monasticism.

F. E. Peters, *Jerusalem* (1985), pp. 152–3

For more than a hundred years after [St Antony of Egypt's] death, men and women inspired by his teachings were coming from the outposts of the Roman Empire to study religion in the desert as in our day they arrive from overseas to study history and economics in the universities. Some of these pilgrims stayed on in Egypt as hermits; some entered the monastic communities already forming in the wastelands beyond the Nile; and some returned to their own countries to establish convents which were to become the depositories of art and science throughout the Dark and Middle Ages. Fathers and doctors of the Church, founders of monasteries and religious orders, monks and nuns, pilgrims and Christians everywhere, all owed something to the Egyptian villager who went to find the Kingdom of God by the mystical road of self-abnegation.

James Wellard, *Desert Pilgrimage* (1970), pp. 89–90

One of the most powerful features of early Christianity was its deep sense of the transitoriness of the present age and its eager waiting for the age to come. 'Here we have no lasting city, but we are looking for the city that is to come' (Hebrews 13:14). We are only pilgrims on the way to 'the Jerusalem above; she is free, and she is our mother'

(Galatians 4:25–26). The vision of a new heaven and a new earth sym-bolized by the Holy City, the new Jerusalem, coming down out of heaven from God' (Revelation 21:1–2) kept the hope aflame in the hearts of the pilgrims amidst earthly trials and persecutions. The New Testament hope for the heavenly Jerusalem, the city that is to come, has to be understood against the obligation prescribed in the Torah for all Jewish males 'to go up' to Jerusalem three times a year for the three festivals of Passover, Weeks and Tabernacles. These pilgrimages were integral to Jewish faith and practice...

In the history of the Church, radical Christians burning with prophetic zeal for the kingdom of God have often deplored the failure of institutional Christianity to recall that Jesus lived the life of a wan-derer and a pilgrim. Born in a manger, rejected by the social structures of security and comfort, Jesus' ministry pervades throughout by the sense of homelessness... He gathered his disciples, not into a secure and stable home, but to share in his work of an itinerant preacher of the kingdom to come and a wandering healer of all kinds of sickness...

The self-emptying of God in the incarnate Christ was God's act of self-exile, the undertaking of a pilgrimage to the heart of created reali-ty. Christ the new Adam, the stranger to the scheme of this world, became the co-traveller with Adam the outcast wandering on the rugged earth and with Cain the murderer, the condemned and solitary wanderer.

K. George, *The Silent Roots:*
Orthodox Perspectives on Christian Spirituality (1994), p. 46

So I saw in my dream that the man began to run. Now, he had not run far from his own door, when his wife and children, perceiving it, began to cry after him to return (*Luke xiv. 26*); but the man put his fingers in his ears, and ran on, crying, Life! life! eternal life! So he looked not behind him (*Gen. xix. 17*), but fled towards the middle of the plain.

The neighbours also came out to see him run; and, as he ran, some mocked, others threatened, and some cried after him to return; among those that did so were two that resolved to fetch him back by force...and in a little time they overtook him. Then said the man, Neighbours, wherefore are you come? They said, To persuade you to go back with us. But he said, That can by no means be. You dwell, said he, in the City of Destruction (the place, also, where I was born): I see it to be so; and, dying there, sooner or later, you will sink lower than the grave, into a place that burns with fire and brimstone. Be content, good neighbours, and go along with me.

OBSTINATE. What! said Obstinate, and leave our friends and our comforts behind us?

CHRISTIAN. Yes, said Christian (for that was his name), because that *all* which you shall forsake is not to be compared with *a little* of that that I am seeking to enjoy (*2 Cor. iv. 18*); and if you will go along with me and behold it, you shall fare as I myself; for there, where I go, is enough and to spare. (*Luke xv. 17.*) Come away, and prove my words.

OBSTINATE. What are the things you seek, since you leave all the world to find them?

CHRISTIAN. I seek an inheritance incorruptible, undefiled, and that fadeth not away; and it is laid up in heaven (*1 Pet. i. 4–6; Heb. xi. 6, 16*); and safe there, to be bestowed, at the time appointed, on them that diligently seek it.

John Bunyan, *The Pilgrim's Progress* (1678)

The idea of pilgrimage is much older than Christianity, but always it has been an expression of the same two main concepts: that of making a pilgrimage by travelling to a specific geographical site, and that of being on a perpetual pilgrimage; the journey is life itself. Both are the pursuit of a greater good than mere existence, and both involve discomfort and hardship, if not a much overworked word, peril. To view life as a pilgrimage is, in part, a description of life as the result of living it...

But only in part, for through all ages an innate sense of longing has shown itself in the hearts of men and women for a better world beyond the present: where the meaning of existence, of the seemingly arbitrary nature of many current happenings, will become clear; where there is justice, peace, love. For Christians, that is the realm where God is shown forth as Creator and Father of all, the origin of his revelation of himself, in time, in the sonship of Jesus Christ – the same Jesus who said to his disciples, 'I go to prepare a place for you.' In our present limited comprehension, we call this habitation heaven, the heavenly Jerusalem.

Margaret Pawley, *Prayers for Pilgrims* (1991), p. xiii

And the Blessed Francis, going into the cave, held converse with God, as Moses did on Mount Sinai, face to face. And God said: 'O Francis, make me a wall between your brethren and the world.' And so Saint Francis put into the Rule the words: 'I order the brothers on obedience to have no place of their own, neither house nor any other thing;

but they shall be as strangers and pilgrims and servants of God in this world.'

Marion Habig, ed., *St Francis of Assisi: Omnibus of Sources* (1964), p. 188

We all go on pilgrimage. It is part of our human yearning to associate places with people we love, with experiences which are precious, with events which are holy, and such places may be imbued with sanctity renewing our dedication, stimulating our devotion and imparting a sense of healing, holiness and peace.

Each year my one pilgrimage from my hut-enclosure is to my home town, Swansea, for there are numerous places in and around that location which are sacred to my childhood, and wandering around the coastline and peninsula evokes memories of joys, sorrows and yearnings which continue to give direction to my life. Last year my sister and I made our annual pilgrimage to the cemetery where mother and father lie, and after tidying and arranging flowers before the simple oak cross, we held hands together and prayed, with some tears. It was a pilgrimage.

Such a pilgrimage to the graveside of a loved one, with its reminder of our mortality, is a reflection of our life's pilgrimage from cradle to grave. All of us are on this journey, and all our pretensions, ambitions, wealth and power come to an end at this place.

The persistence of a sense of pilgrimage is remarkable. I have Catholic friends who regularly go on pilgrimage to Lourdes and other holy places as part of their spirituality. And I have other Welsh Nonconformist friends who would not go near Lourdes, but would make a pilgrimage, say prayers and sing hymns at the graves of William Williams, Pantycelyn, or Ann Griffiths, those saintly hymn writers...

While the faithful people of every tradition go on their pilgrimages with devotion and intense fervour, the saintly ones know that unless God is to be found within their own experience, such pilgrimage is useless.

Brother Ramon SSF, *The Heart of Prayer* (1995), pp. 120-1

My aim here is to set down not the statistical findings but a few testimonies that are fairly typical of the pilgrims' sentiments. Above all, I would like to present a wide range of answers so that the reader may grasp the wealth and complexity of these pilgrims' motivations, feelings and desires. In this domain, researchers often have an unfortunate tendency to reduce and simplify rather than to be attuned to the soul of the people and to convey its originality, which will never be captured and held down by our more sophisticated concepts. Nevertheless I shall try to present the pilgrims' views clearly and coherently.

a) For these men and women, *to be a pilgrim is both a vocation and a grace*. They do not come to Juazeiro through a mere desire or an act of will. Their pilgrimage is all part of a dialogue. They have heard a call and they wish to answer it. Here are a few eloquent expressions of this attitude:

Pedro, aged 33
'I was asked why I went to Juazeiro. I replied: "He calls me and I go." And now, with faith in Padre Cicero and Jesus, I go there every year.'

Julia, aged 36
'Who brings me here – My Papa Cicero and my Mother of Sorrows, of course. This is my twenty-fourth pilgrimage.'

Maria, aged 38
'I last came here twenty years ago. One only comes here when God wills it.'

José, aged 46
'No one comes [to Juazeiro] unless he's invited. Our Lady lights up the pilgrim's heart; this invitation comes from the Mother of God.'

Dolores, aged 54
'I've made twenty pilgrimages to Juazeiro, walking all the way. The first time was in 1940. Each journey takes about three weeks. The Mother of God called me, so I came.'

Stella, aged 60
'I came because Our Lady invited me. I'm not one for making vows.'

The call comes from God, from Our Lady and from Padre Cicero. The very fact of choosing the pilgrim's way is a grace, as a woman of 36 informed me:
'Sure, I came in a truck, but I trust that God will give me the grace to come on foot eventually.'

b) It is not so easy to be a pilgrim…All kinds come to Juazeiro, *for to be a pilgrim is to be a witness, a disciple*, even if one's own interests are at stake.

Carlos, aged 70:

'I came here as a *romeiro*. But I don't know if I'm a true *romeiro*. Because Padre Cicero used to say that two kinds of pilgrims come here: the pilgrims of Our Lady of Sorrows and the bread-pilgrims. So sometime I think "I don't want to be a bread-pilgrim," no ma'am. Padre Cicero used to put it this way: "The pilgrims of the Mother of God, my pilgrims, are those who say in times of persecution: let's go to the help of Padre Cicero, because they're persecuting him. The other kind says: I'm not going there; I don't want to be ill-treated. That's the pilgrim who's scared. In the drought, the bread-pilgrim says: I'm not staying here because if I do, I'll starve; I'll go South to see if I can get food and shelter." That's the way it was in those days, and for my part, I just don't know what kind of pilgrim I am. Today I'm no longer young, but when I was strong, *Ave Maria!* I was always there, ready to face any danger.'

Manuel, aged 45:

'I'd call myself a pilgrim led by the heart. I believe in the heart and I go along with those who are pilgrims and want to visit this holy place.'

Therezinha Stella Guimaraes, 'On the Road to Juazeiro',
Lumen Vitae 32 (1977): 100–1

I'm just the latest in a very long tradition of pilgrims, to Rome and many other places, for any of a dozen reasons. My own reason for pilgrimage was gratitude for a favour granted. Those who went before me have all had reasons of their own. We've all taken to the road with causes, and results, as varied as our routes.

Dennis Larkin, *A Walk to Rome* (1987), p. 249

A pilgrim is a wanderer with a purpose. A pilgrimage can be to a place – that's the best-known kind – but it can also be for a thing. Mine is for peace, and that is why I am a Peace Pilgrim.

My pilgrimage covers the entire peace picture: peace among nations, peace among groups, peace within our environment, peace among individuals, and the very, very important inner peace – which I talk about most often because that is where peace begins.

The situation in the world around us is just a reflection of the collective situation. In the final analysis, only as we become more peaceful people will we be finding ourselves living in a more peaceful world.

In the Middle Ages the pilgrims went out as the disciples were sent out – without money, without food, without adequate clothing –

and I know that tradition. I have no money. I do not accept any money on my pilgrimage. I belong to no organization. There is no organization backing me. I own only what I wear and carry. There is nothing to tie me down. I am as free as a bird soaring in the sky.

I walk until given shelter, fast until given food. I don't ask – it's given without asking. Aren't people good! There is a spark of good in everybody, no matter how deeply it may be buried, it is there. It's waiting to govern your life gloriously. I call it the God-centred nature or the divine nature. Jesus called it the Kingdom of God within.

Peace Pilgrim: Her Life and Work in Her own Words (1983), p. 25

The medieval pilgrim had a clear purpose in mind when he set out for Compostela – he wished to avoid burning in hell. My own motives, I like to think, are more mixed. In four weeks time I am to be married. The arrangements are as ready as they will ever be: the tents are booked, the wine is bought, the music organized. It seemed to me that just as a medieval page would pray and fast before his knighthood, I, an overweight semi-agnostic, should do likewise before my wedding. A pilgrimage would provide an opportunity to think: of my past, of the future and of Olivia. Walking, by its very nature, purges the body and the soul, calms the mind. The medieval monks realized this and offered the pilgrims of their day an indulgence – a pardon from purgatory, an expunging of mental guilt. The act of walking can still help to distil one's thoughts so that all the worries that obscure clarity and peace of mind can rise to the surface and be filtered away. In principle, it is the perfect preparation for marriage.

William Dalrymple, 'A Pilgrim's Progress Ends', *The Spectator* 22 June 1991, p. 14

As Christians, we live in the paradox that we are at once sinners and yet sinners who are justified in Christ. But this formula does not quite express our situation. It hardly makes clear that the Christian life is a movement, a progress, a discipline in which sin is being constantly overcome through grace. That is to say that the Christian life is a way of pilgrimage, summed up in the way of the cross, and it is because the devotion of the Stations of the Cross concentrates this way for us and so helps to shape the whole way of life that we follow, that this devotion can be a useful discipline, conforming our lives to Christ. This also means that as we follow out the devotion, we find ourselves at various levels of identification, just as there are various stages in the Christian life. In our life on earth, we do not pass once and for all from one stage to another, and so in the Stations of the Cross we do not altogether leave one level of identification for another. But through their interaction, we are brought into a better understanding of ourselves in our relation to Christ, and in this devotion as in the Christian life, we are summoned from each level to the one above it and offered the grace whereby each step can be taken.

John Macquarrie, *Paths in Spirituality* (1972), p. 115

When [St Gerald] prayed to God from his innermost heart...he was afraid that God would not listen to him as long as evil thoughts remained in his mind...For his sins, which might perhaps seem trivial to us, weighed heavily on his conscience and he was always thinking of ways to atone for them and secure the remission of them from a merciful God. And so God, in his mercy, showed him the way, that is, the way of prayer...and he developed the habit of going regularly to Rome.

The Abbot of Cluny's *Life of Saint Gerald*, quoted in Jonathan Sumption, *Pilgrimage – An Image of Medieval Religion* (1975), p. 122

Greek Orthodox pilgrims envision their pilgrimage to the holy places as a sloughing off of impurities consequent on the Fall in preparation for death and resurrection. They step out of a world in which they have been deeply involved in sins consequent on mortality and into a world which has, with Christ's life and death, partaken in the process of turning mortal into immortal flesh. Traditionally, Greek and Cypriot pilgrims come to the Holy Land in old age to prepare themselves for good death and for their subsequent assumption into the redeemed world promised by Jesus...

John Eade & Michael Sallnow, eds., *Contesting the Sacred* (1991), p. 108

A man should undertake this voyage solely with the intention of visiting, contemplating and adoring the most holy mysteries, with great effusion of tears, in order that Jesus may graciously pardon his sins; and not with the intention of seeing the world, or from ambition, to be able to boast 'I have been there' or 'I have seen that' – in order to be exalted by his fellow men, as perhaps some do, who in this case from now have received their reward.

The Cavalier Santo Brasca, cited in John Davies, *Pilgrimage Yesterday and Today* (1988), p. 86

Poor Cancer, the word is dark and terrible, full of fear to the medical profession as much as anyone else. I believe it is a constellation; you become simply one of thousands and thousands of stars within it. It is a common everyday disease. A star may be sharp and full of pain, but it may also be a guide, a useful companion on a dark night.

There is a hidden current within every individual. It seeks and stirs, hides and yearns. Sometimes it is bewildered, a mixture of anger and pain and certainty. It may recede, but it never escapes. In moments of crisis it is full of voice.

Make a Pilgrimage. Go to ancient places. Go everywhere there are contemporary seekers. Go in whatever way it works out. Just go!

Jini Fiennes, *On Pilgrimage: A Time to Seek* (1991), p. xi

Whan that Aprill with his shoures soote
The droghte of March hath perced to the roote,
And bathed every veine in swich licour
Of which vertu engendred is the flour;
Whan Zephirus eek with his sweete breeth
Inspired has in every holt and heeth
The tendre croppes, and the yonge sonne
Hath in the Ram his halve cours yronne,
And smalle foweles maken melodie,
That slepen al the night with open ye
(So priketh hem nature in hir corages);
Thanne longen folk to goon on pilgrimages,
And palmeres for to seken straunge strondes,
To ferne halwes, kowthe in sondry londes;
And specially from every shires ende
Of Engelond to Caunterbury they wende,
The hooly blisful martyr for to seke,
That hem hath holpen whan that they were seeke.

Geoffrey Chaucer (*c.* 1340–1400),
The General Prologue to the Canterbury Tales

Soon after, this creature was urged in her soul to go and visit certain places for ghostly health, inasmuch as she was cured, but might not without the consent of her husband. She asked her husband to grant her leave, and he, full trusting it was the will of God, soon consenting, they went to such places as she inclined.

Then Our Lord Jesus Christ said to her: 'My servants desire greatly to see thee.'

Then she was welcomed and made much of in divers places, wherefore she had great dread of vainglory, and was much afraid. Our Merciful Lord Jesus Christ, worshipped be His Name, said to her:

'Dread not, daughter, I will take vainglory from thee, for they that worship thee, worship Me; they that despise thee, despise Me and I will chastise them therefor. I am in thee and thou in Me, and they that hear thee, hear the voice of God. Daughter, there is no so sinful man living on earth, that, if he will forsake his sin and live after thy counsel, such grace as thou promiseth him, I will confirm for thy love.'

Then her husband and she went forth to York and divers other places.

Margery Kempe (*c.* 1373–1439), *The Book of Margery Kempe*

It was assumed that both the senile man and the alcoholic, together with other pilgrims who were visibly unwell, were seeking a cure or amelioration from the pilgrimage. These assumptions were expressed quite unambiguously – for example, 'He's no doubt hoping for a cure'. A middle-aged woman from King's Cross, who described herself as ill, was always conspicuously close to any statue or object which the courier identified as being associated with miraculous cures.

John Eade & Michael Sallnow, eds., *Contesting the Sacred* (1991), p. 45

Shrine officials have always been careful to draw a sharp distinction between religion and magic at Lourdes, especially in the context of the baths. An authoritative French guidebook, for example, explains the symbolic importance of the baths with reference to the sacraments of reconciliation (through confession) and the eucharist:

This water is not magical: it is drinkable, chemically pure, similar to other springs at Lourdes, lacking in therapeutic or radioactive qualities. It sometimes heals but its role is primarily to remind us that we should turn to Him who is the source of eternal life. (Billet and Lafourcade, 1981)

John Eade & Michael Sallnow, eds., *Contesting the Sacred* (1991), p. 64

Many pilgrims, then, decided to go to a particular shrine because they heard about its reputation from neighbours or from others passing through their villages or because they had received dream-admonitions. Others, however, wandered from one shrine to another in search of health, until they felt sufficiently cured. Many English pilgrims went first to Becket's tomb, an indication of his popularity. Sometimes these perambulations in search of health took pilgrims well beyond the coasts of England. An Attenborough man went to Compostela in early 1201 for a cure. He felt some relief while there but after his return in mid-May his condition deteriorated and he spent the next few months 'shrinehopping'. Things grew worse until someone recommended Sempringham, where on 29 September he was cured by the relics of St Gilbert. Another example is the priest who was paralysed while singing Mass. He visited shrines for the next three years begging for health from the saints, *a sanctis sanitatem mendicans*, until at last he was cured at Worcester, some sixty miles from his home. Though they may have agreed that God's power was the same everywhere, the ill, especially the chronically ill, went right on with their quest for health, trudging or riding from shrine to shrine. Perhaps the record is held by the man who visited eighty-seven holy places. While these people moved about (in one case for fourteen years) it was likely that eventually some shrine would receive credit for their 'cure'; on the other hand, perhaps they felt better at every new shrine they visited. Some pilgrims 'chose' their shrine by casting lots; three saints were selected, and the sticks or whatever were drawn three times. Since God controlled all things it was not 'luck' but his will which operated on the lots to pick out a particular shrine. In parts of France early in the present century lots were cast to discover which saint had inflicted an illness and should be placated. But lots are seldom mentioned in the medieval miracles.

Ronald Finucane, Miracles and Pilgrims (1977), p. 85

OG: I have visited Saint James of Compostela; and, on my return, the seaside Virgin so famous with the English; or rather I have revisited her, for I had seen her three years before.

ME: From curiosity I suppose?

OG: Nay, from motives of religion.

ME: This religion, I suppose, has been taught you by Greek literature?

OG: My wife's mother had bound herself by a vow, that, if her daughter had a son born alive, I should in person salute Saint James, and offer our thanks.

ME: Have you saluted the saint only in the name of yourself and your mother-in-law?

OG: Nay, with the devotions of the whole family.

ME: I fancy not a whit less prosperity would have befallen the family if you had left James unsaluted...

Desiderius Erasmus, Pilgrimages to St Mary of Walshingham
and St Thomas of Canterbury (1849), p. 2

I Laurence, Knight of Hungary, have visited Ireland for three reasons. First and chiefly, because I had heard through reports by word of mouth and in writing that if any one had a doubt in the matter of the Catholic faith, and entered the Purgatory of St Patrick in the pre-scribed manner, he could there satisfy all doubts either severally or as a whole...The second reason was that I might say to the serene prince, my lord the King of the Hungarians, that I had visited the place of purgatory referred to...The third reason was that I might see the mar-vels and miracles of the saints of Ireland, for I had heard much of these marvels and miracles, the great diversity of which I had learned from many sources.

Laurence of Pasz, quoted in Shane Leslie, *Saint Patrick's Purgatory* (1932), 34–5

From time to time I need to be made to feel the extent of my helpless-ness, so that I can say, with complete candour, 'I can't cope. This is really beyond me.' It is at that moment of admission that some new and good begins to happen to me. I begin to live from a centre other than my self-protecting, manipulating ego. I begin to *move* in a new direction. My drifting is consecrated into pilgrimage. I begin to live with my longing. Far from finding myself on a masochistic, psycho-logical 'trip', a minor miracle occurs. I am sufficiently 'out of the way' for a while that I get a glimpse of what it might mean to love without strings.

Alan Jones, *Passion for Pilgrimage* (1995), p. 4

All manner of men and women flocked to Whithorn as pilgrims from royalty and nobility, bishops and abbots, to burgesses and peasants, as well as the pedlars, beggars and buskers who were out to exploit them. For many a pilgrimage was a spree, a prolonged day out, the medieval equivalent of the modern holiday. It was a last hope for the maimed and chronic sick, an exaltation of the spirit for the devout, and an act of expiation for the guilty. The courts of justice had the option to require convicted homicides to go on foot to one of the four 'heid sancts of Scotland', of whom one was St Ninian. This recognition of St Ninian by the courts of Scotland represented a notable step forward in the integration of Galloway. The benefits of royal patronage were added.

In 1462 repairs to the cathedral church were once more necessary and King James III, his mother and the prior joined together and sponsored a building fund. They petitioned the Pope that indulgences should be allowed:

to pilgrims visiting on Palm Sunday, Easter, the Feast of the
Nativity of St John the Baptist [Midsummer], Lammas [1
August], and St Ninian's Day [16 September] the church [that
is, Whithorn cathedral] to which we and other Christians even
in sundry realms and lordships, bear singular devotion.

James III and his consort made pilgrimage to Whithorn, more than
once, but their son James IV formed the habit of almost annual, and
sometimes more frequent pilgrimages to Whithorn. His regular visits
made him a major architect of Galloway's integration into Scotland.
    Daphne Brooke, *Wild Men and Holy Places: St Ninian, Whithorn and the
    Medieval Realm of Galloway* (1994), pp. 181–2

One consequence, as Boniface complains, of Roman pilgrimages is that
everywhere in 'Lombardy, Gaul and France' he comes across Anglo-
Saxon prostitutes. It was, in fact, a kind of mass migration on the spiritual plane, and it was in vain that the Irish set themselves against this
development: 'Going to Rome means great toil and brings little profit.
The (heavenly) king whom thou does miss at home, thou wilt not find
there if thou dost not bear him with you. Great is the folly, great the
madness, great the senselessness, great the lunacy. For it is surely
entering upon death to draw on oneself the anger of the Son of Mary.'
The Irish did indeed recognize the veneration of saints and relics, but
belief in the religious significance of particular places played little part
in their piety, and entered not at all into their idea of *peregrinatio*.
Thus, in the fusion of the Irish ideal of pilgrimage with that of the
West in general, we see repeated the process already noticed as regards
the East and the West in the fourth and fifth centuries. The role then
allotted to the Holy Land and Jerusalem is now, in its essentials, taken
over by Rome, whose influence on the development in England is
everywhere palpable.
    Hans von Campenausen, *Tradition and Life in the Church* (1986), p. 247

Between 1050 and 1350, eighty cathedrals, 500 large churches, and
thousands of parish churches were built. It has been estimated that by
the end of the period, there was one church for every 200 people in
many cities. The great thaw, however, was not just a matter of building and adorning churches; it was achieved largely by movement, the
movement of pilgrimage and crusade.
    The medieval pilgrimage has no exact counterpart in our day. It
was neither an extended holiday abroad nor an occasion for sampling

the culture of another locale. Heavenly rewards were sought. Medieval man had a preoccupation with the remission of sins. Unlike modern man, he was deeply impregnated with the fear of natural forces, and he knew he could be helped and healed by the saints at their shrines.

David Sox, *Relics and Shrines* (1985), p. 20

Thus far did I come laden with my sin,
Nor could aught ease the grief that I was in,
Till I came hither. What a place is this!
Must here be the beginning of my bliss?
Must here the burden fall off from my back?
Must here the strings that bound it to me crack?
Blest Cross! blest Sepulchre! blest, rather, be
The Man that there was put to shame for me!

John Bunyan, *The Pilgrim's Progress* (1678)

The British Inter-Church Process of the 1980s, *Not Strangers but Pilgrims* is just one example of using the metaphor of pilgrimage for the search for unity. It is a powerful picture and one which has an interesting and ecumenical pedigree. To an age of inter-continental travel, it is easy to forget some of the aspects of the religious pilgrimage, where the journey was a vital part of the total experience.

Pilgrimage is not like tourism, which sets out to see the sights. It has set before it a significant goal, one that has meaning for the traveller but has not been seen. The road is an unknown road, walked in faith. While not strictly pilgrimage, the stories of Abraham's call, the exodus wanderings and the return from exile are biblical themes which Christian devotion has linked with actual and spiritual pilgrimages. Thus the idea of promise becomes very important. Effort is expended on the long journey, but the end has been given by God, and so the whole journey and arrival are a means of grace. If we continue the picture of ancient pilgrimages, then we can introduce the slowness of the journey (walking pace?) and the dangers and uncertainties of the journey. If Chaucer's *Canterbury Tales* are anything to go by, then we can add *companionship* and *sharing* as dimensions of the pilgrimage, though these were probably more for mutual support and protection than for entertainment.

So we are called to share in an ecumenical pilgrimage. We are called to share in a journey that has been prepared for, undertaken and pioneered by others who have gone before us. The goal is known, though it has not been seen. Companions have been invited and the journey will involve risks, hardships and excitement...We must be concerned with faithfulness as well as faith, for the God who calls comes to us in the Jesus who gives himself for us and says, 'Follow me.'

Christopher Ellis, *Together On The Way: A Theology of Ecumenism* (1990), pp. 136–7

A hundred thousand flocking to Lerins, two hundred thousand to Le Puy, five hundred thousand to Domrémy, a million to Mont-Sainte-Odile, two million to Chartres, three million to Montmartre, four million to Lourdes...True, large figures have come to mean very little today. But how many real pilgrims are there in that camera-laden crowd pressing round the Gypsies' Pilgrimage at Saintes-Maries de la Mer? Are these visitors motivated by a love of folklore or by real faith? How many pseudo-pilgrims stay in the guest-houses merely because they find there, at a very cheap rate, a peaceful climate which has wholly deserted the fashionable tourist resorts, and also good home cooking? Granted all this, God's ways still remain unfathomable. At La Salette I have seen hardened hearts melting like snow in springtime: the beauty of the setting, the heart-rending simplicity of the Weeping Lady's message, the freedom of the mountain heights rediscovered. And the traveller who has come merely to rest his body and mind leaves with a small spiritual flame kindled in his inmost heart by God knows who!

Some may be shocked that the pilgrimage has changed so radically. Formerly it was a series of hardships and mortifications. Today, for many, it is holiday-time, with a car to get you there comfortably and many gastronomic delights on the way. But such an assessment of the modern pilgrimage is a superficial view of an eternal phenomenon. Throughout the centuries, the pilgrimage has constituted for mankind a privileged way of escaping and breaking away from routine. In the Middle Ages the pilgrimage was practically the only way that the poor could emerge from their village, and for the rich man it was a rare opportunity to go abroad under the pretext of defending Christ's tomb. But the truly wise man knows that God lives in him, and that there is no need to cover hundreds of miles by land or sea to meet him...

Jean-Jacques Antier, 'Pilgrimages in France: Religious Tourism or Faith in Action?', *Lumen Vitae* 39 (1984): 373

The goal of our journey is God Himself – not an 'experience', but Himself, the One and only Reality. Each pilgrim, as he sets out on the Way we have been considering, knows that he may say, 'I come from God, I belong to God, I go unto God.' Past, present and future are gathered up in Him and during our life on earth the highest expression of this, our final destiny, is in the act of worship. Here we touch bed-rock; here we know that God alone IS, that He alone matters. Here God manifests Himself in Christ, most majestic and most merciful. Apart from Him there is no meaning in life, no hope, no 'way'. We only exist because of Him. Hence He has the supreme claim upon us, upon our whole being. Gently, but inexorably, God, who is perfect Love, asks from us a total response: all we have and are, and every sphere and activity of human life; for nothing lies outside the scope of His sovereignty.

'Man is a great creature, created for a great obedience': this obedience is offered in worship and wrought out in life. All our worship, whatever form it may take, is our humble, grateful response to this God who has stooped down and come among us, sharing our life in the humblest and most ordinary conditions, 'bone of our bone and flesh of our flesh', quietly living His life according to the will of God, until, through suffering and death, His mission was accomplished.

Olive Wyon, *The Way of the Pilgrim* (1958), p. 123

The pilgrim leaves his home. He is ready to forgo his familiar horizon; he extricates himself from habit, which so easily becomes routine and servitude. He goes off to an 'elsewhere', an unusual and 'extra-ordinary', place, the Other. 'Elsewhere! Elsewhere is the Kingdom of God, peace!'

Who can fail to see that this is an opportunity to break away from the apathy of an inert existence from the servitude of sin and the chains of bad habits? An opportunity, for the person who goes out to the Other, to return as 'another' person...

Francis Bourdeau, 'Pilgrimage, Eucharist, Reconciliation',
Lumen Vitae 39 (1984): 401

We find it very difficult to be full human beings, but we have devised systems that help us to find our place in the world and to transcend our limitations. The cult of the holy place seems to have preceded any other form of reflection on the world: it was the axis for future cosmo-logical speculation. Similarly pilgrimage, the first of our therapeutic quests, has remained an archetype of the later disciplines. The secret of its enduring success must surely be the dramatic simplicity with which it forces us to confront our need to root ourselves healthily and imagi-natively in the past during our search for a spiritual centre of power.

Karen Armstrong, 'A Passion for Holy Places', *The Sunday Times Magazine*
15 April 1990, p. 32

But who, then, is the Centre of the world? That is precisely the question posed to the infant when, after being one with his mother, he begins to distinguish 'others' from 'himself'. When we study children's drawings, we note that their rough sketches of circles coincide with the age at which they are, in fact, beginning to be aware of their individuality. At this stage, conflict is inevitable and one could present a genetic psychology whose starting point would be this notion of the 'Centre' which lies at the very heart of affective space. In so doing, it would become abundantly clear that the path which leads from the self back to the self goes round the world by way of the Other. That is not the aim of the present article, yet we must agree in the light of these reflections that here, too, the pilgrim's quest has its deep roots in a human condition, man's search for the Centre.

It is not without good reason that the place of pilgrimage, which has been called 'a native land twice over', is acknowledged and sought as a *centre*. He who treads the pilgrim's path leaves his home, which Olivier Marc so rightly defines as 'the most perfect expression of the self'. He therefore goes out of himself and, in a manner of speaking, 'decentres himself' in his search for something greater. He who treads the pilgrim's path lives through a kind of existential psychodrama between two affective centres. And here we are touching upon the therapeutic, outward-growing power of the pilgrimage, which has been so aptly analysed by Dupront.

The *peregrinus* is the foreigner, walking over the land of others, seeking the Other.

This emergence from himself is essential to the pilgrim, for without it, he could not rediscover himself in other centres than himself.

Thus, he experiences a fundamental law of human growth: by endeavouring to reach a centre other than himself, he *moves forward* and finally rediscovers himself at that centre.

Anne Dumoulin, 'Towards a Psychological Understanding of the Pilgrim',
Lumen Vitae 32 (1977): 112–3

In all cultures, the meaning of 'road' extends beyond the idea of an actual path to cover a wide variety of concepts. We talk about life's road, the right road, etc., and in all the major religions the word has a figurative sense. For example, the concept is to be found not only in Buddhism and Islam but also in Greek thought, especially in Plato and, later, Hesiod. The latter speaks of two roads, one of which is arduous and leads to virtue, the other being easy and leading to pleasure. The conceptions were close to the meaning of 'road' or 'way' in the Old and New Testaments.

However, just as the road image has a wide variety of meanings in the Christian religion, the idea of *peregrinatio* at first had a figurative meaning. The *peregrinatio pro Christo* conceived in the High Middle Ages did not yet convey the idea of a concrete goal; it simply meant wandering through unknown lands in search of Christ.

In the eleventh century the word *peregrinatio* also acquired the meaning of a journey to sacred places, *peregrinatio ad loca santa*. Visits to Jerusalem and the places where Christ lived were the main components of the *peregrinatio pro Christo*; it was simply a more concrete way of seeking Christ.

Of the three major destinations of these *peregrinationes ad loca santa*, it was the pilgrimage to Santiago de Compostela that kept the idea of road or roads most alive.

'The Santiago de Compostela Pilgrim Routes', *Architectural Heritage Reports and Studies* 16 (1989): 9

The final kind of solitary life was that of the wanderers. Such individuals can be dated to an early period and seem to have survived cenobitical opposition (as in the Rule of St Benedict) fairly well. As has been noted, some early virgins became famous as pilgrims to the Holy Land. The Celtic monastic tradition produced an above average number of such wanderers. Throughout the Middle Ages the wandering tradition continued in different forms. Undoubtedly some wanderers were simply beggars or eccentrics but there were others who led a celibate wandering life for devotional and ascetical reasons. Many became pilgrims to the Holy Land or other great shrines of Christendom, and sometimes the distinction between hermits and everyday pilgrims is rather blurred. Pilgrimage was, of course, a striking phenomenon in the Middle Ages and involved people of both sexes, all classes and every category of life. Not all were 'single ones'. Some, like Margery Kempe who at different times went to Rome, Compostela and the Holy Land, were married with families and their wandering was only a temporary break in an otherwise ordinary lifestyle. However, there do seem to be pilgrims who made the wandering style of dedicated Christian life a more or less permanent occupation.

Philip Sheldrake, *Spirituality and History* (1991), pp. 117–8

Chapter Two

THE PLACE OF THE HOLY

The goal of the spiritual life is to attain holiness. Viewed from one perspective, holiness is not necessarily attached to any physical location. Yet the experience of humankind has always suggested that the spiritual can never finally be detached from the physical. Even though each person's journey is unique, there are certain common spiritual experiences which can be mediated to us by association with holy places.

What makes a particular site a holy place is never finally clear, but believers have come to recognize certain places as helpful to the spiritual life. Pilgrimage can take place without a particular destination in mind, but directionless wandering is a minority experience. Travelling to the holy helps the pilgrim to reflect on that which mediates holiness and so ultimately on God himself. The encounter with places which seem impregnated with the experiences of others can even produce hallucination and other unhelpful spiritual states. Yet these aberrations are insignificant in comparison with the simple testimony of the many who are helped in their spiritual imaginations by being in the presence of that which is felt to be holy.

He has set his foundation on the holy mountain;
    the LORD loves the gates of Zion
    more than all the dwellings of Jacob.
Glorious things are said of you,
    O city of God:
'I will record Rahab and Babylon
    among those who acknowledge me –
Philistia too, and Tyre, along with Cush –
    and will say, "This one was born in Zion."'
Indeed, of Zion it will be said,
    'This one and that one were born in her,
    and the Most High himself will establish her.'

The LORD will write in the register of the peoples:
  'This one was born in Zion.'
As they make music they will sing,
  'All my fountains are in you.'

Psalm 87

A desire to stand on holy ground, to be in a place where the veil
between heaven and earth has grown thin, seems to be a deep human
instinct. I like the way that great scholar of comparative religion Pro-
fessor Mircea Eliade put it when he wrote that 'every pilgrimage
shrine is the archetype of the sacred centre'. In a sacred place we may
experience the transcendent, the 'timeless moment', a universal God,
above the differences of religion or denomination. It is paradoxical
that we should claim God is everywhere and yet seek him in special
places, yet it is a paradox which we, having created, need to accept.

Shirley du Boulay, The Road to Canterbury (1994), p. 6

The spectacle of pilgrims walking barefoot or struggling painfully on
their knees toward their holy places can cause dismay. Such bizarre
behaviour seems obsessive and fanatical, the perverse survival of a
credulity that kept people ignorant and helpless for centuries. Even
religious people can find pilgrims an embarrassment. The Protestant
Reformation abolished pilgrimage with its cult of shrines and saints. It
was seen as a debased superstition: to kiss the ground because it was
'holy' seemed rank idolatry.

But Protestantism is unique in its rejection of pilgrimage. God's
first words to Moses from the burning bush were: 'Take off your
shoes, for the place on which you stand is holy.' The veneration of
holy places seems to have been a primordial religious experience. The
monotheistic religions gave us a religious geography dividing the
world into sacred and profane areas. Some places were radically different because they were closer to God.

Karen Armstrong, 'A Passion for Holy Places', The Sunday Times Magazine
15 April 1990, p. 24

The concept of the sacred is central to the literature on pilgrimage. It
is axiomatic that a pilgrimage is a journey to a sacred place which lies
beyond the mundane realm of the pilgrim's daily experience. Students
of pilgrimage have variously considered this sacred place to be the
cosmic centre...the world beyond this world...or a sacred periphery

which suddenly, transiently, becomes central for the individual, an *axis
mundi* of his faith...As well as being a literal journey, pilgrimage is a
journey of the religious imagination. Here, I assume...that pilgrimage
can be thought of as 'exteriorized mysticism', the private, mystical journey made public, a journey of the spirit which is physically enacted.

John Eade & Michael Sallnow, eds., *Contesting the Sacred* (1991), p. 78

Our first and most obvious discovery is that the pilgrimage is a spatial
prayer. Of course, all our activities are situated in time and space. But
it is clear that the pilgrim's way of proceeding would be meaningless if
it were not a real journey to a holy place, recognized in space as a 'centre'. This movement towards a centre is of prime importance for men
have even sought ways of making a pilgrimage 'on the spot'. Thus, in
the Middle Ages, a maze or labyrinth was frequently marked out on
the floor of the cathedrals and served as a substitute for the pilgrimage
to the Holy Land. The pilgrim who was unable to make the real journey would follow the intricacies of the labyrinth, sometimes on his
knees, until he reached the centre, which symbolized the holy places.

Today some of us cannot help smiling at these astute and econom-
ical practices but, for the medieval mind, a long distance was con-
densed in the labyrinth, and the pilgrim thus had the equivalent of an
adventurous journey full of perils.

And yet here, too, we have a striking example of motion towards a
goal, one of the essential requirements which define the very nature of
the pilgrimage.

Anne Dumoulin, 'Towards a Psychological Understanding of the Pilgrim',
Lumen Vitae 32 (1977): 109

Pilgrimages have a long history in the ancient Near East among Semit-
ic peoples; they are as old as the sacred shrines uncovered by archaeol-
ogists. To these various cultic centres the common man carried a part
of the fruits of his land and livestock to offer it to the gods in homage
and thanksgiving. The sanctuaries were places believed to be chosen
by the gods as special abodes and manifested as such by peculiar natural phenomena (a height, a spring, a tree) or by a theophany, e.g.
Jacob's dream (Genesis 28:10–22).

Some of the Canaanite open-air shrines were merely converted to
the use of the Yahwistic cult, e.g. Sichem, Bethel, and Mamre.
Because of Israel's tribal structure one shrine usually served as the
central sanctuary, at least for partial confederations of the 12 tribes.
The cultic centre acted as politico-religious bond, an inter-tribal focus

to which the federated clans periodically came on pilgrimage. At various times Galgal (Gilgal), Silo (Shiloh), Maspha (Mizpeh), and probably Gabaon (Gibeon) served as such local centres. A description of a pilgrimage to a central shrine is found in the prescriptions for offering the first fruits of the grain harvest (Deuteronomy 26:1–10; cf. 1 Samuel 1:3–7). Jerusalem became the focal point of religious gatherings after King David brought the Ark of the Covenant there. Later Jeroboam I, King of Israel, in order to have his own cultic centres in the Northern Kingdom, separated ᵥfrom Judah, established sanctuaries for Yahweh at Bethel and the city of Dan (1 Kings 12:27–30).

'Pilgrimages', *New Catholic Encyclopedia* (1967)

We came slowly, on our camels, across the Plain of Raha. Straight before us rose, in a precipitous grandeur, Sufsafeh, the steep end of the range of Horeb, to which, tradition says, Moses descended to deliver the law to the people of Israel, after receiving it from the hand of the Lord on the higher peak of Jebel Musa. On the very plain we were crossing the tents of the people of God were once pitched. Here, as the shadows fell, they would perhaps watch from their tent doors, when the day's activity was over, the growing radiance in the mighty pillar of cloud until, through the darkness it shone out like living, consuming fire; awful, yet beautiful; terrible, yet a constant and reassuring sign of the presence among them of Jehovah, Whose Almighty power had brought them out of the land of bondage, and Who was, withal, their Shepherd, merciful and gracious, an Eternal Watcher by night and day, Who neither slumbered nor slept. It seemed impossible to realize that we were on this holy ground at last; we moved on in silence, the speaking silence of a dream.

A. Mary Dobson, *Mount Sinai* (1925), pp. 34–5

At this point, there are special reasons for noticing a pious custom which began in the fourth century, and became of crucial importance ever after, viz., pilgrimages to the Holy Land. As early as the third century, Origen initiated that kind of scriptural knowledge which covers the identification of the traditional sites, traditions which clung to all parts of Palestine and the bordering regions; Eusebius made a Biblical gazetteer summarizing the result of his researches. The queen-mother Helena came as a highly-honoured pilgrim to the Holy Land during Eusebius's lifetime and she inspired the building of churches in Bethlehem and on the Mount of Olives. This and the erection of churches by Constantine's direct orders on sites consecrated by biblical

associations, gave a powerful impulse to the custom of making pilgrimages, and soon to writing records of them.

Hans Lietzmann, From Constantine to Julian: A History of the Early Church
Volume III (1950), p. 302

This creature, when Our Lord had forgiven her sin, as has been written before, had a desire to see those places where He was born, and
where He suffered His Passion, and where He died, and other holy
places where He was in His life, and also after His resurrection.

As she was in these desires, Our Lord bade her, in her mind, two
years ere she went, that she should go to Rome, to Jerusalem and to
Saint James...

Margery Kempe (c. 1373–1439), The Book of Margery Kempe

Yet Jerusalem had pride of place and was not only the goal par excellence chronologically but also the one that most Christians desired to
attain because there was the tomb of the first victor and martyr, Jesus
himself. The title of the first martyr is often given to Stephen, but the
account of his death in Acts, with his forgiveness of his persecutors, is
obviously modelled on that of Jesus and his words – 'Father, forgive
them; for they know not what they do.' In this way emphasis is placed
on the extent to which the death of a follower of Jesus may be linked
to that of his Master. Yet the tomb of Jesus did differ from that of his
saints in that it was empty, and moreover was for a long time inacces-
sible. Hadrian, according to Jerome, had deliberately built a temple to
Venus on the site.

John Davies, Pilgrimage Yesterday and Today (1988), p. 9

But Jerusalem was special. A natural centre of interest to Christians, it
had been elevated further by the heightened veneration of relics, the
popularity of cult centres and the growth of pilgrimages. There had
already been a revival on a large scale of pilgrimages from the West to
Jerusalem, the overland route to which had been partially cleared by
the conversion of Hungary to Christianity and the Byzantine victories
over the mighty Bulgars and Muslims in the late tenth century. Large
numbers of people were regularly departing for Jerusalem with the
encouragement of the monasteries and there was traffic right up to the
eve of the crusade and beyond. Six months before the Council of Cler-
mont, Count Roger of Foix was making preparations for a pilgrimage,
while a knight called Odard, who endowed the abbey of Jumièges in

the spring of 1098, appears to have just returned from Jerusalem: he must have travelled out and back peacefully as a pilgrim at the very time his fellow knights were battering their way through Asia Minor and suffering before the city of Antioch. In fact the attitude of eleventh-century Christians towards Jerusalem and the Holy Land was obsessive. Jerusalem was the centre of the world, the spot on earth on which God himself had focused when he chose to redeem mankind by intervening in history; at the same place, at the end of time, the last events leading to Doomsday would be enacted. In this respect a prophetic tradition, culminating in the reworking around the year 1000 of the Late Roman Tiburtine Sibylline writings, seems to have been very influential. Before the world's end, it was said, a last emperor would be crowned in Jerusalem.

> Jonathan Riley-Smith, *The First Crusade and the Idea of Crusading* (1993),
> pp. 20–1

This concept of Jerusalem as the navel of the world is also found in several ancient descriptions of the city by pilgrims from the West. One such account was dictated around 680 to Adomnan, the abbot of the Scottish monastery of St Columban, by a Gallican bishop whose ship had suffered shipwreck during its return voyage from Jerusalem, erected where a young man returned to life when the Holy Cross was placed on his body. The pillar was positioned so that it cast no shadow at noon on the summer solstice. This story was undeniable confirmation that through Christ's passion and resurrection Jerusalem was both the centre of the world and the navel of the earth and was often repeated. It is found, for instance, in a sermon on the sepulchre of the Lord by Peter the Venerable, the twelfth-century abbot of Cluny, in which he also stresses the importance of the empty tomb for the truth of the Christian faith, since it proves that Christ is not there as a dead body, but rules in the heavens as the living God.

> Adriaan Bredero, *Christendom and Christianity in the Middle Ages* (1994), p. 96

Although Christ is to be found in people rather than in sacred places or objects, it is nevertheless true that Christianity started in a particular place and that it has a theologically significant history which highlights a wide variety of places. God is believed to be active in his world, and although he is everywhere present, certain events are seen as especially significant, because they are revelatory of God's nature and activity.

Supremely, this is true of events in Israel. It follows that it is useful to go there in order to enter something of the context in which

Jesus lived and taught. The road from Jerusalem to Jericho becomes more vivid when it has been experienced, and so the teaching of the parable of the Good Samaritan may be better understood. The fact that sheep wander about looking much like goats may be a helpful subject for meditation. The feel of the place, the climate, the desert and the Sea of Galilee may all contribute insights into the story of Jesus and thus be of importance both in exegesis and to Christian faith in general. The motive is thus educational in the broadest sense with the aim of becoming a better Christian.

Christopher Lewis, 'On Going to Sacred Places',
Theology September 1989: 391–2

To the Christian pilgrim the Holy Land speaks of Jesus and of the Bible nearly all the time. Some places speak of him more vividly and more pointedly than others. At times the pilgrim is aware that he is standing where the Lord once actually stood or walks where his feet once actually trod.

Such is our experience when we walk by the hill road from Bethany over the top of the Mount of Olives and down the other side to Gethsemane and the Kedron Valley.

For this surely is the very same path that Jesus often used in the days of his earthly life. The track winding its way up the hillside from Bethany is without doubt the selfsame route that men ascending that hill have used from the beginning of human time.

John Martin, *A Plain Man in the Holy Land* (1978), p. 25

In the sources, Christian concern with Jerusalem involves the ancient concept of the city as a shrine of pre-eminent holiness, marking the physical and spiritual centre of the cosmos, the spot at which history began and at which it will reach its apocalyptic consummation. The idea of an *umbilicus mundi*, a scale model, as it were, of the universe itself, at which a nation or tribe would gather periodically to renew its corporate life by the observance of the now familiar year-rites was known to many ancient peoples, and the nations converted to Christianity had no difficulty accepting the supreme eschatological significance of Jerusalem and its Temple.

Hugh Nibley, *Jerusalem* (1973), p. 309

The Christian's other Jerusalem is 'the city of the living God, the heavenly Jerusalem...the assembly of the first-born who are enrolled in heaven' (Hebrews 12:22–23), where there is no temple (Revelation 21:22), but where a new covenant is mediated and a new sacrifice offered (Hebrews 12:24). This is the Jerusalem he claims as his mother (Galatians 4:26), and it is her name that he bears (Revelation 3:12). A present yet future reality, this Jerusalem has no man-made foundations, no spatially-defined limits. Its builder and architect is God (Hebrews 11:10), and its citizenship is won not through birth or naturalization, but through faith. Transcending both space and time, this Jerusalem exists whenever and wherever men 'receive gratefully that kingdom that cannot be shaken' by political and social upheaval (Hebrews 12:28), and live in the hope of seeing that heavenly 'city which is to come' (Hebrews 13:14). This Jerusalem is a faltering image of his experience of the Communion of Saints.

J. P. Brennan, *Jerusalem – A Christian Perspective* (1974), pp. 226–7

Sacred sites had long been the objects of pilgrimage. Origen, writing in the middle of the third century, says, 'there is shown at Bethlehem the cave where He was born...and this sight is greatly talked of in surrounding places'. Of Bethlehem again Eusebius writes that it 'is today so famous that other men still hasten from the ends of the earth to see it', and 'to this day the inhabitants of the place who have received the tradition of their fathers confirm the truth of the [nativity] story by showing to those who visit Bethlehem because of its history the cave in which the Virgin bore and laid her infant'. Of Jerusalem he says, 'Believers in Christ all congregate from all parts of the world...that they may worship at the Mount of Olives opposite to the city'. At Paneas there were statues said to be of Christ and the woman with the issue of blood, and a church at Tabgha on the supposed site of the miracle of the loaves and fishes.

D. S. W. Hadrill, *Eusebius of Caesarea* (1960), p. 202

In the first three centuries of the Church's life, the bodies of the saints, especially of those who had been martyred had always been venerated. At the place of their burial, on the anniversary of their death, the local Christian group kept their memory alive by celebrating the Eucharist, followed by an *Agape* or love feast. It was a memorial act of veneration for the dead saints' acts of heroic sacrifice, made all the more vivid by the thought that the remains of their actual physical bodies, that had borne the brunt of the enemy's attack, were but a few feet away helped to make the sense of spiritual fellowship almost palpable, and added force to the joyful acknowledgement in the liturgy, of the living presence of the saints. This kind of veneration Martin was the first to acknowledge, especially for the sense of continuity it provided with the primitive Church and its ways; and Gregory of Tours, his successor and admirer recalls how he caused the body of the first bishop of Tours, Gatien, who had survived the rigours of the persecutions, to be buried in a tomb in the church in Tours.

Christopher Donaldson, *Martin of Tours:*
Parish Priest, Mystic and Exorcist (1980), pp. 143–4

If you make an effort to get to a holy place of pilgrimage, with an open and expectant heart you will find great joy in fellowship of your fellow pilgrims around a place sanctified by prayer and the communion of saints. It was with tremendous anticipation that I heard the following words at the hermit symposium at St Davids in 1975, beginning a week of silence, prayer and fellowship:

> I want to begin with a very simple affirmation. I believe that the question we have come to study here together during these days is one of vital importance not only for the whole Church, but for all mankind. We have come purposely to a place which seems marginal, and we shall be talking about a way of life which, in our time at least, seems particularly marginal. Yet, as I shall hope to suggest, the place of the solitary is only in appearance at the edge; in reality he is the one who stands at the heart of things.
>
> The place where we are meeting, St Davids, may help us to understand a little more of this paradox. Geographically today it is remote and inaccessible, an eminently marginal place. In another age when, however difficult and dangerous sea travel was, it was at least less perilous than travel by land, its position was altogether different. It was one of the focal places of Celtic Christendom, a centre both of cenobitic and eremitic monasticism.

Brother Ramon SSF, *The Heart of Prayer* (1995), pp. 122–3

Alone of the great medieval English shrines, that of Walsingham, has been restored to a position of regular pilgrimage. To a large extent its renaissance is a tribute to the tenacity of an Anglican vicar, and the ingenuity of a Catholic lady. In the high Middle Ages pilgrimages to Marian shrines thrived and none was more important in the British

Isles than Walsingham. In 1061, the lady of the manor, the pious
Richeldi de Favarques, had a vision in which she was transported in
spirit to Nazareth. She was shown the house of the Holy Family and
told to build a replica of it. Two springs of water appeared in the
place where the vision was seen and, close by, the Holy House was
constructed in the form of a wooden hut surrounded by a flint and
stone building.

David Sox, *Relics and Shrines* (1985), p. 69

The town of Juazeiro do Norte lies to the south of the State of Ceara
and now has about 120,000 inhabitants. But in the latter half of the
nineteenth century it was just a hamlet, barely distinguishable from
any other: a halt for the itinerant traders who would shelter from the
burning sun beneath the huge *joa* trees in that dry, tropical region
called the *sertao*.

This region of Brazil, more than 500 kilometres from the coast and
bounded by cattle ranches, farms and hamlets, has developed slowly.
Its administrative relations with the capitals and the ports are its only
contact with the outside world.

It is to this little hamlet of Juazeiro that Padre Cicero Romao
Batista was, at his own request, appointed parish priest in 1872, two
years after his ordination. This Brazilian of the North East, born in
Crato in 1844, of Indian origin, was soon to become one of the most
outstanding popular leaders in the history of Brazil.

In a simple language, he taught his people to live their religion, to
pray the rosary, to give up stealing and killing. As he was not a great
preacher, he was mainly the counsellor and guide of a people steeped
in the anarchy of evil customs, revenge and ignorance. He excluded no
one from his friendship and offered everyone, even the bandits and
the *cangaceiros*, an opportunity to start a new life based on work and
prayer. This won him as many enemies as admirers. Juazeiro being a
shrine that sheltered criminals from the law, some denounced him as
the protector of murderers, while others were impressed by the boldness of his charity and regarded Juazeiro as a haven of hope for all
social outcasts.

The hierarchic Church was also at loggerheads with Padre Cicero.
On the 1st March 1889, an extraordinary event, which some called a
'miracle' and others a 'trick', held the attention of north-east Brazil
and gave unexpected publicity to Juazeiro's dawning religious movement. On that day, as Padre Cicero was giving communion to a pious
woman of the locality, the host suddenly changed into blood. Bearing
in mind the period and the context I have just described, it is not

difficult to imagine the manifold reactions provoked by this incident. The official Church reacted sternly and suspended Padre Cicero from his sacred functions. Nevertheless he continued to affirm till his death that he belonged to the Church, and called upon all the people to emulate his fidelity. Deprived of his sacred ministry, Cicero then assumed political responsibilities. He became the first mayor of the town and even the Vice-Governor of the State of Ceara.

Today, forty years after his death, thousands of pilgrims continue to flock to Juazeiro, squeezed like sardines into uncomfortable trucks, and though the rough journey may take up to five days, no hardship can diminish their enthusiasm and devotion. For them Juazeiro remains a Holy City, the new Jerusalem, the centre of the world, the land of Salvation.

In face of this situation, the official Church remains cautious, but refrains from condemning Padre Cicero and his followers, as it once did.

Therezinha Stella Guimaraes, 'On the Road to Juazeiro',
Lumen Vitae 32 (1977): 98–9

'Although the pilgrim may well have come alone he nonetheless participates in a flux which has elected that *holy place*.' Charles Péguy tells us how he visited Chartres Cathedral on his own and encountered in it the crowds who had been coming there for centuries to pray. And he conveys this by his spontaneous use of *we*; 'You see us walking, we are the foot-sloggers...' He knows, too, that 'others will come to you from distant Beauvais and others again from noble Vermandois'. By revealing to us that grace of ecclesial fellowship, the holy place opens our hearts to encounter. Here we pray as a Church family: the pilgrimage infuses us with brotherly reconciliation, which is both the token and the fruit of God's forgiveness.

Francis Bourdeau, 'Pilgrimage, Eucharist, Reconciliation',
Lumen Vitae 39 (1984): 403

Inis Cealtra was a place of much pilgrimage, even if the saints who originated its monastery are uncertain. It must have been one of the most impressive of the Irish pilgrimages, a lengthy affair spread over four days, from the Friday before Whitsunday to the Monday after. Barefooted the pilgrim went seven times round the island (each circuit would be a mile long), on his way making seven 'rounds', at a series of 'stations', the various churches, the holy well, and so on. It came to an end because, as O'Donovan recorded in the Ordnance Survey letters of 1839, 'some ill-behaved young rascals' took to the habit of carrying off young girls by force from the crowd and thus providing themselves with 'fresh consorts for the ensuing year'. Earlier the island had served as a centre for the harassed Irish Catholics, for in 1609, Sir Arthur Chichester complained to the Privy Council that Jesuits and priests from abroad had flocked to 'Inishgaltaghe...to give absolution and pardons, and they come and go hence with the swallow...making a yearly revenue of poor and rich'. .

Daphne Pochin Mould, *Irish Pilgrimage* (1955), p. 29

The voyage from Ouranoupolis, the last outpost of the 'world', to Daphni, the main port on the Holy Mountain of Athos, makes the feeling of physical separation from the 'world' total. The transition from a profane to a sacred area is marked by the fact that the peninsula, which the visitors are to approach, is regarded by the monks as the Garden of the Virgin, one of the outer signs of which is that no woman is allowed to enter the area. This prescription is sanctified both by legend and by the advice of the holy fathers of the Orthodox tradition.

Therefore, there are no women on board. When approaching Daphni hardly anyone, however, reflects on this matter, since the natural scenery of the peninsula is so absorbing.

Moreover; separation from the world is marked by the fact that the monks use the Julian calendar, a calendar thirteen days behind the Gregorian one. If it was September 9th when the traveller's foot left the boat at Daphni – as it was in my case – the leg would land on the dockside on August 28th. Moreover; the clocks at most of the monasteries point to twelve at sunset, when it is no more than eight o'clock Greek time; the time on the Holy Mountain of Athos being about four hours ahead.

Rene Gothoni, 'The Progress of Pilgrimage on the Holy Mountain of Athos', *Social Anthropology of Pilgrimage*, ed. Makhan Jha (1991), p. 300

European pilgrimage is predominantly Marian. Christ's mother, Saint Mary, is the principal subject at nearly two-thirds of today's shrines. Her significance is followed by that of a multitude of saints whose 1,614 shrines make up 27 per cent of the cases examined. Christ-centred pilgrimage cults are relatively rare, accounting for less than 8 per cent of the shrines. These 453 shrines include 39 focused on the Trinity, usually represented by a carving or painting of the Father, Son, and Holy Ghost. This 'three-in-one' subject usually emphasizes Christ, although in some cases the Holy Ghost depicted as a dove seems to be the subject of special pilgrim attention, whereas God the

Father is apparently the primary subject of devotion at a few shrines. Among secondary subjects, the saints predominate, representing near- ly 70 per cent of the recorded cases. Mary accounts for less than 19 per cent of the shrines with secondary devotional subjects, followed by Christ at 12 per cent of these shrines.

Sidney & Mary Lee Nolan, *Christian Pilgrimage in Modern Western Europe*
(1989), p. 211

The national pilgrimage in honour of Our Lady of the Angels is the most well-known pilgrimage in Costa Rica and the one highest in rank. It is a striking manifestation of the intense devotion of Costa Rican Catholics to Mary, Virgin of the Angels, who, as of September 23, 1824, by decree of the Congress Constituyente of the State of Cos- ta Rica, is and will be in the time to come, the Patroness of the nation. Although it is the virgin of the Angels herself who is Patroness, and not the Image of her under this advocation, the Image is the tangible focus of devotion and the magnet which attracts thousands of pilgrims to her official sanctuary, the Basilica de Nuestra Señora de los Angeles in the city of Cartago, Province of Cartago.

The Image is a dark-stone figure of the Virgin with the Child Jesus on her arm. According to tradition, it was found in 1635, on a boulder in a place called 'La Gotera' in the outskirts of Cartago, by a *mulata* named Juana Pereira. The narrative recounts five instances in which the women and then the parish priest secured the Image only to find it on the boulder again. After each new encounter with the Image – the Little Black One, the Negrita – it was guarded more closely, until, finally, having placed it in the Tabernacle where the Blessed Sacrament was reserved and discovering that the Image had fled once more to the boulder, the priest concluded that the site was the Vir- gin's choice for her church. Because the Image was first found by the *mulata* on 2 August, the day on which the Roman Catholic Church was accustomed to celebrate the feast of Our Lady of the Angels, the stone figure was given that name.

Leslie Ellen Straub, 'Formal Replication in Costa Rican Pilgrimages',
Social Anthropology of Pilgrimage, ed. Makhan Jha (1991), p. 277

Christian pilgrimage in continental Western Europe developed from a desire to be near holy persons who were believed to be especially pre- sent on earth in those places where their physical remains were entombed. As Peter Brown expresses this idea, the early pilgrims were 'not merely going to a place; they were going to a place to meet a person'. Through time, the emphasis on relics was expanded to include images, but the basic idea of visiting a particular place in order to commune more intimately with a holy person remained essentially intact. This Christian emphasis on persons symbolized by objects was, however, superimposed on a much older tradition of pilgrimage to places that were holy in their own right, often because some natural feature such as a height, water source, or grotto was considered to have especially sacred power.

Early Christians on the Continent are thought to have avoided pagan holy places. Churchmen decried the ancient notion that natural site features were sacred, although the old traditions were never fully repressed. But in the Irish Celtic tradition, the ancient holy sites were accepted and Christianized from the beginning of the fifth century. Missionaries, including Saint Patrick, baptized holy wells and mountain heights in the name of the new religion. Gradually continental resistance to old traditions of site sanctity were modified in a syncretism of Christian pagan ideals. The factors leading to this synthesis were numerous. The eastward travels of Irish and British missionaries during the sixth through eighth centuries clearly played a role, as did the association of Syrian and Egyptian holy men and remote sites such as mountain heights, grottoes, and vast deserts. These holy hermits, venerated during their lifetime, were usually buried at places sanctified by their presence, and their tombs continued to draw pilgrims. The intransigence of country people, who refused to give up pilgrimages to the places they had long considered holy, must also have been a factor, especially as missionaries spread the new religion both beyond the bounds of Roman influence and into the never fully Romanized backcountry regions of the former empire.

By at least the sixth century, Christian ideas about shrine location, which emphasized particular sites as holy through sanctification by the saints, converged on Romanized Western Europe from both east and west. Meanwhile, invasions and general chaos encouraged churchmen to remove the bones of the holy dead from their urban-edge tombs to the relative safety of the central city churches. This relocation of holy relics tended in continental Europe to urbanize pilgrimage and further detach it from specific place associations over the short run. Once the principle of holy object mobility was accepted, however, the object could, theoretically, be venerated anywhere. With the addition of miraculous images, any place could become a pilgrimage shrine given the proper set of circumstances.

Sidney & Mary Lee Nolan, Christian Pilgrimage in Modern Western Europe
(1989), p. 291

If one excludes Jerusalem, the bodies of Ss. Peter and Paul in Rome were the primary attraction for Christian pilgrims. Later, alleged tombs of other martyrs came to be venerated, especially that of the Apostle James (son of Zebedee), once his supposed tomb was discovered in Galicia at Campus stellae, hence Compostela, in 830.

Soon pilgrimages acquired varied and diverse goals. The faithful began to venerate the tombs of non-martyrs, e.g. those of the confessors Martin of Tours in Gaul (the most popular of all) and Nicholas of Myra, whose body was transported to Bari, Italy, in the eleventh century, and much later those of Sergius of Radonezh in Russia and the saintly Jean Vianney in the Lyonnais, as well as the tombs of such penitents as Mary Magdalene in la Saint-Baume, Provence.

Pilgrimages were made also to places hallowed as the result of a reputed supernatural apparition. Thus that from the sixth century many pilgrims went to Gargano in Aquila, made famous by an apparition of the archangel Michael. After 710, pilgrims went for the same reason to Mont-Saint-Michel on the borders of Normandy and Brittany.

There were also pilgrimages in honour of the Virgin Mary, Mother of God. Although they originated later than the early pilgrimages to the Holy Sepulchre or tombs of saints in general, certain Marian pilgrimages are obviously very old, dating back at least to the Frankish period so far as the West is concerned; e.g. Ambronay in Burgundy dates from the seventh century at least; Einsiedeln in Switzerland goes back to 954; while Savona (near Genoa, Italy) claims to have received pilgrims as early as the age of Constantine.

'Pilgrimages', *New Catholic Encyclopedia* (1967)

So, in choosing sites for religious settlements different spiritual and practical factors were taken into consideration. Place had a sacred significance. The Christian Celts were as concerned as their ancestors had been about the issue of the sacred landscape and about good and evil places. They accepted that two worlds came together at certain familiar places in the landscape. Christian ascetics therefore sought out places where, in some special way, heaven appeared to meet earth. These boundary or frontier places were sometimes associated with traditional sacred places such as woodlands or wells. Some of the great Christian sites retain references to these links in their names. Thus Kildare derives from the words *Cell Dara* or 'the church of the oak wood'. In other places Christian monuments were raised at traditional tribal burial centres. This is because cemeteries, as we shall see, were rather obvious boundary places – doorways from this material world into the spiritual world.

Philip Sheldrake, *Living Between Worlds* (1995), p. 30

As for Iona, it had been a holy place for both Druids and Christians long before Columba landed there. In the fifth century the Druids are supposed to have come here to escape the persecutions of Imperial Rome, and to have founded a library on the island. In 410, when Fergus II of Scotland became an ally of Alaric the Goth, he added to that library by bringing back books from the plunder of Rome. So it was an established place of learning when Columba arrived. It is probably purely fortuitous that the island's name is the same as the Hebrew word for a dove. For centuries Iona was simply known as the Island, Eo, Hy, Hi or just I, which was expanded to Inis-nar-Druineah, 'the place of the Druids'.

More than twenty years before Columba came to Iona, a Christian cemetery was founded on the island by St Oran of Letteragh, who died in 548. This Reilig Odhrain was the burial place of the kings of Dalriada up to 560, three years before Columba's arrival. There is also a tradition that there was a college of seven bishops on the island at one time, and that two of them met the priest from Ireland and did their best to prevent him from landing.

Shirley Toulson, *Celtic Journeys in Scotland and the North of England* (1995), p. 53

Devotions were not primarily what one read or saw, but what one did. Devout Christians manifested their devotion by saying their prayers, going on pilgrimage, fasting, participating in processions, joining in the activities of confraternities, wearing hair shirts, giving alms, attending sermons, and performing other pious acts...

Although some devotions could take place anywhere, the most important were commonly linked with special locations. Liturgical religion is marked primarily by a sense of special times, and contemplative religion by an effort to transcend both place and time, but devotional religion attends mainly to the veneration of sacred places or to the objects that make these places holy. Indulgences could be secured for those who visited certain churches, chapels, or shrines. At times these shrines would be erected as an imitation of sites in the Holy Land, such as the sepulchre of Christ (the most important of the holy places in Jerusalem, according to fifteenth-century sources). For those who were truly devout, domestic oratories and local churches usually did not suffice for such persons, the very act of travelling to a place of pilgrimage, whether a few miles outside of a town or on the other side of the Alps or across the sea, was a process that helped to define one's destination as a special and sacred location.

Jill Raitt, ed., *Christian Spirituality: High Middle Ages and Reformation* (1987), p. 81

Despite considerable theological objections to the idea of physical relics of Christ, a number of such items have been venerated across Europe: Christ's blood and milk teeth, his foreskin and umbilical cord. Claimants of the latter three were to be found in the pope's own cathedral at the Lateran, and their cult was embarrassing to some pontiffs. Innocent III said, 'What shall we say of the foreskin and umbilical cord which were severed from his body at birth? Were they too resurrected?' Pilgrims at their shrines were told they had been spirited from Jerusalem by an angel and presented to Charlemagne at Aachen. They had been brought to Rome by Charles the Bold.

Relics of the Precious Blood appeared in many places, and their multiplication was sometimes explained in bizarre fashion. Eucharistic hosts had exuded blood when struck by heretics or Jews. Even more controversial were the relics of Christ's blood which were said to have come from his very wounds at Calvary. Mantua had claims to two in its history. A phial containing Christ's blood was reported as early as 804, and Charlemagne asked the pope to investigate its authenticity. The outcome of the inquiry is not known. The memory of that relic was revived when a second phial was unearthed in the garden of the hospice of Sant'Andrea in 1041. This relic is still kept in the crypt of the basilica of Sant'Andrea and was said to have been preserved by Longinus, the Roman soldier who had pierced Christ's side with a spear. The cult took root in the Middle Ages, and the shrine became a popular stopping-off place for pilgrims going to Rome.

David Sox, *Relics and Shrines* (1985), p. 83

The quality of the pilgrim's devotion and behaviour was simpleminded and almost fanatical. [Ignatius of Loyola] was at this point relatively uneducated and theologically naïve. It was enough for him that he was in the Holy Land and in the Holy City. Like other pilgrims of his day, he was not troubled by the uncertainty regarding the exact location of the events of our Lord's life or by the fact that the impression of the Saviour's feet on the supposed rock of ascension was undoubtedly apocryphal. There was no room for hesitation, critical appraisal and judgement, or any suggestion of doubt about these matters. He was transported by the fervour and devotion of the moment, even to the extent of seeing the figure of Christ guiding his way.

William Meissner, *Ignatius of Loyola: The Psychology of a Saint* (1992), p. 116

When I took off my shoes I felt that I was exposed. My modernized and well-protected feet found it hard to walk bare over gravel, stones and heated pavement. The acceptance of all this inconvenience, and in particular of the feeling of being exposed, forms the religious sense of humility and respect. Under the hot Rangoon sun I began to trudge up to the hill where the Pagoda stands. It was a slow climb. Every step was a ceremonially slow step. The sweat on my forehead was, as it were, religious sweat. The time I spent to walk up to the Pagoda was a holy time. When I arrived at the foot of the Pagoda itself, my mind was prepared to see it right in front of me. I recalled how in Japan the Meiji Emperor Shrine in Tokyo, Ise Imperial Grand Shrine in Mie Prefecture and a host of others have long approaches to the main shrine, some as long as a mile or more. No bicycles and no automobiles are allowed. Even the emperor himself must walk from a certain point. The holy must be approached slowly and carefully with respect and humility. The holy must not be approached by motorcycle or helicopter. It must be approached by walking.

Walking is the proper speed and the proper posture that can prepare man to meditate. Thus the universal use of the automobile is, I am afraid, producing a less-meditative mankind! The un-holy (everyday things) may be approached by running or on motorcycle (even if the silencer is broken). But that which is holy must be approached slowly. Such thoughts called to me as I was walking up to the Pagoda.

The God that the Bible proclaims reveals himself to be the holy God. He revealed himself to be holy by becoming *slow* for us. The central affirmation of the Bible is that God does not forsake man.

Kosuke Koyama, *Pilgrim or Tourist?* (1974), pp. 1-3

Chapter Three

PREPARING FOR THE JOURNEY

Preparation for a pilgrimage from which one might not return was not undertaken lightly. Even today, a journey such as the traditional road followed by many English pilgrims, which begins on the French side of the Pyrenees and ends in Santiago de Compostela (a distance of approximately six hundred miles), if undertaken on foot, requires some planning and forethought. But it is clear that whatever the complexities of planning the route and obtaining transport where necessary, the pilgrim almost always has in mind the more delicate task of spiritual preparation.

The blessing of those in spiritual authority is not just helpful in a practical sense but is spiritually important. Prayers for a safe journey feature strongly in pilgrimage narratives. But alongside these more obvious prayers and preparations is a strong sense of the need to set matters right with those who have wronged you and those whom you have wronged. Absolution for past sins even before setting out is often an element in the spiritual preparation.

This kind of preparation calls to mind the typology of pilgrimage as preparation for that final journey that each person must take in death. Such a serious review of one's life to date helps to make pilgrimage a point at which the direction of a person's life might be significantly altered. Direction for a pilgrimage can therefore impact the direction of one's future. Preparation for pilgrimage is therefore also preparation for a new kind of life.

Calling the Twelve to him, he sent them out two by two and gave them authority over evil spirits.

These were his instructions: 'Take nothing for the journey except a staff – no bread, no bag, no money in your belts. Wear sandals but not an extra tunic. Whenever you enter a house, stay there until you leave that town. And if any place will not welcome you or listen to you, shake the dust off your feet when you leave, as a testimony against them.'

They went out and preached that people should repent. They drove out many demons and anointed many sick people with oil and healed them.

Mark 6:7-13

Rich pilgrims often made generous donations to the poor before leaving. The cartularies of monasteries, from the eleventh century onwards, are full of deeds recording the gifts made by departing pilgrims and crusaders. A donor could have the best of both worlds by making his gift conditional on his not returning alive. Then, when he returned home, he could demand the usufruct of his property for the rest of his life, after which it would become the unencumbered possession of the Church. When Aimeric II, count of Fézensac, gave some windmills to the canons of Auch in 1088 as he was about to leave for the Holy Land, he insisted that 'if I come back alive from Jerusalem, I can have them back until my death'. If the knight never returned, the monks were required to give a pension to his widow and sometimes even to his children...Pilgrims probably adopted this roundabout procedure in order to ensure that their lands were safe in their absence. Some of them may also have borrowed the cost of the journey from the monks and left the lands with them as a pledge.

Jonathan Sumption, *Pilgrimage – An Image of Medieval Religion* (1975), p. 169

The pilgrim may bring with him no money at all, except perhaps to distribute it to the poor on the road. Those who sell their property before leaving must give every penny of it to the poor, for if they spend it on their own journey they are departing from the path of the Lord. In times past the faithful had but one heart and one soul, and they had all their property in common, owning nothing of their own; just so, the pilgrims of today must hold everything in common and travel together with one heart and one soul. To do otherwise would be disgraceful and outrageous...Goods shared in common are worth much more than goods owned by individuals. Thus it is that the pilgrim who dies on the road with money in his pocket is permanently excluded from the kingdom of heaven. For what benefit can a man possibly derive from a pilgrimage undertaken in a spirit of sin?

Liber Sancti Jacobi, cited in Jonathan Sumption, *Pilgrimage – An Image of Medieval Religion* (1975), pp. 124-5

Poor or rich, pilgrims first had to make plans for their journey, since they could not stride out on pilgrimages whenever the fancy took them, no matter how common the activity may now seem to us. Major pilgrimages required considerable preparation. Even pilgrimage to local shrines involved at least a minimum of planning. These journeys demanded the right opportunity, sufficient means as an alternative to begging, and the right season – obviously farming peasants could not wander off at critical periods in the agricultural cycle. The 'pilgrimage season' in England was thought to include the feasts of Christmas, Easter, Whitsun, and St Michael's (29 September) or, alternatively, the Easter week, Whitsun, and 'after the harvest (autumpnum) because then men – having a holiday from their labours – can go on pilgrimage more freely'.

Ronald Finucane, Miracles and Pilgrims (1977), p. 48

'He that be a pilgrim,' declared the London preacher Richard Alkerton in 1406, 'oweth first to pay his debts, afterwards to set his house in governance, and afterwards to array himself and take leave of his neighbours, and so go forth.'

His first act, if he was a man of substance, was to make his will... In Normandy local custom required every landowner to make a will which would automatically be executed if he did not announce his return within a year and a day. Some pilgrims also made private agreements with their wives as to how long they should leave before remarrying. The Church did what it could to ensure that the terms of the pilgrim's will were respected. In Spain, for instance, it made his companions responsible for looking after his personal effects. Failing companions, the local clergy were expected to keep them for a year and a day and, if they remained unclaimed, to sell them and apply the money to endowing masses for the repose of the dead pilgrim's soul.

Jonathan Sumption, Pilgrimage – An Image of Medieval Religion (1975), p. 168

May the almighty and everlasting God, who is the way, the truth, and the life, dispose thy journey according to his good pleasure. May he send his angel Raphael to be thy guardian in thy pilgrimage; to conduct thee on thy way, in peace, to the place wither thou wouldest go, and to bring thee back again in safety on thy return to us...

J. Wicham-Legg, ed., The Sarum Missal, Edited from
Three Early Manuscripts (1916)

The pilgrim should prepare himself to pardon the injuries done to him; to restore everything belonging to others; and live according to the law, because without this first and necessary disposition every hope and every fatigue is in vain.

The Cavalier Santo Brasca, cited in John Davies,
Pilgrimage Yesterday and Today (1988), p. 42

We begin our pilgrimage with a call to repentance. Repent and return to the Lord! There is one table, one Commonwealth. In this, we are, with all the people of the world, *graced*...The life of grace rests on our willingness to place ourselves 'under the mercy' (as the old phrase has it). The mercy of God enables us to abridge ourselves of our super-fluities, delight in each other, rejoice *together*, mourn *together*, labour and suffer *together*. There is not one of us who is not 'well connected', joined as we are in one communion and fellowship in God's Common-wealth. The Church is the sacrament of this Commonwealth, which is a community of all for all. The Church is the place where the wonderful story that will make us into one People is told over and over again. It is a Love Story about the mending of broken bones; it is a Passion Story about the joy of homecoming.

Alan Jones, Passion for Pilgrimage (1995), p. 12

THE HOLY LAND – BEGINNING THE PILGRIMAGE

Lord Jesus Christ,
you were a pilgrim in this Holy Land.
Now you lead and guide us
on our pilgrimage to the heavenly Jerusalem.

As we follow in your steps,
we ask the grace to keep our eyes on you.
Open our hearts that we may find you,
not only in ancient stones,
but in your people
and in each other.
Let your words be a fire
burning within us.
Write your Gospel upon our hearts.
Give us a spirit of prayer
lest we return full of facts
but not of grace and love.

Lord, teach us to pray
in the very land where you taught your disciples.

Stephen Doyle OFM, cited in Margaret Pawley,
Prayers for Pilgrims (1991), p. 106

Why are Christians not reminded more often that the Eucharist was
born of a *pilgrimage*? It was born during the Passover pilgrimage to
Jerusalem. Remember: Jerusalem was full of pilgrims. And Jesus' enemies feared that crowd: 'Not during the feast, lest there be a tumult
among the people' (Matthew 26:5). That is why Judas looked for an
opportunity to get Jesus arrested 'without the people knowing' (Luke
22:6).

Jesus himself had come up to Jerusalem *as a pilgrim* for the feast of
Passover: 'Go and make preparations for us to eat the Passover' (Luke
22:8). In fact, in the Gospel of Luke, Jesus' risky ascent and last pilgrimage to Jerusalem begins much earlier, at the end of chapter 9:
Jesus knows that his enemies are lying in wait for him, but 'he resolutely takes the road to Jerusalem' (Luke 9:51). This pilgrim's way
therefore runs through the whole Gospel, and the Last Supper is the
high point of the journey: 'They set off and prepared the Passover.
And when the hour came, he took his place at table, and the apostles
with him.' Only for that reason – since it was at that supper that the
Eucharist was instituted – each Mass we celebrate with the desire to
identify with the sentiments of Christ Jesus must be lived with a pilgrim soul.

Francis Bourdeau, 'Pilgrimage, Eucharist, Reconciliation',
Lumen Vitae 39 (1984): 395–6

A pilgrim who left without making amends to those he had wronged
could not possibly make a sincere confession, and without a sincere
confession, it was generally agreed that his pilgrimage would be worth-
less. 'In order that my devotion may be the more acceptable to God,'
reflected Odo, duke of Burgundy, before joining the crusade in 1101,
'I have decided that I should set out at peace with everybody.' Accord-
ingly he wished to make amends for the damage he had done, in a lifetime of violence, to the abbey of St-Bénigne de Dijon. He begged
forgiveness in the nave of their church for the trespass he had committed against their lands and the insults he had heaped upon their heads.
'And my promises of amendment and offers of compensation have
been accepted by the monks of St-Bénigne; they have pardoned and
absolved me and have agreed to pray for me, and I may keep my

promises and enjoy a safe journey to the Holy Land.' Bertrand de Moncontour, who had seized some land belonging to the abbey of the Trinity of Vendôme, wished to go to the Holy Land in 1098 but 'realized that the path of God would be closed to me while such a crime remained on my conscience'.

Jonathan Sumption, *Pilgrimage – An Image of Medieval Religion* (1975), pp. 170–1

O God, our own God, true and living Way: as you went with your servant Joseph on his travels, so, Master, guide this your servant on his present journey. Protect him against trying circumstances, bad weather and every stratagem that may be directed against his welfare. Give him peace and strength; grant him the prudence he needs if he is to act as he ought, in accordance with your commandments. Bring him back home rich in the goods of this world and in heaven's blessings.

For kingship, power and glory are yours, Father, Son and Holy Spirit, now and always, age after age. Amen.

Walter Mitchell, *Early Christian Prayers* (1951), p. 148

In the Middle Ages the pilgrim received a special liturgical blessing before setting out; he would have already put on a special dress reminiscent of a penitent, with a broad-brimmed hat, a wallet, or pouch, slung across his back, and a long iron-shod cane or 'pilgrim's staff' in his hand. Before leaving, he would have been advised to put his affairs in good order, return any money unjustly acquired, making provisions for the support of his family in his absence, and give alms while retaining enough money to defray the expenses of his often long and costly journey. Furthermore, to claim the privileges to which the authentic pilgrim was entitled (for a pilgrim was protected by many conciliar decrees and was, in a certain sense, assimilated into the clergy) the pious traveller had, in fact, to get written authorization of his bishop (or abbot, if he were a monk). By the twelfth and thirteenth centuries only the production of such testimonial letters (*testimoniales*) enabled him to escape being classified as an adventurer or pilgrimage profiteer. An ordinance of King Richard II of England in 1388 indicated that any pilgrim without such *testimoniales* risked arrest.

'Pilgrimages', *New Catholic Encyclopedia* (1967)

INSTRUCTIONS TO PILGRIMS

FIRST ARTICLE. Should any pilgrims come thither without express leave from the pope, and have thereby incurred the pope's sentence of excommunication, such persons must present themselves to the father guardian after Mass, and he himself would absolve them from their guilt by virtue of the Apostolic authority committed to him...The cause of the excommunication is that after the Christians were driven out of the Holy Land some bad Christians remained behind therein, and associated themselves with Saracens, swearing allegiance to them.

Anonymous, cited in F. E. Peters, *Jerusalem* (1985), p. 427

May God shield us by each sheer drop,
May Christ keep us on each rock-path,
May the Spirit fill us on each bare slope,
    as we cross hill and plain,
Who live and reign One God for ever. Amen.

Martin Reith, *God in Our Midst: Prayers and Devotions from the Celtic Traditions* (1975), p. 38

A special order of ceremony for pilgrims, as opposed to ordinary travellers, was now coming into existence. This usually took the form of blessing the pilgrim's pouch and mantle and presenting him with his staff from the altar. The ceremony has its origin in the blessing conferred on knights departing with the first crusade, and is referred to in 1099 as a 'novel rite'. Behind the 'novel rite' is the pronounced tendency of the Church in the eleventh century to stimulate lay piety by assigning to laymen certain defined spiritual functions. Those who fulfilled these functions were clothed with a special, almost ecclesiastical, status; they enjoyed spiritual privileges and ultimately secular ones as well. Hence the religious ceremony which now almost invariably accompanied the dubbing of a knight. Indeed, the ritual presentation of the pilgrim's staff bears a striking resemblance to the dubbing of a knight and to the ordination of a priest. To the more austere pilgrim, the act of putting on his travelling clothes might have the same significance as taking the monastic habit. One such pilgrim was Rayner Pisani, an Italian merchant who experienced a sudden conversion during a business trip to Tyre in about 1140. Rayner took his pilgrim's tunic under his arm to the Golgotha chapel in Jerusalem and, in full view of an astonished crowd, removed all his clothes and gave them to the beggars. He then placed his tunic at the altar and asked the priest serving the chapel to invest him in it. This the priest did, and Rayner passed the remaining twenty years of his life as a hermit in Palestine.

Jonathan Sumption, *Pilgrimage – An Image of Medieval Religion* (1975), pp. 172-4

Ignoring for the moment the dresses worn by Chaucer's merry band, we find that in early days the costume of a professional pilgrim consisted of a long, coarse, russet gown, with large sleeves, sometimes patched with crosses, a leather belt round the shoulders or loins, with a bowl, bag and scrip suspended from it, a large round hat decorated with scallop-shells, or small leaden images of the Virgin and saints; a rosary of large beads, hung round the neck or arm, a long walking staff (a bourdon), hooked like a crosier, or furnished near the top with a hollow ball, or balls, which were sometimes used as a musical instrument.

Jonathan Sumption, *Pilgrimage – An Image of Medieval Religion* (1975), p. 121

This hymn was sung by a pilgrim in setting out on his pilgrimage. The family and friends joined the traveller in singing the hymn and starting the journey, from which too frequently, for various causes, he never returned.

> Life be in my speech,
> Sense in what I say,
> The bloom of cherries on my lips,
> Till I come back again.
>
> The love Christ Jesus gave
> Be filling every heart for me,
> The love Christ Jesus gave
> Filling me for every one.
>
> Traversing corries long and wide,
> The fair white Mary still uphold me,
> The Shepherd Jesus be my shield,
> The fair white Mary still uphold me,
> The Shepherd Jesus be my shield.

Oliver Davies & Fiona Bowie, *Celtic Christian Spirituality* (1995), p. 128

In medieval times pilgrimages were a mass phenomenon, which inspire admiration and even astonishment in today's observers, considering the low population figures of the time. Chroniclers reported a stream of many thousands of pilgrims in one day, often many times more than the total population of the largest places of pilgrimage themselves.

The resultant problems of traffic, food and lodging have been recorded for us in documents and accounts, in the form of hundreds of sober facts. For example, many treaties concerning the transport of pilgrims from Aix-la-Chapelle, concluded between the guilds of Rhine boatmen, between the Lake of Constance and the Lower Rhine, have been preserved. As an old French proverb tersely says, *Point de marine sans pèlerinage* (no navy without pilgrimages).

When the holy coat of Treves was first displayed in 1512 on the orders of the emperor Maximilian I, the authorities of the city sought the help of bakers, butchers and fishmongers in the wide swathe around the city. They had so many people to feed that they did not know how to do so. In 1475 the town of Erfurt was faced with such insurmountable problems of housing and feeding the mass of pilgrims streaming from central to southern Germany towards Wilsnack that the town council saw no way out other than barring them from the town. Caesarius of Heisterbach (*c.* 1180–1240) reported with astonishment that he had never seen so many people in his life as he did in the Marburg in 1233 on his pilgrimage to the tomb of Saint Elizabeth.

'The Santiago de Compostela Pilgrim Routes', *Architectural Heritage Reports and Studies* 16 (1989): 94

By a law of Edward III English pilgrims were compelled to embark and return by way of Dover, 'in relief and comfort of the said town'; and...at the request 'of the Barons of Dover', who alluded to this ordinance, [Richard II] commanded that all pilgrims and others, excepting soldiers and merchants, should embark either at Dover or Plymouth; but at no other port without special licence of the King. It has been suggested that these restrictions arose partly from a desire to check the practice of smuggling, at which certain pilgrims are said to have been adept.

Sidney Heath, *Pilgrim Life in the Middle Ages* (1911), p. 159

In God's name we are sailing,
His grace we need:
May his power shield us
And his holy sepulchre protect us.
Kyrie eleison.

Cited in John Davies, *Pilgrimage Yesterday and Today* (1988), p. 54

Before starting out a pilgrim of St James, it is necessary to choose the road. Our twelfth-century French fellow-pilgrim, Aymery Picaud of Poitou, whose advice we follow implicitly, tells us in his Guide, which is intercalated in the *Codex Calixtinus*, that there were in the twelfth century four roads through France to Spain by which the pilgrims travelled.

The first road was called the Via Tolosana and was the usual way of approach to Spain for pilgrims travelling from Italy and Provence. It began at Arles which with its avenue of tombs called les Alyscamps and the Cathedral of St Trophyme and passed by St Gilles, the centre of a famous pilgrimage, and on through the Camargue, the rough hills of the Cevennes, through Toulouse with its Cathedral of St Sernin, which was a rival to Santiago de Compostela itself, and on by the Somport Pass into Spain.

The second road, which was called Via Podiensis, was the most severe of all, and was patronized mainly by the Burgundians and the Germans. Aymery Picaud describes how its remote town of Le Puy, perched on its precipitous rocks, was celebrated for its miraculous Virgin, who was venerated even by the Moors from Cordoba. From the mountainous solitude of Aubrac the pilgrims visited the sanctuary of St Foy of Conques and descended into the fertile lands of the Romanesque Abbey of Moissac, and from there on to Ostabat at the foot of the Pyrenees, whence they ascended into Spain by the Port de Cize. Ostabat was the frontier meeting-place of the second and two following roads.

The third road, which was called the Via Lemosina, crosses obliquely the central mountain range high above its forests and fertile slopes sacred to the memory of St Mary Magdalene. The pilgrims crossed the Loire at Nevers and journeyed through the plains of Berry and halted at shrines of St Leonard, the redeemer of captives, whose chains festoon his tomb, and St Martial of Limoges, who in the eleventh century was even included among the Apostles. From there the road undulates through the pleasant hills of Perigord and Chalosse to Ostabat and the Pyrenees.

The fourth road, which was called the Via Turonenis, was the natural artery linking France to Spain, and followed roughly the line of the Paris-Madrid railway. By that road travelled the pilgrims from England, Flanders, Paris and its region, and its principal stages were at the Orléans: Tours, where was the tomb of St Martin, the Apostle of Gaul: Poitiers, the fief of St Hilaire: Saintes, the Sanctuary of St Eutrope: Blaye, where pilgrims knelt at the tomb of Roland the martyr, and Bordeaux, the resting-place of St Seurin. From there the pilgrims wended their way through the monotonous desert of the Landes of Dax, Ostabat and the Pyrenees.

Walter Starkie, *The Road to Santiago* (1957), pp. 81–2

Give me my scallop-shell of quiet,
   My staff of faith to walk upon,
My scrip of joy, immortal diet,
   My bottle of salvation,
My gown of glory, hope's true gage,
   And thus I'll take my pilgrimage.
                Sir Walter Ralegh (*c.* 1552–1618), 'The Passionate Man's Pilgrimage',
                     The Faber Book of Religious Verse (1972), p. 76

After wearing his crown and making his offering at the main altar, the Emperor of France returned to the hall of his palace in Paris...'Lords,' said the Emperor, 'listen to me. If it pleases God, you will visit a far off kingdom to seek Jerusalem and the land of the Lord God. I wish to worship the cross and the sepulchre. Thrice have I dreamed this, so I must go. And I shall seek out a King of whom I have heard. You will take several hundred camels, laden with gold and silver, enough to last seven years in that land. I shall not return until I have found him.'
   ...The Emperor of France had his companions make ready, equipping them nobly and giving lavish gifts of gold and silver. They carried no shields, lances or sharp swords, but staffs of ash tipped with iron, and hanging scrips. Their horses were shod front and rear, the servants padded the saddles of both mules and pack-horses and filled up the trunks with pure gold and silver, with vessels and coins and other equipment. Folding chairs of state were taken and white silk tents...The king rode on until, reaching a plain, he turned to one side and called to Bertrand: 'What a noble body of men these pilgrims are: out in front there are eighty thousand men. Their leader must be a man of great power!'

   Glyn Burgess, ed. & trans., *The Pilgrimage of Charlemagne* (1988), pp. 34–5

May God free me from my wickedness,
May God free me from my entrapment,
May God free me from every gully,
From every tortuous road, from every slough.
May God open to me every pass,
Christ open to me every narrow way,
Each soul of holy man and woman in heaven
Be preparing for me my pathway.

                Avery Brooke, ed., *Celtic Prayers* (1981), pp. 60–1

Having ruled the [Saxon] nation for thirty-seven years, Ini also abdi-cated...He then set out to visit the shrines of the blessed Apostles ...wishing to spend some of the time of his earthly pilgrimage in the vicinity of the holy places, hoping thereby to merit a warmer welcome from the saints in heaven...Many English people vied with one anoth-er in following this custom, both noble and simple, layfolk and clergy, men and women alike.

The Venerable Bede, *Ecclesiastical History of the English Church and People* (731)

A sure sign that Western pilgrimage to the Holy Land was not only becoming common but had, for some, commercial possibilities that might be exploited is the preservation from the sixth century of two works that might fairly be called guidebooks to the area. Neither the anonymous *Breviarius* nor the *Topography of the Holy Land* attributed to a certain Theodosius, the latter accompanied by maps, makes a claim to be a learned work nor even a personal or religious statement, but both had their use and each contributed to the fund of informa-tion that was accumulating in the West and being passed on, copied, and reintegrated into newer accounts. Pilgrims, it appears, were begin-ning to read up on the subject before setting out for the Holy City.

F. E. Peters, *Jerusalem* (1985), p. 154

No doubt the most comfortable way to carry out a pilgrimage was to pay someone else to go. Pilgrimage by proxy was far from rare, and not uncommonly money was provided in wills to pay for this service – when it would be most needed. In the fifteenth century, Margaret Est bequeathed money to Thomas Thurkeld for pilgrimages to St Thomas of Canterbury and other specified shrines 'yf my goodys wyll stretch so ferr for his costs'. Professional pilgrims, known as 'palmers', were available to discharge other peoples' vows or simply to bring back bits of the Holy Land or Rome; they might take someone's ring along to touch it to famous shrines in distant places. Unless they went on Cru-sade – ever less likely as the Middle Ages drew to a close – a journey to Jerusalem or even to Spain or Italy was probably beyond the means of most English folk, although it is surprising to see how readily some took up the mendicant life for the sake of foreign pilgrimage. General-ly speaking, though pilgrim ships continued to depart until the early sixteenth century, for most English people domestic shrines had to suffice. Even here the problem of expenses could not be avoided.

Ronald Finucane, *Miracles and Pilgrims* (1977), p. 46

Our journey was to start from the cathedral itself, but first, following the tradition of the medieval pilgrims, we went to St John's, the oldest surviving parish church in Winchester. Here the vicar, Canon Robert Teare, read a short and ancient service, the *Itinerarium for Pilgrims*. He invoked the blessing of the Archangel Raphael – one of the seven archangels who stands continually in the presence of God – then read the Benedictus and a few prayers. He prayed for God's protection, for:

> a support in setting out, a solace on the way, a shadow in the heat, a cover from the rain and cold, a chariot in weariness, a protection in danger, a staff in slippery places, a harbour in shipwreck, that under your guidance they may happily reach the place whither they are going, and at length return to their homes in safety.

Shirley du Boulay, The Road to Canterbury (1994), p. 20

There are doubtless places of pilgrimage within reach of your area that you could undertake as an individual or with a group from your church or prayer group...Let me illustrate by telling you of one of my favourite pilgrimage places. It is the church, cell and holy well of St Issui at Patricio in the Black Mountains, just below Offa's Dyke in Wales – just a few miles from Llantony Abbey. If you look at your map, find the A465 between Hereford and Abergavenny. You will find marked the village of Llanfihangel Crucorney. From there the road ascends and narrows until you reach the high place of Patricio with an overwhelming and panoramic view of grandeur and serenity.

If you approach from the A40 Brecon to Abergavenny road, take the turn to Crickhowell and Llanbedr which will bring you to Patricio. Geographical directions sound mundane and pedestrian, but if you are fit enough to do the last few miles by foot, or even if you have to take your vehicle up to the holy well which lies in the dingle a few hundred yards below the church, you will soon be caught up to heaven.

The church at Patricio is simple, beautiful and with a silence which is palpable. The lovely medieval rood screen remains because the iconoclastic reformers missed the church in the mountains. The foundation began way back about the seventh century when Issui, a hermit, set up his wattle or wooden cell in the dingle, through which runs Nant Mair (St Mary's stream). He sanctified the well by baptizing pilgrims and filling the whole place with prayer. The approach to the well is marked by a pilgrim stone bearing the Maltese cross, and in the spring enclosure there are small niches which once held the figures of saints.

The desert tradition carries stories of attacks upon hermits, and here it was no different, for Issui was murdered by an ungrateful traveller, but because of his saintly reputation the well became a place of pilgrimage and evidenced healing qualities. In the early eleventh century a continental pilgrim was so grateful for the healing of his leprosy at the well that he donated the gold to build a church on the hill above the well, dedicated to St Issui. This is now the chapel-cell which has been refurbished and was rededicated and opened for prayer by the Bishop in 1991. The present main church was built on to the eastern aspect of this chapel cell.

I've often made a pilgrimage to this holy place with its stone seat and preaching cross outside the church, and its wide, expansive view of the lower Grwyney Fawr with the Usk in the far distance, and I've often coveted the hermit cell for myself!

Brother Ramon SSF, *The Heart of Prayer* (1995), pp. 126–7

I experienced both stages of becoming a pilgrim between the ages of 20 and 23. My father had been, in an unusual way, miraculously healed at Lourdes when he first came into the world: because he was practically stillborn, his mother (my grandmother) made a vow that if he lived, he would go to Lourdes himself to thank the Virgin Mary. The baby was sprinkled with Lourdes water, of which there was an abundance in the house, as in most Christian homes of the time (1896). And the miracle – if indeed it was one – came to pass. The baby lived. But despite his mother's scoldings, he subsequently refused to go on the pilgrimage promised in his name. And for a very simple reason: he did not believe in it. Then he died when I was still a child. I did believe in it. That is why, at the age of 20, yielding to my grandmother's pleas, I went to Lourdes (1948) in my father's place, as it were. I was in any case intrigued by that manifestation of faith which I would be observing for the first time.

Jean-Jacques Antier, 'Pilgrimages in France: Religious Tourism or Faith in Action?', *Lumen Vitae* 39 (1984): 367–70

Bless to me, O God, the earth beneath my foot,
Bless to me, O God, the path whereon I go;
Bless to me, O God, the thing of my desire;
Thou ever-more of ever-more,
Bless thou to me my rest.
Bless to me the thing whereon is set my mind,
Bless to me the thing whereon is set my love;

Bless to me the thing whereon is set my hope;
O thou King of Kings,
Bless thou to me mine eye!
As thou wast before at my life's beginning,
Be thou so again
At my journey's end.
As though wast besides at my soul's shaping,
Father, be thou too at my journey's close.
Be with me at each time, lying down and arising,
Be with me in sleep, companioned by dear ones.

Avery Brooke, ed., *Celtic Prayers* (1981), pp. 48–51

Rucksacks, I discovered, are sold by the litre. I chose a strong blue one, thirty-five litres, with a mass of exciting, hidden pockets. The young men in the camping shop in Shepherd's Bush told me it was far too small for three months; it was simply a day sack. But I couldn't have handled anything bigger. Once strapped to it I felt different; there was great freedom in the feeling of it. I couldn't wait to be off, on the move. Different beds. Different places. Different people. Keeping only the company of strangers...

Finally I was alone in the departure lounge at Brittany Ferries at Portsmouth, waiting for the 11.30 night crossing to Caen. I sat there surrounded by excited, boisterous school children and several families. Anxiously I kept checking and rechecking; passport, glasses, Visa card, penknife, pencils, camera. I had brought another bag, with even more zip pockets: it was for books, film, maps and things. I began to realize that all this double checking might become feverish and neurotic. I had once had a great friend, an Austrian psychoanalyst, who earlier in his life had had a nervous breakdown. He had told me, 'I used to check and recheck letters I had written, opening them again and again, finally I even called the Post Office to open up the post box; I knew then the anxiety was master of me.' I kept thinking of this. I realized that I must never let practical anxieties overwhelm me. Nothing mattered. No loss was irredeemable. Even death would not be a real disaster, as it was the one certain event in life. Why worry? It was only a book, a puff of thin air, less than a spider's web in a rusty bucket.

Jini Fiennes, *On Pilgrimage: A Time to Seek* (1991), pp. xii–xiii

The walk began at Roncesvalles on 21 July 1988. The group of pilgrims comprised 60 men and 50 women ranging in age from 76 down to 12, with an average age of 37 for the men and 32 for the women.

Sixty-five per cent of the group were academics or university students; 11 were secondary school-leavers, 14 had received a primary education and 5 had followed vocational training courses.

The project was presented to the pilgrims as an undertaking in which the two parties concerned were working towards complementary goals, with one party offering the will and desire to make the journey to Compostela, and the other, the City of Pamplona, providing the basic facilities necessary to the project's success.

A team of professionals was responsible for the organization, which was divided into three sectors:

material organization and basic facilities;
organization of cultural and artistic activities;
organization of concurrent events, and relations with relevant institutions and the media,

the whole being overseen by a general co-ordinator.

The walkers were accommodated overnight in tents, owing to the difficulty in lodging 150 people in villages with fewer than 100 inhabitants.

The camps were set up where indicated by the mayors of the localities we could be passing through, which necessitated a prior approach and facilitated our knowledge of the places concerned before we left Roncesvalles. The basic facilities and supplies team looked after catering.

Two vehicles transported the logistical equipment, with certain people assigned to the task of assembling and dismantling the camp every day. A medical team and another team responsible for relations during the walk with villages, institutions and the media accompanied the walkers. A mobile office gave information about the walk and audio-visual screenings relating to the route and to Pamplona.

The cultural activities were open to the inhabitants of the towns and villages in which they took place; in all, some 10,000 people took part in events along the route.

'The Santiago de Compostela Pilgrim Routes', *Architectural Heritage Reports and Studies* 16 (1989): 112

The following is a blessing for a journey. Tenth century or later. Middle Irish.

May this journey be easy, may it be a journey of profit in my
   hands!
Holy Christ against demons, against weapons, against killings!
May Jesus and the Father, may the Holy Spirit sanctify us!
May the mysterious God be not hidden in darkness, may the
   bright King save us!
May the cross of Christ's body and Mary guard us on the road!
May it not be unlucky for us, may it be successful and easy!

Oliver Davies & Fiona Bowie, *Celtic Christian Spirituality* (1995), p. 38

Chapter Four

THE COMPANY OF OTHERS

Many of those who have been on various kinds of pilgrimages report that there is a great difference between travelling on one's own and travelling in the company of others. In very simple terms, travelling alone allows a sufficient degree of solitude that a pilgrim can better find himself and God along the way. The talk of others can be a distraction. Yet these two conditions are not diametrically opposed. Those who travel together can arrange for times of silence when each will be free to think their own thoughts and explore their own questions. Similarly, those who travel alone are never entirely so. They meet other pilgrims or travellers along the way. They have conversation in the various lodging houses or hostels as they journey. Indeed these chance encounters may turn out to be a significant element in the overall experience of pilgrimage.

Clearly, the question of personal safety might be sufficiently acute that travelling in groups or organized parties can be advisable. But the larger and more organized the group, the greater the danger that one will have only left home physically but not emotionally, spiritually and socially. The company of others can act to insulate one from the actual journey. It is possible to simply take our own environment to another place and so hardly be on pilgrimage at all. The serious pilgrim will often choose to walk, at least for large portions of the pilgrimage, to avoid simply being a tourist, packaged and delivered.

———————

'Look,' said Naomi, 'your sister-in-law is going back to her people and her gods. Go back with her.'

But Ruth replied, 'Don't urge me to leave you or to turn back from you. Where you go I will go, and where you stay I will stay. Your people will be my people and your God my God. Where you die I will die, and there I will be buried. May the LORD deal with me, be it ever so severely, if anything but death separates you and me.' When

Naomi realized that Ruth was determined to go with her, she stopped urging her.

Ruth 1:15–18

> Bifil that in that seson on a day,
> In Southwerk at the Tabard as I lay
> Redy to wenden on my pilgrimage
> To Caunterbury with ful devout corage,
> At night was come into that hostelrie
> Wel nine and twenty in a compaignie,
> Of sondry folk, by aventure yfalle
> In felaweshipe, and pilgrimes were they alle,
> That toward Caunterbury wolden ride.
> The chambres and the stables weren wide,
> And wel we weren esed atte beste.
> And shortly, whan the sonne was to reste,
> So hadde I spoken with hem everichon
> That I was of hir felaweshipe anon,
> And made forward erly for to rise,
> To take oure wey ther as I yow devise.

Geoffrey Chaucer (*c.* 1340–1400), *The General Prologue to the Canterbury Tales*

Off we went, we three pilgrims, to Canterbury, as so many have over the years. It was a good quick journey and Chris made up for her very early start! We parked where we had planned, and walked through the beautiful gardens to the cathedral enjoying magnolia, spring bulbs, primulas and blossom. The sun shone and everything seemed to sparkle with delight on this special day. We were really excited and joined the other pilgrims making their way to the cathedral door...Then the Archbishop entered and shouted: 'The Lord is Risen' and there was a great roar: 'He is risen indeed'. It was at that moment that my blood tingled with excitement. What a privilege to be there...Christ was there with us. God had led us to this holy place.

As I wrote in my diary, 'A truly memorable Easter – a goal of our pilgrimage well and truly achieved.' And Chris put up her poster from Turvey Abbey – 'He is Risen'.

John Key, *Journey to Resurrection* (1995), pp. 69–70

At the very beginning of the *General Prologue* the pilgrims exude an air of *felaweshipe* (26, 32), and the narrator, who senses it too, tells us he and the rest made a *forward* to rise early the next morning and depart. Then to further emphasize the fellowship of this group of pilgrims, Chaucer has the Host propose a contest of tales…A more spiritual motivation for pilgrimage would have generated a true Christian fellowship among the pilgrims…

Christian Zacher, *Curiosity and Pilgrimage: The Literature of Devotion in Fourteenth-Century England* (1976), p. 88

There was a heavy mist when I started out next morning. When the sun broke through I was in a sheltered forest. At 3.00 p.m. I came to Mailly-le-Château, where I found a hotel opposite the thirteenth-century church. Ian Tweedie had advised me to stay at a hotel or pension at least once a week for a long rest and cooked meals. I followed his advice on this occasion, I did not feel the need of a hotel rest again until I was within two days of Rome.

For eighteen hours I lived the sybaritic life and enjoyed every minute of it. I washed and dried out all my clothes, including the sleeping bag, and started on the last 20 kilometres to Vézelay at 9.30 a.m. Although it was the hottest day so far, I was now walking easily along tracks and side-roads through the most beautiful country and I did not tire until I was within a few kilometres of Vézelay. I called in at a café, where I sat with a group of French holidaymakers, who included in their number an earnest student of psychology with a sharp eye for any manifestation of abnormal behaviour. I was obviously an answer to prayer, walking in mid-afternoon on the hottest day of a very hot summer with a 15.5 kilo pack on my back. After plying me with preliminary questions, she moved into the diagnosis. 'And are you walking alone?' 'Yes,' I said. 'Perhaps Monsieur prefers being alone to being with people,' she suggested hopefully. 'No, I enjoy both being alone and being with people.' A shadow of disappointment swept across her face, but she was a determined student. 'I see,' she said after a pause, 'when you are alone you want to be with people, and when you are with people you want to be alone.' 'That is partly true,' I replied, 'solitude helps me to appreciate company and company helps me to appreciate solitude, but there's a time for speaking and a time for being silent.' She looked puzzled and disappointed and I was dismissed with a curt 'Bon Voyage'.

Gerard Hughes, *In Search of a Way: Two Journeys of Spiritual Discovery* (1994), p. 83

In 1987, I joined the group of pilgrims from the parish church of San Ramon, in the town of that name which is the centre of the canton.

They were setting out for the sanctuary in Barrio Los Angeles six kilometres away, carrying with them the parish church's image of the Virgin of the Angels. Following the announcement of a communal intention for the pilgrimage of prayer for peace, the group walked along a customary route through outlying settlements and past fields of cardomom, sugarcane, coffee, bananas, and corn. People prayed and sang hymns the entire way except when climbing the final – and steepest – hill, at which time they were asked to meditate in silence. Some participants paused *en route* to buy refreshments, but the group as a whole did not stop until it reached its destination where pilgrims who had come, unaccompanied by any image, from approximately twenty-three other settlements in the canton, were waiting.

Leslie Ellen Straub, 'Formal Replication in Costa Rican Pilgrimages', *Social Anthropology of Pilgrimage*, ed. Makhan Jha (1991), p. 279

Our conductor organized his passengers, placing fat ones like myself next to slender ones and vice versa, and making sure that the parish priest had a seat to himself, if possible. Then came last-minute recommendations and requests from a long queue of housewives and others who clustered around the door chattering volubly, while the woman at the head of the queue gave her recommendations to the collector mostly by word of mouth. The sallow-faced *cobrador* had to commit these to memory: six yards of suiting, four dozen coat and trouser buttons, a key of pure alcohol, a pestle and mortar, five packets of shampoo powders and so on, not to mention the man with guns who handed him a hare and a few brace of partridge to sell on the way. When I expressed my admiration of his powers of resistance and his memory he answered resignedly: 'One has to be a jack-of-all-trades, Señor, and possess, besides, a good dose of patience and sympathy, especially for the *novias*, who hand me their love-letters; I have to deliver them personally to the *novios*, and on my return deliver the answer orally to the girls, as their parents generally won't allow them to receive letters from boyfriends. More complicated are the business messages I have to carry for farmers in the village and for lawyers, scrawled in pencil on bits of paper that the devil himself could not make out. The trouble never ends, but, as they say, patience and shuffle the cards; 'tis a good job and enables me to see the world and I'd sooner brave it than be quill-driving in an office.'

Walter Starkie, *The Road to Santiago* (1957), p.153

A young pilgrim at Rocamadour:

> Here you feel that the pilgrim people are on their way to the
> promised land: two hundred young people, who only yesterday
> were strangers to each other, are about to pray together and to
> share what constitutes their life. Together, they'll feel joyful in
> Jesus Christ. Here we shed our prejudices; friendship and
> esteem are born of this new view of life. Hands stretch out to
> each other; the guitars sing of hope, joy, reconciliation. Like
> Jesus, we've walked all the way; we've dropped our masks and
> discovered truth. Tomorrow we'll build a Church open to
> everyone. That's what the pilgrimage is about.
>
> Jean-Jacques Antier, 'Pilgrimages in France: Religious Tourism or
> Faith in Action?', *Lumen Vitae* 39 (1984): pp. 376–7

The crowds of young people who have been coming for years to the hill
of Taizé are very diverse. Nevertheless, they are, for the most part, char-
acterized by two main features: the search for the meaning of their life,
in silence and contemplation; and the concern to share their spiritual and
material goods, especially with the most deprived. *Prayer and sharing*:
these two main axes of faith are precisely the values which the pilgrimage
strongly emphasizes. So in summoning the young to a world pilgrimage
of reconciliation, we are doing nothing new. Rather we are enlarging to
the scale of God's people the experience which many are already living,
and have been living for years. To go out to one another, beyond the
barriers which usually separate us, and to go forth together to encounter
God in prayer – is this not the true meaning of the Christian pilgrimage?

Our word 'parish' comes from the Greek *paraikos*, which means
precisely 'pilgrim, passing stranger'. Is not every Church, in fact,
called to be the 'pilgrim's house', centred on prayer and sharing, a
place of welcome and communion for everyone? In so far as she fulfils
that vocation, keeping nothing for herself but living, in the image of
her Lord, as the servant of universal reconciliation, the Church gives
us a glimpse of the goal of the pilgrimage, the future city (Hebrews
13:14), already breaking into our present life.

> Brother John of Taizé, 'Pilgrimage Seen through the Bible',
> *Lumen Vitae* 39 (1984): 393

The thesis of this book is that Irish Christians are being called by God
to a new fellowship, a new *koinonia*, a pilgrimage together which will
unite Catholic and Protestant in a single witnessing, serving community.

It is not a pilgrimage which attempts to take shortcuts, to experience prematurely the fullness of communion which the churches are not yet ready to enter. But it *is* a breaking down of the enmity, a choosing of life, a step towards an island that works.

And this *koinonia* already exists.

We have looked at some of its manifestations, in interchurch groups of people who are committed to their churches, but also committed to each other, and to the quest for justice, for peace, for communion. Their numbers are not great and many Irish Christians know little about them. But they represent something *new* in the history of Ireland. For the first time since the Reformation, considerable numbers of Irish Christians from both traditions have come together in a series of interlinked groups committed to their faith and to their own traditions, yet looking to a common future and already enjoying a foretaste of what life in a 'complete' Ireland might be like.

Their *koinonia* is committed to common witness to the faith, not merely in their pursuit of justice and peace – though that is part of the witness – but in the proclamation of the good news of Jesus the Christ, and the sharing of the Messianic lifestyle with all those, outside or within the churches, who do not know it. They are not interested in proselytism, which they reject; but they are vitally concerned that more and more people should experience the fullness of a Christian life anchored in personal commitment to the Lord of the church. Committed to the proclamation of the liberating word, they share in the prophetic ministry of Christ.

They are committed to the unity of Christians, and long for the day when that unity will be expressed by common participation in the bread and wine of the eucharist. But meantime while firmly grounded in their own traditions, they share in each other's worship and prayer to the maximum possible extent. There are features of one another's traditions which they cannot accept. But they know that when they hear the Word read and preached, and when they attend each other's eucharists, it is the same Lord who is truly present to each of them. And so, already, they share in the same pilgrim lifestyle, looking to the future with hope because the present has enabled them to set each other free. Committed to the liturgical and corporate life of the church, they share in the priestly ministry of Christ.

Robin Boyd, *Ireland: Christianity Discredited or Pilgrim's Progress?* (1988),
pp. 124–6

I met an elderly man, Burgos, who was one of the founders of the pilgrimage and has never missed one since. He has a venerable white beard, his eyes are sunken. 'They'll have to bury me on that road,' he says. Now a group of children has come, about fifty of them, as an advanced guard. And, in summary, I have seen in this pilgrimage the only possible classless society. The industrialist, the merchant, the professional man, beside the Indian, next to the worker. On the road, they walk, suffer, and pray together. In the inns, they throw themselves down side by side on the same piece of ground. And even their dress is the same.

'Fifty Years of Guadalupan Pilgrimage', cited in Victor and Edith Turner,
Image and Pilgrimage in Christian Culture (1978), p. 97

Once initiated into the 'order' of pilgrims, he signified his attachment to a new way of life by wearing a uniform, as distinctive in its own way as the tonsure of a priest. 'When the debts be thus paid and the meine is thus set in governance,' continued Richard Alkerton in 1406, 'the pilgrim shall array himself. And then he oweth first to make himself be marked with a cross, as men be wont to do that shall pass to the Holy Land...Afterwards the pilgrim shall have a staff, a sclavein, and a scrip.' The staff, a tough wooden stick with a metal toe, was most distinctive as well as the most useful part of the pilgrim's attire. The 'sclavein' was a long coarse tunic. The scrip was a soft pouch, usually made of leather, strapped to the pilgrim's waist; in it he kept his food, mess-cans, and money. Such was the attire of every serious pilgrim after the end of the eleventh century. Much later, probably in the middle of the thirteenth century, pilgrims began to wear a great broad-brimmed hat, turned up at the front, and attached at the back to a long scarf which was wound round the body as far as the waist.

The origin of this curious garb is not at all clear. The staff and pouch were used by the migrant monks of Egypt in the fourth century, but they were obvious and sensible accessories for any traveller on foot, not only for pilgrims and not only in the Middle Ages. The tunic, on the other hand, whose practical usefulness is not as readily apparent, seems to make its first appearance at the beginning of the twelfth century. Canute, setting out for Rome in 1027, 'took up his scrip and staff as did all his companions', but there is no mention of the tunic. St Anselm, in 1097, 'took a scrip and staff like a pilgrim', but again, no tunic. Orderic Vitalis, writing in about 1135, said that he could remember a time when pilgrims were indistinguishable from other travellers, except by their unshaven faces. Indeed it is probably about this time that the normal clothing of the traveller took on a sudden rigidity and became peculiarly the garb of the spiritual traveller.

Jonathan Sumption, *Pilgrimage – An Image of Medieval Religion*
(1975), pp. 171–2

LUKE: Dwell with us, sir, if ye might,
For now it grows towards the night,
The day is gone that was so bright,
    Let rest prevail:
Meat and drink is but your right
    For thy good tale.

JESUS: I thank you both for this good cheer,
At this time I may not dwell here,
My way to walk is still severe,
    Where I must tread:
I cannot bide so near,
    As ye have said.

CLEOPAS: Now, as I hope no more to smart,
At this time we shall not part,
Unless you thrust us through your art
    Further away:
Unto the city with good heart,
    Now wend our way.

LUKE: Thou art a pilgrim, as we are,
This night thou fare as we fare,
Be it less or be it more
    Thou shall assay:
Then tomorrow thou prepare
    To wend thy way.

JESUS: I will abide with you awhile.

CLEOPAS: Sir, ye are welcome, though small our skill,
Such as we have lacks any guile.

The Pilgrims, from *The Wakefield Mystery Plays*, ed. Martial Rose (1961), pp. 409–10

Let all guests that come be received like Christ, for he will say: 'I was a stranger and ye took me in.' And let fitting honour be shown to all, but especially to...pilgrims. As soon, therefore, as a guest is announced, let the superior or some brethren meet him with all charitable service. And first of all let them pray together, and let them unite in the kiss of peace. This kiss of peace shall not be offered until after the prayers have been said, on account of the delusions of the Devil. In the greeting of all guests, whether they be arriving or departing, let the greatest humility be shown. Let the head be bowed or the whole body prostrated on the ground, and so let Christ be worshipped in them, for indeed he is received in their persons...

The Rule of St Benedict, quoted in G. R. Evans & J. R. Wright,
The Anglican Tradition: A Handbook of Sources (1991), p. 76

Popes and secular rulers early realized their duty to organize pilgrim roads and erect hostels and to ensure, as far as possible, the safety of the pilgrims. In Rome, for example, Pope Symmachus concerned himself with pilgrim safety as early as the sixth century and the famous Schola Saxonum was in existence in the eighth century. In the sixteenth century the staggering influx of Holy Year pilgrims in the city of Rome prompted St Philip Neri's work there. On the most dangerous parts of the journey refuges were built: Novalesa (on the road through the Mont-Cenis Pass) was encouraged by Emperor Louis the Pious (825); and Roncesvalles, a hostel for pilgrims to Compostela, was perhaps the most renowned of all such hospices and was showered with favours by the kings of Navarre. Certain orders were created expressly to aid pilgrims, such as the Knights of St James in Spain, the Knights Templars, and the Knights of Malta, who were initially intended to aid poor, unarmed, and sick pilgrims. The seal of the Templars bore the figure of a knight aiding a *pauper et peregrinus*. From the thirteenth century there appeared all over Christendom a great number of confraternities whose aim was to assist pilgrims. One of the most famous of these was that of Altopascio founded in Tuscany. Its influence in Paris is marked by its church of Saint-Jacques 'du Haut-Pas', at the starting point of the Paris stage on the road to Compostela. A shrine-city like Lourdes today, or the hostels for pilgrims (in the widest sense of the word) founded in Chartres or Vézelay by Pax Christi, are modern extensions of the efforts and the spirit of the medieval hospitallers.

'Pilgrimages', *New Catholic Encyclopedia* (1967)

Arrangements were made for the comfort of this throng of pilgrims. They brought with them introductions, and were received on the way in the Bishop's houses, in monasteries and in guesthouses. Pope Symmachus (498–514) had established three hospices in Rome, at St Peter's, St Paul's and St Laurence's; and Belisarius, the general of Justinian, built and magnificently endowed a hospice in the Via Lata. In the time of Charlemagne there was a special guest-house for the Franks, the Schola Francorum; and other little national colonies were formed – Saxons, Frisians, Lombards – in the precincts of St Peter's. Here also were two great fountains for the pilgrims to wash in, stalls at which to buy food and 'objects of piety', and a place under the arcades of the Atrium where, from the earliest days, the poor were fed on the feast day of St Peter.

Ansa, wife of the Lombard king Desiderius, built a hospice about 740 on Mount Garganus, on the Adriatic. Paul the Deacon put up an inscription on it:

Go on thy way safely, pilgrim from the western shores, who seekest the temple of blessed Peter and the rock of Garganus and the blessed cavern. Safe under his protection thou shalt not fear the robber's dagger, nor cold nor storm in the dark night: the queen has provided you with spacious shelter and with refreshment.

Ethel Ross-Barker, *Rome of the Pilgrims and Martyrs* (1913), pp. 25–6

The rich put up at abbeys as honoured guests or at inns where, as one traveller commented, one should take care 'for love of the fleas, that they may not leap on your legs, for there is a peck of them lying in the dust under the rushes...'

Monasteries provided hospitality and charity to poor pilgrims who could not afford inns; this charitable work was an accepted routine as well at hospitals, episcopal households and other ecclesiastical establishments. These institutions of the Church were reinforced by the Christian virtue of charity practised by laymen. One well-off family put up twenty of Becket's pilgrims at a time, a Norwich tanner supported a blind man in his house along with many others too poor to fend for themselves and a baker at Canterbury cared for poor and sick pilgrims for the sake of Christ. Wealthy Lincoln citizens supported destitute pilgrims and when one was cured at St Hugh's shrine his benefactors were fetched to witness the cure of their protégé. Not all private charity was voluntary; when her washerwoman became crippled the lady of a village near Arundel Castle ordered some of her peasants to shelter and care for her. Private charity might not go on indefinitely: Samson cared for a paralysed man for a year but when he could no longer afford him he had him taken to the city gate – at Old Sarum, which can be a bitterly cold and windy place during the winter – where the ill usually lay; here the sick man remained another year until St Osmund cured him.

Ronald Finucane, *Miracles and Pilgrims* (1977), p. 47

Few pilgrims travelled alone after the eleventh century, whatever their destination. The growing popularity of pilgrimages made it easy to find companions. Indeed, on the busy roads to Rome and Santiago it was impossible to avoid them. Pilgrims were exhorted to choose their friends with care, for there were regular reports of travellers killed or robbed by their companions. Particularly notorious was the stretch of road to Santiago which ran from Saintes to the Pyrenees. Here, theft was a well-organized industry. In one incident a blind man was robbed by his companions of his money, his horse, and all his luggage, and left without a guide at the side of the road. The 'companions' were of course professional thieves of the sort described in the *Liber Sancti Jacobi*, who dressed as pilgrims or priests in order to gain the confidence of their victims. 'Take care, then, not to join up with bad companions,' warned the French jurist Beaumanoir, after telling of a pilgrim who was hanged as a felon on being found in the company of thieves; 'for however pleasant they appear, you never know what evil will befall you.'

Jonathan Sumption, *Pilgrimage – An Image of Medieval Religion* (1975), pp. 196–7

You must choose good company – that is, the holy devout community, where you participate in so many advantages, and where especially you are with holy lovers of God, by whom God is most loved and honoured, and from whom you feel that you receive the greatest help, and through whom your heart is most united and elevated in God, and whose words and society most draw you and advance you toward God. But with these persons shun your repose and the inclination of your senses. And closely observe, with regard either to myself or to others in whom you seek sincere practice of virtue, who they are that help you to improve, and consider what their life is. For there are all too few on earth today in whom you can find true fidelity: for almost all people now want from God and men what pleases them and what they desire or lack.

Mother Columba Hart, trans., *Hadewijch: The Complete Works* (1980), pp. 78–9

Sources tell of mob scenes at many medieval shrines, especially on certain dates (e.g. Holy Saturday at the Holy Sepulchre), with everyone wanting to be the first to reach the holy places; many were trampled in crowds carried away by misguided eagerness. The figures given by medieval sources seem astonishing; yet modern statistics tend to corroborate the huge numbers involved in pilgrimage statistics. Villani states that, during the first Holy year in 1300 Rome had a steady 200,000 inhabitants above normal. 100,000 pilgrims are said to have congregated in Turin for the first solemn exhibition of the Holy Shroud in 1512. But then there were 300,000 pilgrims in Puy in 1853, close to 160,000 in Aachen in 1881, and at least 1,200,000 in Kiev in 1886 (the railroad had opened that year). Einsiedeln had 150,000 pilgrims a year at the beginning of the twentieth century. Lourdes had 8,000,000 in 1958, the centenary of the apparitions. The initial number of pilgrims in Lisieux (St Thérèse Lisieux) still exceeds 1,000,000. In India a

week-long exposition of the arm of St Francis Xavier in Goa attracted
several million pilgrims who, incidentally were not all Christians.

'Pilgrimages', *New Catholic Encyclopedia* (1967)

This upswing in popularity climaxed in the wake of a series of children's pilgrimages to the site in 1475. Reminiscent of similar events,
especially the notorious juvenile processions of Mont-Saint-Michel
that had commenced from South Germany in 1456, these journeys to
Wilsnack were criticized for their disruptiveness. Groups of youths
making their way along the route to the shrine were greeted alternately
with horror and enthusiasm. Even as town authorities tried to force
the children to disband and return home, others interpreted the processions as a sign of divine grace and aided the participants. By the
summer of 1475, the traffic to the shrine was thick, as hundreds of
peasants, vagabonds, and day workers joined the youthful bands. At
towns along the way, late medieval chroniclers tell us, the processions
were often greeted as a kind of plague. At Erfurt, for example, the
town locked its gates to the approaching pilgrims, refusing to fulfill
the traditional Christian duty of providing the travellers with food and
lodging. Yet even though the town council prohibited its own youth
from joining the processions, one chronicler recorded that 310 children left the city.

Despite the hyperbole that marked the written accounts, it must be
admitted that events like these would be bound to result in a degree of
chaos. As the ranks of faithful making their way to a shrine suddenly
swelled, they passed through towns and villages ill prepared to provide
food and accommodation. Yet an increase in poverty and the landless
was also beginning to afflict Germany in the late fifteenth century. In
discussing Wilsnack and other mass pilgrimages, commentators sometimes linked the surge in these cults' popularity with the generally
hard economic times. Referring to the pilgrim as 'common people' or
'the poor', chroniclers drew explicit connections among bad harvests,
dearth, and the episodic outbreak of 'pilgrimage' fever ...Wilsnack
provided for many a way of earning a living through begging on the
pious journey. We will never know for certain how widespread such a
practice was, yet begging remained a widely respected act of ascetic
devotion in late medieval Germany. Certainly, not all who begged
along the route to Wilsnack did so because of need. As a sign of apostolic poverty, the begging of alms remained a sacrificial act that many
believed made their journeys more pleasing in the eyes of God.

Phillip Soerfgel, *Wondrous In His Saints: Counter Reformation
Propaganda in Bavaria* (1993), p. 47

One of the most extraordinary features of the Middle Ages, and the direct outcome of pilgrimages, were the wandering bands of penitents. These companies were numbered by hundreds, and each of them possessed some individual characteristic. Some were composed of the poor only, others were limited to men, while one or two were made up entirely of children. Occasionally a brotherhood would arise with membership extended mainly to those who held peculiar opinions. The great majority, however, were free to all Christians without distinction of age, sex, rank, or opinion, though each of them had some particular form of discipline for their adherents.

Thus every now and then these bands of people would journey from shrine to shrine, praying and mortifying as they went, and gathering recruits along the way. After exciting interest for a short time the larger number of these associations would dissolve as suddenly as they appeared; a few survived for years, while one or two underwent periodical revivals down to comparatively recent times.

The most persistent of these bands of fanatics were the dancers, the palmers, and the flagellants.

The dancers made their first appearance at Aix-la-Chapelle in 1373, when they were composed of a ragged set of wanderers who made begging and vagrancy a profession. They had a secret system of initiation, they practised all kinds of abominations. Wandering about in bands of thirty or forty, their apparent poverty, their earnestness, and their frantic fanaticism gave them an extraordinary hold on the multitude.

Wherever they went their singular reputation caused large crowds to assemble to watch their performances, and thousands who went as sightseers became infected by the mania, which came to be regarded in the nature of a contagious disease that was even more dreaded than the plague.

Everywhere the dancers became the centre of a writhing mass of humanity making violent motions of worship, offering prayers in the form of convulsive shrieks, and acting as though they would take heaven itself by storm. Their hysterical ravings were regarded as prophetic. It was quite in vain that the axe beheaded hundreds of these maniacs, or that the gibbets broke down with the weight of their bodies.

Sidney Heath, *Pilgrim Life in the Middle Ages* (1911), p. 96

I have seen them in Latin America, travelling in impossible conditions, their feet torn and bleeding, their eyes bruised with fatigue like those of miners emerging from the coal pit, dazzled, haggard but radiant at the long-awaited sight of daylight.

In Europe I have come across them at Lisieux, Sainte-Anne d'Auray, Lourdes, Montserrat and Banneux, and though their travelling conditions are less daunting, they, too, return every year like migratory birds, flocking to the shrines, the pilgrimage centres, which they still visit in thousands, even in this secularized age.

Anne Dumoulin, 'Towards a Psychological Understanding of the Pilgrim', *Lumen Vitae* 32 (1977): 108

Today Lough Derg attracts more pilgrims than ever before. They come in thousands all through the period when the island is open, June 1st to August 15th, in special trains and buses and in their own cars, which crowd the new car park cut in the moor by the lake side. The medieval pilgrimage lasted a month, but the time spent on the island has steadily decreased, first to six days when the pilgrimage became popular rather than visionary and for the few; then in 1813 to the present three-day routine. The penitential standards of the early Church have however been maintained, as nowhere else in Europe.

Daphne Pochin Mould, *Irish Pilgrimage* (1955), p. 121

The pilgrims returned to Santiago in goodly numbers – not quite like the good old days, but still impressive. During the special pilgrimage of 1971 when the saint's day of 25 July fell on a Sunday (that occasions a special holy year), three million people visited the shrine. Despite Santiago's being, as Kendrick puts it 'a very satisfactory bit of history', the pilgrims continue to pray at St James's shrine. It is lavishly appointed as only the Spanish manage so well. The high altar is of alabaster, jasper and silver, and encloses a statue of the seated apostle, James. This is the goal of the pilgrim, the end of the journey. The statue has been rather cynically described by Richard Ford in his noteworthy 1845 guidebook: 'The face is painted – the expression is cubby and commonplace, with a bottle-nose and small twinkling eyes, more like a pursy minor canon than a captain-general, a destroyer of sixty thousand Moors at one time.'

Never mind, a costly silver cape set with diamonds and other gems now almost completely covers the figure. Across a flight of stairs the pilgrim passes behind the statue and embraces it. This is the high point of the pilgrimage to Santiago, and one who ascends those stairs has joined an impressive number.

David Sox, *Relics and Shrines* (1985), p. 191

Regardless of distance, there is an important difference between pilgrimage perceived as an individual act and pilgrimage undertaken as a corporate enterprise. In the former case...the relationship between a pilgrim and the holy person to whom the shrine is dedicated is a highly personal 'I/Thou' association. The timing of the journey is not necessarily determined by any special day or activity at the shrine, and the group with which the pilgrim chooses to travel is not directly related to the purpose or meaning of the pilgrimage.

Communal pilgrimage, in contrast, is essentially a 'We/Thou' relationship. Health and salvation from catastrophe may lie at the roots, but it is the community rather than the individual that seeks protection or pays homage. Pilgrims approach the shrine in an act of corporate thanks for salvation from plague, war, natural disaster, or as a community act of tribute and devotion. In difficult times they ask for deliverance, not solely as individuals, but for a community which they see as an extension beyond the span of their personal lives. The sense of community underlies many pilgrimages and inspires individual participation even in a modern age.

There are long-distance pilgrimages in which the devotees travel more as members of a corporate body than as individuals. The pilgrims may represent a particular community such as a diocese, a village, an urban neighbourhood, or the congregation of a parish church. Each pilgrim may have personal reasons for making the journey, but all share the collective view that their shrine visit will benefit the entire community. For example, participants in the fiftieth anniversary pilgrimage from Liverpool to Lourdes, whom we encountered in 1980, said that the primary purpose of their journey was to affirm a special relationship between their English city and the French shrine, although some individuals in the group expressed personal reasons for joining that particular annual delegation.

Sidney & Mary Lee Nolan, *Christian Pilgrimage in Modern Western Europe* (1989), p. 38

With the opening of the Suez Canal in 1869, a further impetus was given to travel in the Near East and that in fact was the very year that Thomas Cook led his first party to Jerusalem...

In 1867 he made a preliminary sortie to the eastern Mediterranean but did not actually go as far as Jerusalem. The following year he planned a full-scale organized tour to set out just before Christmas but then decided to postpone it in the hope that congregations might be encouraged to give their ministers extra large Christmas boxes to enable them to afford the journey. 'It would be a glorious thing for all ministers and students of divinity to visit the lands from which they draw so much of their pulpit inspirations.'

Then in the Spring of 1869, fifty-two people formed his first party: sixteen ladies, thirty-three men, Cook himself and two assistants. They divided into two groups, one starting from Beyrouth and the other from Jaffa. When it is recalled that by the turn of the century, only thirty-one years later, Thomas Cook and Son had enabled some twelve thousand people to visit the Holy Land, then the firm's contribution to the re-emergence of Protestant pilgrimage cannot be overestimated.

John Davies, *Pilgrimage Yesterday and Today* (1988), pp. 147–8

So what of today, the age of cynicism, video games and easy transport? Has the golden thread of pilgrimage been broken? Far from it. While the line between tourism and pilgrimage is still thin (is a quick visit to a local shrine during a fortnight's sunny holiday a pilgrimage?) we still have that ancient need to take to the road, to seek out the sacred. Every year over 10,000 go to Santiago de Compostela as accredited pilgrims, walking, biking or riding, while another one and a half million arrive in coaches and cars. In 1992 five and a half million people travelled to Lourdes and Walsingham receives 20,000 in organized groups alone, not to mention those who come unannounced. At its peak Medjugorje received 80,000 pilgrims every day and pilgrims flock to Fatima, San Giovanni, Croagh Patrick, Lough Derg, Knock as well as to communities like those founded on Iona or at Taizé. Yet this enthusiasm is not reflected in regular churchgoing. It is almost as if pilgrimage becomes even more popular as churchgoing declines; as if pilgrimage meets today's spiritual needs in a way more formal churchgoing does not.

Shirley du Boulay, *The Road to Canterbury* (1994), p. 85

We have a choice, if we wish to know God, between learning from the friends of God and learning from the common notion. I would choose to learn from the friends of God. The common notion is a way of interpreting whatever happens, but it does not seem to arise out of any actual communication between God and man. The friends of God, on the contrary, walk and speak with God, experience a love that is 'from God and of God and towards God'. The to-and-fro with God in which they live seems to be the only real knowing of God that man has reached. To actually know God ourselves we will have to enter ourselves into the to-and-fro. Maybe from that vantage point we may be able to see the common notion in a new light. It too has to do with experiences: floods, storms, earthquakes, afflictions, and if in fact everything that happens whatsoever.

John Dunne, *The Reasons of the Heart* (1978), p. 2

'...it's primarily a religious book. In a way, I suppose you could say it's terribly fanatical, but in a way it isn't. I mean it starts out with this peasant – the pilgrim – wanting to find out what it means in the Bible when it says you should pray incessantly. And what you should say if you do...All he carries with him is this knapsack filled with bread and salt. Then he meets this person called a starets – some sort of terribly advanced religious person – and the starets tells him about a book called the 'Philokalia'. Which apparently was written by a group of terribly advanced monks who sort of advocated this really incredible method of praying.

'...Anyway, so the pilgrim learns how to pray the way these very mystical persons say you should – I mean he keeps at it till he's perfected it and everything. Then he goes on walking all over Russia, meeting all kinds of absolutely marvellous people and telling them how to pray by this incredible method. I mean that's really the whole book.'

J. D. Salinger, *Franny and Zooey* (1964), pp. 31–2

Anyone could join a confraternity – man, woman, priest – who could produce proof that they had actually been to Santiago de Compostela. To aid pilgrims in this respect (as well as to encourage further business) the canons of the cathedral in Santiago from the fourteenth century took to issuing a certificate to arrivals. This was called a *Compostela*.

Edwin Mullins, *The Pilgrimage to Santiago* (1974), p. 20

Chapter Five

A HARD ROAD

There is almost an expectation that a pilgrimage needs to contain a challenging physical ingredient in order for it to be a pilgrimage at all. It is as if the physicality of the experience is part of the defining experience of a pilgrimage. Without the hardship, a journey, even if undertaken for spiritual motives, comes much closer to a holiday or outing. So, in a strange way, the pilgrim rejoices in the dangers, difficulties and hardships. The toil of the journey enables the pilgrim to identify with the sufferings of Christ.

There seems also to be a strange relationship between the spiritual and the physical. To challenge the physical dimension, by denying the usual tendency to indulge the needs or desires of the body, can allow the spiritual space in which to grow. Clearly there is not an inevitable connection between hardship and spiritual growth but the growth of the spirit can come in such a way. Christians sometimes refer to this connection as the mortification of the flesh.

The same kind of idea lies behind the concept of penance. At one level it would seem ridiculous for the creator of the universe to require a truly repentant person to undergo physical hardship. Yet the spiritual does not always operate at the purely cerebral level. The experience of physical hardship and even pain can be therapeutic from a psychological and spiritual perspective. Many of those who go on pilgrimage embrace the hardships as a legitimate part of the experience and not merely as an inconvenience. Thus for some, the physical encounter is at least in part a matter of penance. For many it is a stimulus towards spiritual growth.

As they were walking along the road, a man said to him, 'I will follow you wherever you go.' Jesus replied, 'Foxes have holes and birds of the air have nests, but the Son of Man has no place to lay his head.'

Luke 9:57–58

The *Guide for Pilgrims to Santiago* catalogues the full range of catastrophes which could overcome the traveller on the roads in the twelfth century. It is both a historical guide and a route-book, offering its readers information about towns and hospices, a few useful words of the Basque language, an architectural description of Santiago cathedral, and precise directions on how to get there. The pilgrim is warned that the eight-mile ascent to the Port de Cize, the principal pass over the Pyrenees, is a steep climb; that in Galicia there are thick forests and few towns; that mosquitoes infest the marshy plain south of Bordeaux where the traveller who strays from the road can sink up to his knees in mud. Some of the rivers are impassable. Several pilgrims had been drowned at Sorde, where travellers with horses were ferried across the river on hollowed-out tree trunks. Other rivers were undrinkable, like the salt stream at Lorca, where the author of the Guide found two Basques earning their living by skinning the horses who had died after drinking from it. Pilgrims were in theory exempt from the payment of tolls, but nevertheless the Guide reports that the local lords exacted payment from every traveller in the Béarn. At the foot of the Port de Cize, pilgrims were searched and beaten with sticks if they could not pay the toll. The author demanded immediate action by the bishop and the king of Aragon, but it was more than half a century before the extortionists suffered retribution at the hands of Richard Cœur de Lion.

   Jonathan Sumption, *Pilgrimage – An Image of Medieval Religion* (1975), p. 177

Of course, certain individuals fared less fortunately; and sometimes they were in part to blame. The wearing of green, the colour sacred to descendants of the Prophet, was always disastrous. Biddulph saw a Christian's shoes removed in the street because they were tied with green shoe-strings, and another, 'wearing green Breeches under his Gowne (being espied) had his Breeches cut off, and he was reviled and beaten'.

   Wilfred Blunt, *Pietro's Pilgrimage* (1953), p. 96

A long journey in the Middle Ages was not a thing to be lightly undertaken...The condition of the roads was the first obstacle. Europe relied throughout the Middle Ages on the networks of roads bequeathed to it by the Roman Empire. This network was far from comprehensive, but new roads did appear from time to time in response to changing needs. Thus the Roman road from Lyon to the south-west was diverted in the eleventh century through the hard granite mountains of the Ségalas to take it past the abbey of Conques; when the pilgrimage of Conques was forgotten, in the fourteenth century, travellers returned to the old road. In France, the roads were never allowed to fall into complete disrepair, as they were in parts of England. Nevertheless travel was not easy and even an experienced rider could not expect to cover more than thirty miles in a day. The Seigneur de Caumont, who rode from Caumont to Santiago in 1418, was reduced to six miles a day in the Pyrenees and the Asturias, but he was capable of doing twenty-seven when the terrain was good.

Jonathan Sumption, *Pilgrimage – An Image of Medieval Religion* (1975), p. 175

He [the old pilgrim] was dressed in a rough unbleached habit and walked bare-foot: by his side was his long staff and his broad-brimmed hat with the traditional shell. He remained for a long time absorbed in prayer, murmuring ejaculations in a voice that echoed through the silent church. When he rose to leave I followed him and asked him whether he, too, was on his way to Compostela.

'Yes, I am,' he answered, 'but I hope my two feet will carry me there, for I'm getting old and feeble and there are days when rheumatic pains pierce me like knives.'

…The old man was so much the embodiment of the medieval pilgrim with his habit, his broad hat, his long staff and bare feet that I felt ashamed of my modern clothes and my well-shod feet.

Walter Starkie, *The Road to Santiago* (1957), p. 231

Walking completely barefoot, clothed in a simple tunic, and with scarcely a penny on them, he and his companions set out for Rome rich in the abundance of their poverty. They rode on horseback rarely or never, and used their mule only to help weak and infirm pilgrims whom they met on the road.

Sulpicius Severus, *Dialogi*, cited in Jonathan Sumption,
Pilgrimage – An Image of Medieval Religion (1975), p. 127

At that time when the sky rapidly bends
Toward the west, and our day starts to fly
Beyond, to people who wait for the sun,
Feeling in distant lands alone and dry,
The tired old woman to her journey lends
A doubled step, and hurries, hurries on;
And as she is, alone,

At the end of her day
Sometimes is glad to stay
A little while, and rest and so forget
The pain by which her past road was beset.

Petrarch (1304–74), 'Rima Sparse No. 50',
Petrarch: Sonnets and Songs, trans. A. Armi (1968), p. 77

May God give those who call this pilgrimage an easy exercise the power of feeling its sorrows, that they may learn to have the compassion for pilgrims to the Holy Land which they deserve. It requires courage and audacity to attempt this pilgrimage. That many are prompted to it by sinful and idle curiosity cannot be doubted; but to reach the holy places and to return to one's home active and well is the especial gift of God.

No one should think visiting the holy places to be a light task; there is the intense heat of the sun, the walking from place to place, kneeling and prostration; above all there is the strain which everyone puts on himself striving with all his might to rouse himself in earnest piety and comprehension of what is shown him in the holy places, and to devout prayer and meditation, all which cannot be done without great fatigue, because to do them fitly a man should be at rest and not walking about. To struggle after mental abstraction whilst bodily walking from place to place is exceedingly toilsome.

Felix Fabri, The Wanderings of Felix Fabri, cited in John Davies,
Pilgrimage Yesterday and Today (1988), pp. 73–4

'A cold coming we had of it,
Just the worst time of the year
For a journey, and such a long journey:
The ways deep and the weather sharp,
The very dead of winter.'
And the camels galled, sore-footed, refractory,
Lying down in the melting snow.
There were times we regretted
The summer palaces on slopes, the terraces,
And the silken girls bringing sherbet.
Then the camel men cursing and grumbling
And running away, and wanting their liquor and women,
And the night-fires going out, and the lack of shelters,
And the cities hostile and the towns unfriendly
And the villages dirty and charging high prices:

A hard time we had of it.
At the end we preferred to travel at night,
Sleeping in snatches,
With the voices singing in our ears, saying
That this was all folly.

T. S. Eliot, 'Journey of the Magi',
The Complete Poems and Plays of T. S. Eliot (1969), p. 103

Pietro had set his heart upon climbing Jebel Katherin [Sinai]; he saw with dismay that the fine weather seemed to be breaking. His fears were realized, for after a sleepless night he rose to find the ground white, with every sign of more snow to come. The guide now flatly refused to take part in so foolhardy an enterprise, and his pessimism soon infected the rest of the party.

Wilfred Blunt, *Pietro's Pilgrimage* (1953), p. 65

Forgive my not writing. I have been on the Mons Jovis: on the one hand looking up to the heavens of the mountains, on the other shuddering at the hell of the valleys; feeling myself so much nearer to heaven that I was the more assured that my prayer would be heard. 'Lord,' I said, 'restore me to my brethren, that I may tell them not to come to this place of torment.' Place of torment it is indeed, where the marble pavement of the rocky ground is ice, and you cannot safely set a foot down; where, strange to say, though it is so slippery that you cannot stand, the death into which you are given every facility to fall, is certain death. I put my hand on my scrip to scratch out a word or two to your sincerity, behold I found my ink bottle filled with a dry mass of ice. My fingers refused to write, my beard was stiff with frost, and my breath congealed in a long icicle. I could not write.

John of Canterbury, *Epistolae Cantuarienses*, cited in John Davies,
Pilgrimage Yesterday and Today (1988), p.47

Prayers for peace throughout all Ireland were offered at Masses on the summit of Croagh Patrick on Sunday when about 40,000 people – many in their bare feet – made the annual national pilgrimage. Dry shale, after the recent fine weather, squally showers that fell from dawn, and a slippery descent, made the pilgrimage this year particularly hazardous on the three and a half mile climb of the 2,510 ft mountain...There were 15 accident victims, and six cases were

detained at the Co. Mayo Hospital, Castlebar. All were carried down
on stretchers by the Knights of Malta.

Connaught Telegraph, 3 August 1972, cited in J. Preston, ed., *Mother Worship*
(1982), p. 149

There was a time when I was walking out of town at sunset and a
well-to-do couple in a big house called me over. They had read about
my pilgrimage and felt it was their Christian duty to warn me that
ahead on the way lay a very wicked place called 'South of the Border'.
They just wanted to warn me not to go near that place. They did not
offer food or shelter, however, so I walked on for several hours.

It was a very dark night with a heavy cloud cover and all of a sudden it started to rain. Big drops were coming down, and I was carrying a lot of unanswered mail. I looked for a place where there might
be a shelter and nearby I saw a combination gas station, restaurant and
motel. I ducked under the roof over the gas pumps and started to put
the unanswered mail into the front of my tunic so it wouldn't get wet.
The man from the gas station came running out and said, 'Don't stand
out there is the rain, come into the restaurant.' The man in the restaurant said, 'Oh, we read all about you, and we would like to offer you a
dinner or anything you want.' By that time I realized where I was. I
was in 'South of the Border'.

Peace Pilgrim, Her Life and Work in Her Own Words (1983), p. 45

We had a thorough storm, which obliged us to shut all close; the sea
breaking over the ship continually. I was at first afraid; but cried to
God, and was strengthened. Before ten I lay down: I bless God, without fear. About midnight we were awakened by a confused noise of
seas and wind and men's voices, the like to which I have never heard
before. The sound of the sea breaking over and against the sides of the
ship, I could compare to nothing but large cannon, or America's thun-
der. The rebounding, starting, quivering motion of the ship much
resembled what is said of earthquakes.

John Wesley (1703–91), 'The Heart of John Wesley's Journal',
in Anne Freemantle, *The Protestant Mystics* (1965), p. 143

The following curious law was enacted during the reign of Richard I
for the government of those going by sea to the Holy Land: 'He who
kills a man on shipboard shall be bound to the dead body and thrown
into the sea; if the man is killed on shore, the slayer shall be bound to

the dead body and buried with it. He who shall draw his knife and strike another, or who shall have drawn blood from him, to lose his hand; if he shall have only struck with the palm of his hand without drawing blood, he shall be thrice ducked in the sea.'

Sidney Heath, Pilgrim Life in the Middle Ages (1911), pp. 155–6

After a month at sea, the Negrona docked safely at Famagusta, Cyprus, where the governor disembarked. The plan was for the ship to continue on to Beirut, from whence the pilgrims could make their way overland to Jerusalem. But the plague was then raging in Beirut, so Ragazzoni, the ship's captain, aborted the voyage. The pilgrims had to disembark and make their way to Salinas (modern Larnaca) where they met the other, tardy, pilgrim ship. The captain, Jacopo Alberto, had determined that he would go no further with only thirteen pilgrims on board, but the arrival of the additional eight and the fees they were willing to pay for passage apparently changed his mind. The revenues were sufficient for him to allow Inigo free passage. They set sail on 19 August and came within view of Jaffa by the twenty-second. A storm kept them from landing, however, until 25 August. (*Vita* 44)

'Throughout this time,' Inigo recalled, 'our Lord appeared to him very often, which gave him much strength and consolation; but he thought that he saw something that was large and round, as though it were of gold. This kept appearing to him from the time he left Cyprus until they reached Jaffa.' (*Vita* 44)

William Meissner, Ignatius of Loyola: The Psychology of a Saint (1992), p. 113

It is terrible how boring the conversation generally is when people have to be so long together as we are now. Just as toothless old folk have to turn the food round and round in their mouths, so the same remark gets repeated over and over again, till the last one has to spit it out. There were four priests on board, and although the crossing lasted eight or nine hours (for me an eternity) the experienced travellers found it an unusually quick crossing. This gave each of the priests the opportunity first of all to remark that skippers in general disliked to have clergy on board because it brought contrary winds; but now the truth of this was now disproved.

Søren Kierkegaard (1813–1855), Søren Kierkegaard's Pilgrimage to Jutland,
trans. T. Croxall (1948), pp. 29–30

Hee onely can behold
    With unafrighted eyes
The horrours of the deepe,
    And terrours of the Skies.

Thus, scorning all the cares
    That fate, or fortune brings,
He makes the heav'n his booke,
    His wisedome heev'nly things,

Good thoughts his onely friendes,
    His wealth a well-spent age,
The earth his sober Inne,
    And quiet Pilgrimage.

Thomas Campion (1567–1620), *The Works of Thomas Campion*,
ed. W. Davies (1969), p. 43

Negotiations for passage to Venice were difficult. The ship owners were asking fifteen ducats per head. Inigo had no money, so his companions tried to persuade the owners to take him aboard for nothing. They refused, and other shipmasters were no more accommodating. Finally the pilgrims were able to contact the governor through a Franciscan friar at the convent of St John de Montfort, and he persuaded one of the shipmasters to lower the price of passage – and to allow Inigo free passage. They set sail on 1 November.

About the second day out, they ran into a terrible storm that forced them back to Salinas, on Cyprus. They set sail again on 12 November, were driven off course by a violent headwind, and reached Rhodes on 20 November. Because of the weather, they could not set out again until 27 November. Another fierce squall battered the ship. The pilgrims prayed together and made vows to St Roch, fearing that they were doomed to a watery grave. They struggled into a small Cretan port on 12 December. That winter was one of the most severe in the Mediterranean in living memory. The rest of the voyage they had to endure winter storms, heavy snow, and a hurricane that tore the mainsail. Through it all the vessel struggled on and finally made port at Parenzo. There they switched to a light bark that carried them to Venice, where they landed on 12 January, three and a half months after they had left Jaffa.

William Meissner, *Ignatius of Loyola: The Psychology of a Saint* (1992), pp. 116–7

The outward voyage was for those days uneventful. Twice, admittedly, the galleon was in imminent danger of shipwreck; once, through the negligence of a Jewess, it was within an ace of destruction by a fire which took firm hold of the rigging. Soon, too, a variety of diseases broke out, and the congested conditions on board favoured their dissemination. For doctor there was only the ship's barber – 'a man of such prepossessing appearance, that even in perfect health I would have sickened if he had felt my pulse'. Pietro and his servants, however, escaped the infection, though of the five hundred persons on board twenty or thirty were struck down every day, 'nor did Death fail of his tithe'.

Wilfred Blunt, *Pietro's Pilgrimage* (1953), p. 10

...the necessities of a journey are continually apt to reduce this scrupulousness to a very indifferent observation of such rules. For instance, it is impossible for a woman to accomplish so long a journey without a conductor; on account of her natural weakness she has to be put upon her horse and to be lifted down again; she has to be supported in difficult situations...whether she leans on the help of a stranger, or on that of her servant she fails to keep the law of correct conduct; and as the inns and hostelries and cities of the East present many examples of licence and of indifference to vice, how will it be possible for one passing through such smoke to escape without smarting eyes? Where the ear and the eye is defiled, the heart is too, by receiving all those foulnesses through eye and ear, how will it be possible to thread without infection such seats of contagion?

Gregory of Nyssa, cited in H. Wace & P. Schnaff, eds., *A Select Library of Nicene and Post-Nicene Fathers of the Christian Church, Vol. V: Gregory Of Nyssa* (1893), pp. 382–3

The principal hardship was accommodation; and while it was conceded that tents were not absolutely necessary, they were advised, especially if ladies were included in the excursion. Women, one notes, were an additional complication in nineteenth-century travel in Egypt, whence the recommendation that 'where ladies are of the party, particularly on the Nile, the servants should be supplied with drawers, and an order given that the boatmen never go into the water without them'.

However, the guides and camel-drivers who led the party to the Wadi Natrun were enveloped in their hooded cloaks and hence were unlikely to offend modesty. Tents, on the other hand, gave privacy.

Otherwise travellers had to sleep in the waiting rooms of railway stations, or in the huts of the Egyptian Salt and Soda Company...

James Wellard, Desert Pilgrimage (1970), p. 19

During my pilgrimage through Arizona I was arrested by a plain-clothes policeman while mailing letters at the local post office in Benson. After a short ride in a patrol car I was booked as a vagrant. When you walk on faith you are technically guilty of vagrancy. Yes, I've been jailed several times for not having any money, but they always release me once they understand.

There is a great deal of difference between a prison and a jail. A prison is something big that maintains some kind of standards. A jail is a little affair that doesn't maintain much of any standard. And this was a jail!

They put me into a huge inner room surrounded by cell blocks in which they locked me with women, four to a cell for the night. As I walked in I said to myself, 'Peace Pilgrim, you have dedicated your life to service – behold your wonderful new field of service!'

Peace Pilgrim, Her Life and Work in Her Own Words (1983), p. 33

The provincial addressed him kindly and told him that he had learned of his good intention to remain in the holy places, and had given the matter careful thought. From the experience he had of others, he thought that it would not be wise. Many, he said, had entertained a like desire, some of whom had been taken prisoner, others died, and that his Order had been later obliged to ransom those who had been taken captive. For this reason, he should get ready to leave the next day with the other pilgrims. His answer was that he had made up his mind to stay, and was determined to let no reason prevent him from sticking to his resolve, giving him honestly to understand that although the provincial did not agree with him, if it was not a matter that obliged him under pain of sin, he would not give up his purpose out of any fear. To this the provincial replied that they had authority from the Apostolic See to dismiss or retain, and to excommunicate anyone who refused to obey. In his case they judged that he would not remain. (*Vita* 45–46)

The account is striking insofar as it tells us something of the intense devotion Inigo experienced and the fierce determination with which he pursued his aims. The driving force was undoubtedly the wish to follow in the Lord's footsteps, not merely in the geographic locale of Christ's earthly life but to imitate the very pattern and mode of that life in its intimate details. His near fanaticism would brook no interference and count no cost too great to achieve its aims – even the threat of prison and death.

William Meissner, *Ignatius of Loyola: 'The Psychology of a Saint'* (1992), pp. 114–5

There were many moments when fatigue was just a physical thing, aches and bruises, mosquito bites, the back, a grizzly red charge, gripping the base of the spine; and often from the cancer scare itself, violent shooting pains; only to be expected the radiologist had said after the burn up and that long infection. But physical pain however acute and persistent is always somehow a remove from self. You can observe it, move it, alter it, or you can abide within it, thrashing about, tense, angry and apparently powerless, but there is always choice; there is always an outside feel, with regard to pain and bodily fatigue.

There seems to be another fatigue. A clouded, uneasy, dry, but sharp fatigue; a fatigue of the spirit. Here you may be overwhelmed. Suddenly the field of choice blurs; it goes under, although with enormous effort it can always be retrieved; almost always.

Jini Fiennes, *On Pilgrimage: A Time to Seek* (1991), p. 167

I sat waiting in the little square near the post office, brewed a cup of coffee and then stretched out on a bench in the hot sun in a daze, not very sure whether I really had been on the road for over four weeks, had covered half the distance to Rome and was now in Grenoble. I lifted my boots from the ground beside the bench. The thick vibram soles with which I left Weybridge were now without tread and there was little rubber left. My arms and legs were mahogany-coloured and the soles and heels of my feet were extremely hard.

But the more important change was within me. I felt a great sense of peace, the peace of at-oneness, and I prayed that I would never lose it but grow in it. In this peace I felt I was seeing more, hearing more, living more fully...

Gerard Hughes, *In Search of a Way: Two Journeys of Spiritual Discovery* (1994), p. 112

As this path on the high mountain of perfection is narrow and steep, it demands travellers who are neither weighed down by the lower part of their nature nor burdened in the higher part. This is a venture in which God alone is sought and gained, thus only God ought to be sought and gained.

Obviously one's journey must not only exclude the hindrance of creatures but also embody a dispossession and annihilation in the spiritual part of one's nature. Our Lord, for our instruction and guidance along this road, imparted that wonderful teaching – I think it is possible to affirm that the more necessary the doctrine the less it is practised by spiritual persons – that I will quote fully...He states in the eighth chapter of St Mark: *They who wish to follow my way should deny themselves, take up their cross and follow me. For those who save their soul shall lose it, but the one who loses it for me shall gain it* [Mark 8:34–35].

John of the Cross (1540–91), *The Ascent of Mount Carmel, John of the Cross: Selected Writings*, ed. Kieran Kavanaugh (1987), p. 94

How can we follow this 'Way'? and 'lead this Life'? Journey will mean very different things to each one of us according to our vocation; but one point comes out very plainly in the Gospel story and particularly in the Gospel of St Luke, that the 'way' of Jesus was a living and a moving way. There was no stagnation; no withdrawal from the demands of life, although there were many periods of solitude and unrecorded experience. Wherever He was, He was always 'on the way'...

We too are called, whatever our life may be, to be always 'on the way' – the way that leads to God, the way of uttermost love and service to men. When we offer ourselves to God in worship we promise to follow wherever He may lead, without knowing what this will involve. Sometimes we shall feel afraid, like His disciples on the road up to Jerusalem. Sometimes we shall feel that we have lost sight of the track, like travellers in the Sahara when a sandstorm has blotted out the route. But we learn to keep on, regardless of feeling afraid or uncertain or perplexed. All these temptations to fear and anxiety can be met by casting ourselves more resolutely than ever into the arms of God, who has pledged Himself to bring us through.

Olive Wyon, *The Way of the Pilgrim* (1958), pp. 124–5

So here I am, a pilgrim through life, restless indeed, looking, searching all the time for that which will make me truly and fully myself. That is natural, and I discover that it is only when I can delight in that which is most beautiful, in that which is the fullness of goodness, and only when I am united to that which is most loveable that I am truly myself and so truly human.

...The way is often rough for a pilgrim and hard going, but pilgrims must keep going resolutely and courageously. They are lost if they stop looking for the right way to reach their destination. But there is one who is on the look-out to guide us; it is the Son of God who is the way, the truth and the life.

Basil Hume, *To Be A Pilgrim* (1984), p. 39

To reach satisfaction in all
    desire its possession in nothing.
To come to possess all
    desire the possession of nothing.
To arrive at being all
    desire to be nothing.
To come to the knowledge of all
    desire the knowledge of nothing.
To come to the pleasure you have not
    you must go by the way in which you enjoy not.
To come to the knowledge you have not
    you must go by the way in which you know not.
To come to the possession you have not
    you must go by a way in which you possess not.
To come to be what you are not
    you must go by a way in which you are not.
When you turn toward something
    you cease to cast yourself upon all.
For to go from all to the all
    you must deny yourself of all in all.
And when you come to the possession of the all
    you must possess it without wanting anything.
Because if you desire to have something in all
    your treasure in God is not purely your all.

John of the Cross (1540–91), *The Ascent of Mount Carmel, John of the Cross: Selected Writings*, ed. Kieran Kavanaugh (1987), pp. 78–9

When I set out on pilgrimage, I was inspired by simple views about the future. In the political realm there was a mood of optimism. The war to end war had been fought; the League of Nations had been established; and a new world order was thought to be emerging. We foresaw an era of international amity, based on freedom and justice for all peoples.

In the world of mission there was a comparable mood. Triumphalism was the keynote of the missionary movement:

Jesus shall reign where'er the sun
Doth his successive journeys run;
His kingdom stretch from shore to shore
Till moons shall wax and wane no more.

We knew that we were engaged in a difficult undertaking, but had no doubts about the victory of Christ's kingdom on Earth and within human history.

The hopes for a new world order have been demolished by the spread of barbarism and the threat of the collapse of civilization. We do not know what the world is coming to. But Christians do know what has come to the world, and it is their primary duty to proclaim it. When Jesus took his final farewell of his disciples, they were naturally curious about the political future and asked him about it. Jesus told them that that was none of their business; their given mission was to preach the gospel to the uttermost parts of the Earth. Those are still the marching orders of the church, the mandate of the world mission. Our planet Earth may end with a bang in meteoric collision or nuclear holocaust. It may end with a whimper as society slides down into squalid disintegration. Or there may be something quite different in store for the future. It is not given us to know these things. We do know however, that Christ's kingdom is not of this world and does not depend on the survival of any civilization or even the survival of the planet itself.

C. W. Ranson, *A Missionary Pilgrimage* (1988), p. 193

The pilgrim's progress today passes through a world of beauty and opportunity. Yet it also winds through valleys of death and cruelty never previously explored. The pilgrim cannot pass by the hungry masses or those who clamour for justice and the recognition of their human dignity. The pilgrim's mind and heart are fixed on far horizons but must never ignore or make light of injustice, pain and deprivation here in the passing world. Each day provides for the pilgrim the tasks that have to be undertaken.

...The pilgrim is confronted with daily evidence of a world of sin and division. Here God is dethroned and empty idols are held in honour. False prophets clamour for attention. Belief and unbelief struggle for ascendancy.

Today's world is threatened by new and terrible dangers. Humankind has fashioned weapons which could bring final destruction to our planet. Our race meanwhile multiplies and most face hunger and poverty while the privileged enjoy prosperity unimagined by previous generations.

The pilgrim is not helpless in the presence of such menace and hardship. The divided world can be united and healed. There is an immense work to be done to reconcile divided Christianity, to bring peace and understanding to those who fear and fight each other. There has to be a restoration of family life and the fostering of stable and united communities. These are tasks which involve us all in our different walks of life. They do not distract the pilgrim, nor deflect us from our goal. They are themselves the road we must pursue in our search for God and the fulfilment of His will.

Basil Hume, *To Be A Pilgrim* (1984), p. 157

A pilgrimage made from devout motives was an imitation of Christ. Dangers and adversities encountered on the way were accepted as a participation in his Passion. The robbers into whose hands one could fall were likened to the soldiers who stripped Christ and divided his clothing among them.

Such comparisons are particularly found in the written Lives of the saints. It was an essential part of the story if one whose holiness was described and whose canonization was sought had made a pilgrimage to Jerusalem. Such a pilgrimage was proof that the saint had exercised the virtues of asceticism and perseverance. In this respect the saints were compared to Old Testament figures: the patience of Abbot Poppo of Stavelot, which according to his hagiographer had equalled martyrdom, was likened to that of Job. The pilgrimage of another abbot was compared with Abraham's departure from Ur of the Chaldees. Of course, these saints also did special works of penance on the way. St Gerlach (d. 1170), the hermit from South Limburg, travelled barefoot and wore a hair shirt under his outer garments.

Adriaan Bredero, *Christendom and Christianity in the Middle Ages* (1994), p. 96

Oh misery me on my pilgrimage to Lough Dearg!
Oh King of Belfries and bells.
For keening thy woes and thy wounds
Not a tear can I drag from my eyes.

Shane Leslie, *St Patrick's Purgatory* (1961), p. 10

I fasted for some forty days on bread and buttermilk,
For passing round the bottle with girls in rags or silk,
In country shawl or Paris cloak, had put my wits astray,
And what's the good of women, for all they can say
Is fol de rol de rolly O.

Round Lough Derg's holy island I went upon the stones.
I prayed at all the Stations upon my marrow-bones,
And there I found an old man, and though I prayed all day
And that old man beside me, nothing would he say
But fol de rol de rolly O.

All know that all the dead in the world about that place are stuck,
And that should mother seek her son she'd have but little luck
Because the fires of Purgatory have ate their shapes away;
I swear to God I questioned them, and all they had to say
Was fol de rol de rolly O.

A great black ragged bird appeared when I was in the boat;
Some twenty feet from tip to tip it stretched right out,
With flopping and with flapping it made a great display,
But I never stopped to question, what could the boatman say
But fol de rol de rolly O.

Now I am in the public-house and lean upon the wall,
So come in rags or come in silk, in cloak or country shawl,
And come with learned lovers or with what men you may,
For I can put the whole lot down, and all I have to say
Is fol de rol de rolly O.

W. B. Yeats, 'The Pilgrim',
The Collected Poems of W. B. Yeats (1965), pp. 360–1

Each year, on the day set aside by the Catholic Church for the festival of the Holy Trinity, which, fluctuating with Easter, usually falls in the days between spring and summer, thousands of pilgrims from all the tributary valleys of the Simbrivio climb to the chapel situated in the mountain cleft known as the Tagliata del Monte Autore. Within this chapel lies the ancient sanctuary which the earliest inhabitants dedicated to the numen of the distressed (*Nume Indigete*), which dwelt in the River Simbrivio. The votive offerings found near this holy site make it clear that a heathen cult was once practised in this spot where the roads from the two slopes of the Apennines meet. And indeed, elements of the pre-Christian liturgy have survived the ritual of the long and arduous pilgrimage to this shrine.

The pilgrims, arriving at the edge of the hallowed ground, must cross the Simbrivio at the point where it flows into the Aniene. Here they kneel down and cross the bridge backwards on their knees; in devout awe they throw stones to the left and right over the parapet, raising their hands in so doing as if to exorcise the evil spirits which might be lurking in ambush at the entrance to this zone sacred to the deity.

Joseph Campbell, ed., *Spirit and Nature: Papers from the Eranos Yearbooks*
(1955), p. 214

For St Charles, pilgrimages were religious exercises in the strictest sense of the word. He exerted every effort that all idea of even legitimate diversion be removed from this devotional practice. It was to be only a succession of prayer and penance. Ordinarily he did not undertake a pilgrimage of importance without first informing his people of it. Often he made it an occasion to invite them to a general Communion, thus adding solemnity to his departure. He himself would distribute holy Communion in the cathedral on the Sunday before his departure. In one of his invitations he wrote: 'We earnestly desire, by means of the general Communion, to be accompanied in our journey by all the people of Milan.'

Once on the road, he found means of increasing his penances and discomforts, although at that time travelling was quite devoid of comfort. He preferred to go on foot, sometimes even barefoot, as the inhabitants of Jesi testified. They had the good fortune to receive the saintly Cardinal in their city when he was on a pilgrimage to Loreto, and they noticed, when he was on his knees in their church, that there were no soles on his shoes. 'It cannot be estimated,' said the historians of that time, 'how great was the edification of all on seeing a gentleman of noble birth make such a long journey barefoot.' His food also served as a means of increasing his penance. When he was on a pilgrimage, his meals were like those of Lent and Advent, that is, he ate only nuts, apples and olives. On his first journey to Turin to venerate the Holy Shroud, when he and his party arrived the first evening at Trecate, after walking a good twenty-five miles and that fasting, he insisted on reading to the others while they ate. And only after they had finished, at the urgent request of Father Adorno he finally ate an apple and drank a glass of wine. And this was his entire dinner. Lanfranco Reina, one of his servants and frequently his companion on pilgrimages, assures us that almost always on such journeys the saint ate nothing but bread, nuts and raisins.

Cesare Orsenigo, *The Life of St Charles of Borromeo* (1945), p. 302

Chapter Six

ALONG THE WAY

Almost no matter where a pilgrim begins their journey, they will be bound to experience a wide diversity of landscapes. In part, this experience is determined by the means of transport. But whether walking, travelling by train, plane, bus or ship, the sense of wonder at new environments is evident. The smell of food, the beauty of flowers, the strange sights – sometimes occasioned by the people who are observed along the route – all add something to the sense that the pilgrim is on the way. There is gratitude too for the welcome, the hospitality and acts of kindness offered to the pilgrim along the route.

Inevitably some pilgrims' accounts read like a travelogue. The famous sights are noted. Particular places of prayer are visited as part of the journey itself. Details become important and sometimes significant. The closer that the pilgrim comes to the destination, especially when the end of the journey is the Holy Land itself, the more the sense of anticipation is heightened.

But even when the formal destination is reached, the journey continues. It is supplemented, especially in the case of Jerusalem, with a number of other small journeys. Whether it is to encounter the Stations of the Cross, or to visit particular holy sites that are part of the destination, the wonder of the journey is maintained.

———

'When you enter a house, first say, "Peace to this house." If a man of peace is there, your peace will rest on him; if not, it will return to you. Stay in that house, eating and drinking whatever they give you, for the worker deserves his wages. Do not move around from house to house.

When you enter a town and are welcomed, eat what is set before you. Heal the sick who are there and tell them, "The kingdom of God is near you."'

Luke 10:5–9

This preoccupation with Christian hospitality meant the increasing availability of an alternative, and explicitly Christian, framework for travel around the Roman empire, which imposed its own pattern on a journey, in contrast to that provided by the existing state facilities; the existence of such a Christian network was frankly acknowledged in a canon of the council of Nîmes which sought to prevent the abuse, 'on the pretext of pilgrimage', of the charity of local churches. The 'Pilgrims' Road' through Asia Minor provides some confirmation of this development of the Christian context for the journey...There is explicit recognition of the organization of Christian hospitality in this area in the pagan programme of charitable works which Julian despatched to his high priest in Galatia, endeavouring to evoke the same concern among pagans by recalling the Homeric tradition of hospitality to strangers. Charity should not be the preserve of the 'impious Galileans'.

Edward Hunt, *Holy Land Pilgrimages in the Later Roman Empire AD 312–460*
(1982), p. 65

Now the Emperor journeyed with his great band of men...Leaving France they travelled through Burgundy, across Lorraine, Bavaria, and Hungary, through the lands of the Turks and the Persians and of that accursed people, crossing the great river at Lycia. On rode the Emperor through the area of Troy, through the woods and the forest, and they entered Greece. They saw the hills and the mountains of Romania, and, moving swiftly on towards the land where Christ suffered martyrdom, they caught sight of the ancient city of Jerusalem.

Glyn Burgess, ed. & trans., *The Pilgrimage of Charlemagne* (1988), p. 35

The Pacific is very blue. Many small white clouds are floating over it, several thousand feet below us...We – the planeload of people on Pan American: the silent Hawaiian soldier, the talking secretaries, the Australians, the others who like myself had to pay for excess baggage. Lesson: not to travel with so many books...

The moment of take-off was ecstatic. The dewy wing was suddenly covered with rivers of cold sweat running backward. The window wept jagged shining courses of tears. Joy. We left the ground – I with Christian mantras and a great sense of destiny, of being at last on my true way after years of waiting and wondering and fooling about.

May I not come back without having settled the great affair. And found also the great compassion, *mahakaruna*. We tilted east over the shining city. There was no mist this morning. All the big buildings went by. The green parks. The big red bridge over the Golden Gate. Muir Woods, Bogeda Bay, Point Reyes, and then two tiny rock islands. And then nothing. Only blue sea.

I am going home, to a home where I have never been in this body, where I have never been in this washable suit (washed by Sister Gerarda the other day at the Redwoods), where I have never been with these suitcases...

Thomas Merton, *Asian Journal* (1973), p. 4

It was like Switzerland, and the sun shone in and it was lovely and warm. The basket work chairs were most comfortable. I bought some food in the town to make our tea, and afterwards had a walk. The crocuses were out and the daffodils in tight bud! We were back to early spring – wonderful! It had been a long drive, and Chris was tired, but we were finished with motorways, and into the austere beauty of the Scottish mountains. How lucky we were to see them in snow, out of cloud, and in clear crisp sunshine. As the sun set, we watched the train on its way to Fort William and Mallaig, and heard the other half of the train passing near the house as it made its way to Oban and the Mull ferry. The next day there was no hurry. We chatted to the proprietor over our porridge and big cooked breakfast and admired the big trout caught in the nearby river by his son...

The last time we'd come to Iona we'd had a boat trip up the loch. Oban was its usual busy self but so different from London. We went to the ferry terminal to get the tickets for the ferry and to book places on the ferries up to the Western Isles for later. We were so near to Iona now surely nothing could stop us! We had a happy afternoon exploring the Bridge over the Atlantic, the Isle of Seil, and the Highland Arts Studio. There they plied us with shortbread and fudge, and we watched a video, and were tempted to buy presents and souvenirs. In the evening I walked down to the shore from the B&B we'd booked into, walked quite a distance and then sat to watch the sun set, over Mull. Chris was very tired and watched the TV news – John Curry had died of AIDS at 44.

Saturday was the day we crossed the sea to Iona. It is always exciting, going on a ferry, especially when you haven't been on one for a while. We had an earlyish breakfast, and then called at the shops for a film, and an alarm clock – our other one had broken. The ferry was fine, Chris managed the steps from the car deck and we looked out at the views, sipping coffee. The sea was like a mill pond, and the weather a bit cloudy but quite bright and clear. Then off we went on the single track road over Mull, with the car wheel still scraping and creaking a bit. Even Chris was excited enough to take a photo of snow capped Ben More. We stopped at Bunessan for a drink, and a photo of the memorial to Mary MacDonald who wrote 'Child in the Manger' set to the tune we know better for 'Morning has Broken'.

But Chris was getting agitated. She wanted to get to the ferry terminal at Fionnphort and get the luggage sorted out for the crossing. So after a bit of lunch we parked as near to the ferry as possible, and Chris began to sort, while I asked about times of ferries. We had a while to wait. Chris told me what there was to take: two large suitcases and several bags. I said, 'Chris, how can we take all this. You know how unsteady you are, and I can't carry it all.' I might as well have saved my breath. 'No I'm going to have a rest to get my strength up,' she said, but she was looking very agitated. I could see her falling with that lot but it was no use arguing.

Then a coach driver came up. 'Waiting for the ferry? There's one coming over now, especially for my party. They'll take you as well.' I persuaded Chris to come – sitting there thinking about it was making her worse. I couldn't help her. We staggered down the road with our loads, me first to make sure the ferry waited for us. The sea was sloshing round the bottom of the ferry ramp – it was easy to get a shoeful. Chris was making a supreme effort, and then the ferryman was helping her. She collapsed on to a seat and the ferry was off.

John Key, *Journey to Resurrection* (1995), p. 75

Farnham is one of the few towns directly on the Old Road [Pilgrims' Way], which seldom passes through settlements. Travellers sought dry going underfoot, while settlements, built after the roads were first etched across the countryside, needed water and tended to arise close to springs, usually found to the south of the Way. The lie of the hills round Farnham has given it an important position at the convergence of roads, most relevant for us being that here the Pilgrims' Way from Winchester joins the Harrow Way from Stonehenge. For thousands of years travellers reaching Farnham would have been able to determine the broad contours of the road ahead with confidence, for a ridge of chalk hills offers the traveller a route from which he would be unlikely to deviate. First the Hog's Back and then the rolling chalk ridge of the North Downs Way would lead us to Canterbury, and on, if we so chose, to Dover.

Shirley du Boulay, *The Road to Canterbury* (1994), p. 67

At the western end of the west Somerset flatlands, between Queen's and King's Sedge Moor, rises a five-hundred-foot tor, conical and precipitous. On its narrow top stands the tower of St Michael, all that remains of the original church that collapsed in the thirteenth century. From here, where the last abbot of Glastonbury was put to death, the view is immense. Looking westward, there is a smaller hill nearby named Chalice, for reasons that presently appear, and to the south are some other hills like beehives. Immediately below is Glastonbury on an almost imperceptible rise, the roofs and streets of the little town close about the abbey that once dominated them. The rise is the Isle of Avalon, swelling above the once submerged marshes of the Vale that spreads out and away to the Bristol Channel some fifteen miles distant as the heron flies. North runs the high ridge of the Mendips with its faults, caves and dwellings of pre-history: far to the south-west are the Quantocks.

D. Hall, *English Medieval Pilgrimage* (1965), pp. 45–6

The heathland, the sun, the light wind and the charm of the day again tempted us to stop and stretch out on the heath for a while. We chose as our resting place the open grassy area marked by a noble granite cross, the Wilberforce Monument, where Bishop Samuel Wilberforce, the son of the Member of Parliament who devoted his life to the abolition of the slave trade, was killed by falling from his horse. It says something for the luminosity of this day that though my notes remind me yet again of the agony in my back I have no recollection of aches and pains, just sheer delight in my surroundings. And, after a few moments, amusement at seeing a couple emerging sheepishly from one of the farm buildings opposite us, brushing the straw off their clothes and trying to look as if they had been admiring its architectural interest.

Shirley du Boulay, *The Road to Canterbury* (1994), pp. 116–7

The beauty of the Northumbrian coasts where the hills rise in folds to the Cheviots is austere; often, even in summer, it is suddenly hidden by sea mists sweeping in over grey water. There is nothing to be seen then but puffs of spray from the breakers on the offshore island of Farne. The islands are sanctuaries, especially for eider-duck, St Cuthbert's bird, and colonies of seals live there. The cry of gulls, the chorus of wild geese on the saltings of the mainland and the call of curlew wheeling in the mist are the overture to the curtain rising on Lindisfarne, Ynys Medicante, Holy Island.

D. Hall, *English Medieval Pilgrimage* (1965), p. 76

The tower frowns now on the acres of subtopia creeping over that part of Hertfordshire, but if one approaches up Holywell Hill in summer there is an illusion still of the abbey dominating a wide and wooded countryside.

At the foot of the hill the road crosses the narrow trickle of the Ver, then climbs acutely and narrowly to the town's centre between medieval buildings, mostly refaced. Halfway up the hill on the right is the fourteenth-century pilgrim's hostel, lately rescued from centuries of filth and neglect. A hundred yards further on the left is the turning up to the place where St Alban, the protomartyr of Britain, was executed.

D. Hall, *English Medieval Pilgrimage* (1965), p. 185

At dawn I set off for the interior by coach. We crossed the whole of the Algerian coastal strip, which is every bit as beautiful as the loveliest Mediterranean scenery, and arrived at Saïda at about ten o'clock.

An hour's rest, a change of coaches and off again towards the South. Along the way the vines gradually became less frequent and the cold grew more intense. The grasslands of the plateau appeared. We reached Géryville, the last town of any size, close to four in the afternoon. As arranged, I went to the Mission of the White Fathers. I spent the night in the Mission itself in a humble bed near a lit stove. The weather is threatening and I am worried that I won't be able to leave because the roads may become impassable.

Carlo Carretto, *The Desert Journal* (1992), p. 18

I caught the bus to Mâcon from the market place; it was a meandering country bus. It was a brilliant day. Vigorous, white clouds moved fast in a strong, blue sky. There were rolling hills and deciduous forests, white Charolais cattle, and dark brown goats, in meadows of rich, long grasses full of flowers; cowslips, and buttercups, but no primroses. Everywhere leaves were unfurling fast. Their fresh brilliant green was in keen contrast to the dark grass. A real Vivaldi spring day. Piping energy in everything except perhaps the cows.

The country buses in France are so good, but so empty. On this particular journey there was only myself and a young girl who was going to Mâcon to buy a christening robe for her sister's baby. I told her that I was going to Taizé and the driver overhearing this said that I should get out at Cluny, where there were three buses every day into Taizé. Grateful for his advice I got out at Cluny. It was really hot. There was the sense of full, still, midday heat; closed shutters; cooking smells and snatches of conversation coming from behind open doorways, the dark, cool interior hidden by a beaded curtain. There was no one about.

Jini Fiennes, *On Pilgrimage: A Time to Seek* (1991), p. 84

Thirty kilometres from ∙Darmstadt I came to the village of Brensbach where I called in at a baker's shop for bread and to inquire about lodgings for the night. The womàn gawked at me and Mungo, both snow-covered, ignored my order because she first wanted to know why in heaven's name I was walking in this weather with such a machine. When I explained that I was on my way to Jerusalem on foot, she took my order, but refused payment. I then asked her about lodgings in Brensbach and she told me there was nothing hereabouts, but why did I not try the 'Pfarrer', which can mean either the Catholic priest or the Protestant minister. I braced myself for an interrogation and rang the Pfarrer's bell. A cheerful-looking young man answered, listened to my request, did not ask to see any papers, but begged me wait a moment while he consulted his wife upstairs. In a moment he was back again, welcoming me in for supper and offering me a bed for the night. Supper was an excellent meal, enlivened by the company of their three very chatty little children. Later that evening Christoph, the Pfarrer, and Claudia, his wife, sat talking till late, telling me among other things of their experience of ecumenism in Germany today.

Gerard Hughes, *Walk to Jerusalem* (1991), p. 85

The pilgrimage of M[aster] Robert Langton, clerke, to saynt James in Compostell and in other holy places of Christendome, with the name of every town and the space betwene them, as well by fraunce and spayne as the dutche way and other londes. And of the relykes and wondres in certayne townes and compendiously ordred as it appereth playnly in this present boke.

...Langton follows the standard route in Spain. But at Leon he turns north to Oviedo, to San Salvador, across the Parjares pass. He then takes the coastal road to Betanzos and La Coruña where he slaves up 'a breakback hill' to Compostella. At Padron he talks of St James's boat of stone in which the saint arrived at the little port: 'Also ye maste of stone under ye auter of the church wherin is the measure of his foot'. Langton then made a circle down into Andalusia, back up through Valencia, into Italy and home through Germany.

Robert Tate, *Pilgrimages to St James of Compostella from the British Isles during the Middle Ages* (1990), p. 21

The long first stage out of Paris took the pilgrim thirty miles to Étampes. It is a dreary stretch, and must always have been; but at least it was flat – Oh so flat – and easy on tender feet. Étampes is a bleak strip of a town, with cobbled streets and a clutch of medieval churches of which the oldest is Notre-Dame-du-Fort – not that such a fortified chunk of masonry can have raised the spirits of many pilgrims as they knelt in one of the vast transepts opening on to the nave of the ogre's fortress. Nonetheless, the south portal is a reminder that Chartres is no farther off than Paris: slender pillar-figures on either side of the entrance, and carved arches above, together make up a shadow of the great west door at Chartres, though here at Étampes all the heads of the figures were lopped off during the French Revolution and the rest stand in the strongest need of a clean. An air of morose decay prevails.

Edwin Mullins, *The Pilgrimage to Santiago* (1974), p. 17

The mountain route from the Col de Cize slaloms down to Roland's split rock and the remnants of Charlemagne's church. It was midday – which is lunchtime for Frenchmen, but Spaniards eat at two in the afternoon – so I had a couple of hours to while away, and walked up the pilgrim road into the quiet mountains.

It was hot, suddenly very hot. I shed layers of clothes and tied them round my waist. Outcrops of rock glistened with iron in the sun. Huge beeches clustered in sheltered places, and vivid moss flourished in their shade. On the moss sat a grey-uniformed Guardia Civil, his improbable hat like a black bandage with wings pressed over a military haircut. He gazed at me and grunted when I said good afternoon. Self-consciously I went at the same slow pace, half expecting him to reappear from behind every tree, until the track zig-zagged up on to the open hillside.

Edwin Mullins, *The Pilgrimage to Santiago* (1974), p. 118

The sun was already setting and the shadow on the mountain was growing longer and longer. Like a man aroused from sleep, I turned back and looked towards the west. The boundary wall between France and Spain, the ridge of the Pyrenees, is not visible from there, though there is no obstacle of which I knew, and nothing but the weakness of the mortal eye is the cause. However, one could see most distinctly the mountains of the province of Lyons to the right and, to the left, the sea near Marseilles as well as the waves that break against Aigues Mortes, although it takes several days to travel to this city. The Rhône River was directly under our eyes.

> Epistle of Petrarch, 26 April 1336, cited in Christian Zacher, *Curiosity and Pilgrimage: The Literature of Discovery in Fourteenth-Century England* (1976), pp. 38–9

Of all my days of walking, the most memorable was April 28th, when I was walking from Fuzine in the mountains of the Novi Vinodolski on the coast, passing from the winter snow and bare trees of the mountains, through spring, as I descended, to summer weather by the sea.

For the first four kilometres to a village called Lic, there was no problem apart from the cold. At Lic my map had a clearly marked yellow road leading south to a village called Kastelj. I searched for this road without success. The first man I asked could speak Italian. When I showed him the map he shrugged his shoulders and told me the road did not exist. This I could not believe, so I tried an elderly couple. They examined the map with interest, then gave me directions, she pointing east and he to the west. They began quarrelling with each other, so I left them to it and asked the next passer-by, a smartly dressed young woman, with a confident, didactic manner. She bade me follow, which I did. She led me into the local shop. When I said, 'But where is my road?' she pointed clearly to the road to Fuzine, whence I had come. The shopkeeper, noticing my difficulty, came out from behind his counter leaving the shop unattended. He, too, assured me that the splendid road on my map existed only in the minds of the planners and he pointed to a path across wasteland leading to hills in the distance and said that I would eventually find a forest track which would bring me out on to the main road.

> Gerard Hughes, *Walk to Jerusalem* (1991), pp. 149–50

Mandeville's *Travels* is in part a record of a pilgrimage to the Holy Land, but it is in greater measure the account of a curious man's exploration of the earth. And the book is not simply a diary-like summary of successive experiences (as, for example, Marco Polo's), but a consciously arranged sequence of adventures. Structurally, the book breaks into two parts, and these reflect the differing motivations of the traveller. The first part recounts the pilgrimage routes through the known world from Europe to Palestine: the second and slightly longer part describes the marvels of the unknown world that stretches beyond Jerusalem to the lands of Prester John, the Great Chan of China, and the Terrestrial Paradise. The changing nature of Mandeville's itinerary corresponds to (and indeed demonstrates) the author's actual motives for travelling. In the linear narrative of the book, the devout pilgrim metamorphoses into the wide-eyed curious wanderer.

Christian Zacher, *Curiosity and Pilgrimage: The Literature of Discovery in Fourteenth-Century England* (1976), p. 131

In 333 a Christian traveller from Bordeaux made the journey by land from the Atlantic coast of Jerusalem, and compiled (for the benefit of future pilgrims) a detailed record of the stages and distances en route, both there and back (the so-called Bordeaux itinerary). The result is a very complete itinerary of his route: up the valley of the Garonne and into Narbonensis via Toulouse, on through the Cottian Alps into northern Italy and Milan; thence on the highway across to Aquileia and into the Balkan provinces. The Daube towns – Emona, Poetovio, Mursa, Cobalae, Sirmium, Naissus, Sardica – pass by along the route to Constantinople…On from Constantinople, his road took him through the provinces, of Asia Minor to the Cilician Gates and Tarsus; thus he traversed the route which linked the new capital with its eastern provinces the road which came to be labelled by Sir William Ramsay (in recognition of these new travellers) as the 'Pilgrims' Road'. He passed then via Antioch, capital of the eastern diocese, along the coast road already mentioned to Caesarea, and the northern approach to Jerusalem. There was a variant on the return journey; from Constantinople he followed, not the Danube route, but the old Via Egnatia through Thrace and Macedonia, thence across the Adriatic to the heel of Italy (Hydruntum). His way northwards followed the Via Appia to Rome, then on through central Italy to the Adriatic coast at Ariminum, where he branched along the 'Via Aemilia' north-eastwards to Milan, to rejoin his outward route.

Edward Hunt, *Holy Land Pilgrimage in the Later Roman Empire AD 312–460* (1982), p. 55

To return to St Willibald and his brother pilgrims, we find that after attending to the obsequies of their father they hastened over the wide regions of Italy, and arrived safely at Rome and stood before the glorious Basilica of St Peter, the great apostle.

The two brothers suffered greatly from fever at Rome, where they remained until the spring of 723, when, with one companion, they set out for 'the delectable and desirable city of Jerusalem'. Their journey lay by pleasant paths and sunlit valleys – rich in religious and histori- cal associations – by Terracina, Gaeta, and Naples, spending three days in Sicily, and crossing the Adriatic to Albania, and thence to Chios and Samos to Ephesus.

From here 'they walked two miles along the coast to a town of great size called Figila. They were there one day, and having begged some bread, went to a fountain in the midst of the city, and sitting beside it on the margin of the basin they dipped the bread in the water and so ate of it.'

The journey was continued on foot along the coast to Patara, where the winter was passed; then crossing over to Tortosa, they visited Ortha, where they attended a service officiated over by a bishop of the Greek Church. Proceeding to the tower of Emessa, they would enter territory in the occupation of the Saracens, on whom they appear to have made a favourable impression. From Emessa they set out for Damascus, where they visited the scene of the conversion of St Paul:

> And having prayed there, they went on their pilgrimage into
> Galilee, until they came to the place where Gabriel first came
> to Blessed Mary with the salutation, 'Hail, full of grace!' A
> church now stands there, and the village in which the church
> is is Nazareth. The heathen would many times have destroyed
> the church, but the Christians have ransomed it. There having
> commended themselves to the Lord, they walked on, and came
> to the village of Chana, where the Lord turned water into
> wine. A great church stands there, and in the church an altar,
> composed of one of the six water-pots which the Lord com-
> manded to be filled with water which He turned into wine,
> and of the wine they partook.
>
> Sidney Heath, *Pilgrim Life in the Middle Ages* (1911), p. 151

The land of Egypt is long but it is narrow; for men may not inhabit it on breadth for deserts, where great default is of water and therefore it is inhabited on length endlang [along] the foresaid river. For they have no moisture but that the foresaid river [Nile] ministers; for it rains not there, but the land is overflowed therewith certain times of the year, as I said before. And for there is no troubling of the air through rains, but the air is there alway fair and clear without clouds, therefore there were wont to be the best astronomers of the world. The foresaid city of Cairo, in which the sultan dwells, is beside the city of Babylon, as I told before, nought but a little from the foresaid river of Nilus towards the deserts of Syria.

Malcolm Letts, trans., Mandeville's Travels (1957), p. 32

Mercifully, the area to the north, where Jesus spent most of his public life, remains calm and unspoiled, and the several New Testament lakeside locations are lovely. The ancient site of Capernaum, Jesus' second home, with its remains of the third-century synagogue has been tastefully maintained. The Sea of Galilee – though hardly a sea – lives up to the expectations of a place well remembered from childhood Bible stories. Even Hollywood could not have come up with anything more convincing. It is hard to believe that the lake is 675 feet below sea level, and it is vital to Israel, being the largest reservoir of fresh water in the country. Galilee's water makes the deserts to the south bloom with vegetation, and the province itself is a region of lush land full of flowers and fruits. Olives, dates and pomegranates are everywhere.

Another place where the visitor may easily receive a spiritual feeling of a different sort is the barren wilderness east of Jerusalem and Bethlehem. There are few more memorable drives than that of coming up to Jerusalem from the Dead Sea at sunset. The bedouin scurry to light their fires and bring in their wandering goats; there is an eerie quiet in this region. Stopping in the desert or by the Dead Sea at night and experiencing the quiet is unforgettable.

David Sox, Relics and Shrines (1985), p. 213

In Egypt are places where the earth bears fruit eight times in the year. And there they find in the earth the fairest smaragds [emeralds] that are overwhare; and that is the cause that they are so good cheap there, forbye in other places. Also, if it falls that it rains once in the summer, then all the land of Egypt is full of mice. At the city of Cairo they bring to the market men and women that are of other countries born and sell them commonly, as men do beasts on other countries. Also there is in the city of Cairo a common house ordained and made full of holes, as it were hens nests: and thither the women of the country bring eggs of hens and geese and ducks and lay them in the nests. And certain persons are ordained to keep that ilk house and to cover them with warm horse dung; and through the heat of the horse dung the eggs bring forth birds without sitting of hen or any other fowl. And at the end of three or four weeks the women come that brought thither eggs and bear away the birds and bring them up as the manner of the

country asks. And thus is all the country replenished with such manner of fowl. And thus they do als well in winter as in summer.

Malcolm Letts, trans., *Mandeville's Travels* (1957), p. 35

The nearer the *peregrini* are brought to the Holy Land, the more their
progress is slowed by the increasing number of shrines and holy
places lying in their way. Mandeville has so far described two promi-
nent overland routes from western Europe, one leading through Egypt
and the other bypassing it, and now, in chapter VIII, he pauses to
insert an alternate itinerary for pilgrims who desire a speedier journey.
This route leads from Italy and includes stopovers in Sicily (the site
of Mount Etna and volcanoes that 'ben weyes Helle'), Crete, Rhodes,
Cyprus, Constantinople, Alexandria, and finally the new Babylon.

Christian Zacher, *Curiosity and Pilgrimage: The Literature of Discovery in
Fourteenth-Century England* (1976), p. 137

Above [the Templar buildings] the area is full of houses, dwellings and
outbuildings for every kind of purpose, and it is full of walking-places,
lawns, council chambers, porches, consistories and supplies of water in
splendid cisterns. Below it is equally full of wash-rooms, stores, grain
rooms, stores for wood and other kinds of domestic stores.

On the other side of the palace, that is on the west, the Templars
have built a new house, whose height, length and breadth, and all its
cellars and refectories, staircase and roof, are far beyond the custom of
the land. Indeed, its roof is so high that, if I were to mention how
high it is, those who listen would hardly believe me.

Theoderic, cited in J. Wilkinson, J. Hill, & W. Ryan,
Jerusalem Pilgrimage 1099–1185 (1988), p. 294

Indeed a thin ridge comes down from Libanus and projects into the sea
like a tongue. It has a hill at its east end on the top of which the founder
fixed the city. This city is extremely small in circumference, but it is
nevertheless most beautiful with its high walls and beautiful buildings.

After that comes what is called Jebelet and after that Berytus, a
large city and well populated, surrounded with meadows. It is outstanding for the excellence of its port, but in fact the harbour is not
natural but artificial. It is embraced by the city in a crescent, and on
the horns of the crescent are built two great towers. A chain is
stretched from one to the other, and confines the ships inside the harbour. This forms the boundary between Syria and Phoenicia.

Then comes Sidon and its harbour, celebrated in a song as 'The Twin', whose situation the writer *Leucippe* has so well described. If you stay there you can see how the real harbour and the entry strait agree with the written description. About three bowshots outside the city is a Church enclosed by a long roofed colonnade, and against the apse of the Church lies a stone on which, according to the common report, Christ the Saviour of the World, stood and taught to the multitudes.

John Phocas, cited in J. Wilkinson, J. Hill, & W. Ryan,
Jerusalem Pilgrimage 1099–1185 (1988), p. 318

And on the other side of this lake [Gennesareth] to the north-east there is a very high and very large mountain on which the snow lies throughout the summer. It is called Lebanon, and it produces the incense of Lebanon and white incense. From this Mount Lebanon flow twelve rivers, six flowing to the east and six to the south. These rivers flow into the Lake of Gennesareth and six rivers flow to Great Antioch, and this place is called Mesopotamia, which means the place between rivers. Between these rivers is Haran from which Abraham went out. The Lake of Gennesareth is filled with much water by these rivers, and from this lake flows a great river into the Sea of Tiberias, and from that sea flows the Jordan as I have stated before when speaking of the Jordan, and it is indeed so. I could not reach Mount Lebanon on foot myself for fear of pagans, but the Christians who lived there and were our guides told us of it in detail and would not let us go to the mountain because of the many pagans there.

Daniel the Abbot, cited in J. Wilkinson, J. Hill, & W. Ryan,
Jerusalem Pilgrimage 1099–1185 (1988), p. 160

At its highest level, the pilgrim's life in Jerusalem was conceived as a continuously repeated drama of the life of Christ. The rituals which he performed, more than a mere Passion play, had something of the regenerative qualities of the celebration of the Eucharist. In this idea lies the distant origin of the modern liturgical practice of the Roman Catholic Church known as the 'Stations of the Cross'. Already in 1231 the exact route which Christ was believed to have followed from Pilate's prison to Calvary was marked out in the streets of Jerusalem. Some seventy years later Ricoldo of Monte Croce 'followed the path which Christ ascended when he carried the Cross', which took him past the house of Pilate, the place where Simon of Cyrene was made to help him, and thence to the Golgotha chapel in the basilica of the

Holy Sepulchre...The journey of the ideal pilgrim could be presented, as Franco Sacchetti presented it at the beginning of the fourteenth century, as an elaborate allegory of the life of Christ from the Nativity to Resurrection. The pilgrim's entry into a roadside hospice was likened to the incarnation of the womb of the Blessed Virgin. The dangers of the route found their counterpart in the Passion of the Lord. The pilgrim may be betrayed and killed by his companions as Christ was betrayed by Judas and killed by the Jews...It is a naïve picture which must have been offered to countless groups of pilgrims departing to the Holy Land. Yet it conceals one of the profoundest sentiments of an age which reduced all spiritual ideas to images. At a popular level men sought to associate themselves with the life of the Saviour, to express literally their conviction that he had saved them by his death. They wished to tear down the barrier of remoteness that separated a man of the thirteenth century from the events of the first.

Jonathan Sumption, *Pilgrimage – An Image of Medieval Religion* (1975), p. 93

Chapter Seven

SAINTS BEFORE

Although for a few pilgrims, the act of simply wandering (no matter if the destination is known or not) is enough, for most, the sense of treading ground made holy by past events is crucial. The sense of the holy is gained first from an awareness that great events, especially the miraculous, have taken place in a particular location. Thus, all of the places which are specially mentioned in Scripture as sites where Jesus ministered are important. But that original import is reinforced by an awareness that the pilgrim is part of a previous multitude, a community of the saints, who have added their testimony of prayer to that which originally took place.

Many claim to sense in the numinous realm an atmosphere of awe and wonder, even if the immediate physical surroundings detract from an immediate awareness of the holy. The witness of others thus gives the actual route as well as the destination a particular importance. Walking in the footsteps of Jesus, the saints of old and the community of the faithful helps the process of reflection.

In this sense, the observance of tradition, whether in the form of ancient liturgy or popular custom helps the pilgrim to identify with ancient events. These past wonders thereby become appropriated by the pilgrim. The past becomes present. The experience of the pilgrim in actually walking in the way of others enables them to become a participant in all that has happened. The pilgrim becomes one with all who have gone before.

———————

Therefore, since we are surrounded by such a great cloud of witnesses, let us throw off everything that hinders and the sin that so easily entangles, and let us run with perseverance the race marked out for us.

Hebrews 12:1

PLIABLE. And what company shall we have there?

CHRISTIAN. There we shall be with seraphims and cherubins, creatures that will dazzle your eyes to look on them (*Isa. vi. 2; 1 Thess. iv. 16, 17.*). There also you shall meet with thousands and ten thousands that have gone before us to that place; none of them are hurtful, but loving and holy; every one walking in the sight of God, and standing in His presence with acceptance for ever. In a word, there we shall see the elders with their golden crowns (*Rev. iv. 4*); there we shall see the holy virgins and their golden harps (*Rev. xiv. 1–5*); there we shall see men that, by the world, were cut to pieces, burned in flames, eaten of beasts, drowned in the seas, for the love they bare to the Lord of the place, all well, and clothed with immortality as with a garment (*Rev. iv. 4; and xiv. 1–5; John xii. 25; 2 Cor. v. 2–4.*).

John Bunyan, *The Pilgrim's Progress* (1678)

There is an atmosphere which stems from the community started by St Columba so many years ago, when Iona, far from being isolated, was a great centre for the boat traffic up the West Coast of Scotland. Scottish Kings are buried there, and over the years a great peace and tranquillity has been built up in a very beautiful place. The worship at the abbey each day is well thought out and full of creativity, and participation involves young and old, and the volunteer staff. The abbey lends itself to worship which is innovatory, and there are services of great beauty and depth. The symbols of the wild goose and dove are to do with the Holy Spirit, and often an Atlantic gale will rattle the big door and blow around the Abbey, the wind invoking the Spirit. The white doves flying round the abbey are reminders of St Columba, for Columba means dove. It is a place where the imagination is stimulated by the beauty of nature, the great variety of the people, the old stones of the Abbey and the ruined Nunnery, and the strange remnants of the Hermitage. The stone crosses stand in silent tribute as they have stood for hundreds and hundreds of years.

John Key, *Journey to Resurrection* (1995), p. 77

The Celtic monks themselves would join in the 'rounds' and traditions would soon grow up of the founder saints having made and originated the pilgrimage in all its detail. The pilgrims would feel that they were walking in the track of the saints, which, in fact, to all intents and purposes, they were and are doing. By the time that Manus O'Donnell wrote his 'Life of St. Columcille' in 1532 this was a well-established idea, with all its details worked out. Manus, for instance, tells how

Columcille went to Aran and how he and the other saints of the island were 'making the round' of the churchyard of Aran, saying their prayers and their office. In the course of the round, they came to a huge stone marking an ancient tomb and nobody knew whose it was. Then Columcille told them it was that of an abbot of Jerusalem, who had heard of the fame of the Irish saints and come to Aran to see for himself, and died there.

Daphne Pochin Mould, Irish Pilgrimage (1955), p. 64

For me as a humble pilgrim of today the vision of the Sanguesa portal was a profoundly moving experience, for it enabled me to understand the universal significance possessed by the pilgrimage to Santiago de Compostela in those early centuries. Here, not more than one day's foot-slogging from the royal capital, Jaca...at Sanguesa, which was then as it is still today, a tiny town and a mere station on the pilgrim road, the wandering builders and craftsmen halted and enriched the wayside shrine with art forms they had brought ...We modern pilgrims, artists, painters, architects, plod our way along the road of St James, but our names are written in water, whereas those anonymous masons and stone-cutters of eight hundred years ago, when they tarried in this narrow street where I linger today, left as a token of their passing some tiny individualized figure or ornament, which, in a flash, illustrates the universal significance of the pilgrimage.

Walter Starkie, The Road to Santiago (1957), p. 157

St Chad's well, by which that saint and bishop had his oratory, still exists in a little garden adjoining St Chad's Church at Lichfield, although the relics and bones of the saint, which had been carefully hidden and preserved during the Reformation, have been enshrined in the altar of the Roman Catholic Cathedral of St Chad, at Birmingham, one of the finest architectural creations of Pugin, as it is one of the least known. This little well at Lichfield was frequented in olden days by a vast number of pious devotees, and even to-day it is customary for the clergyman, attended by the churchwardens and a great concourse of children, to visit this well on Holy Thursday (Ascension Day)...

Sidney Heath, Pilgrim Life in the Middle Ages (1911), p. 103

Now I pray to Thee, God the Father eternal, through this pilgrimage of Thy dear Son, that He may watch over us on this our pilgrimage through this vale of tears, and safeguard us from the satanic enemies

of our souls, and cast down the idols, that is the domination of sin in
our hearts, that we meet with Christ Our Lord through this pilgrimage, and be called back to the promised land, Amen.

C. Leeu, *Thoek van den Leven Ons Liefs Heeren Jhesu Christi* [*The Book of the Life
of Our Dear Lord Jesus Christ*] (1488), cited in R. Falkenburg, *Joachim Patrini:
Landscape as an Image of the Pilgrimage of Life* (1988), p. 98

Does the road wind up-hill all the way?
  Yes, to the very end.
Will the day's journey take the whole long day?
  From morn to night, my friend.

But is there for the night a resting place?
  A roof for when the slow dark hours begin.
May not the darkness hide it from my face?
  You cannot miss that Inn.

Shall I meet other wayfarers at night?
  Those who have gone before.
Then must I knock, or call when just in sight?
  They will not keep you standing at the door.

Shall I find comfort, travel-sore and weak?
  Of labour you shall find the sum.
Will there be beds for me and all who seek?
  Yea, beds for all who come.

Christina Rossetti, 'Up Hill', in *Goblin Market, The Prince's Progress
and Other Poems* (1884), p. 194

When I reached St Gilles I went first of all to the cathedral where all
Jacobean pilgrims halt to make their devotions to one of the most lov-
able saints in all the calendar...Around the abbey a large city grew up
later under the patronage of the last Count of Toulouse, who came
originally from St Gilles, and it reached the zenith of its power in the
twelfth century, when the Knights Templar and Hospitallers were in
their heyday, and its port carried on a flourishing trade in the
Mediterranean. The Abbey, which belonged to the Order of Cluny,
had received privileges from the Pope, giving it quasi-independence,
and its fame was universal owing to the pilgrimage from all over
Europe to the tomb of St Gilles in the crypt of the cathedral.

Walter Starkie, *The Road to Santiago* (1957), p. 92

...the history of the ancient trackway, which is, in many parts, of far greater age than the earliest pilgrim, is still involved in obscurity. There are so many tracks the pilgrims may have taken, so comparatively few portions we know they actually did tread. There were innumerable detours from the direct course, robber-infested districts to be avoided, rivers and streams to be crossed, and visits of devotion to be paid to the numerous holy places that sprang up like mushrooms on either side of the main track. At the same time, if we use a little imagination and trust to the instinct of locality, it is possible to define what was the probable route followed by the majority of the wayfarers.

It is generally admitted, all writers are agreed on the fact, that the trackway itself is of greater antiquity than the events which give it the greater part of its present-day interest. The 'holy road' to Canterbury was merely the renascence of an older highway that led in the same general direction; a harrow or hoary old road to which the feet of multitudes of devout pilgrims gave a new lease of life...

Sidney Heath, *Pilgrim Life in the Middle Ages* (1911), p. 169

The imagination of the pilgrim is well stimulated even before he or she makes the journey to the shrine. Pilgrims are usually familiar with the essential details of the life-story of their saint, namely that for most of his life he bore the wounds of Christ's crucifixion on his body, that he suffered physically, that he was mistreated and misunderstood by the church authorities, and that through him many miracles were and still are performed. The pilgrim's journey to San Giovanni Rotondo is, then, a classic journey to 'the centre'. That Pio bore the stigmata, like St Francis before him and like Christ himself, transforms the mountain of the Gargano into Mount La Verna (where Francis received the stigmata) but also, more importantly, into Calvary.

John Eade & Michael Sallnow, eds., *Contesting the Sacred* (1991), p. 90

One of the cardinal sins in medieval Europe was avarice...Poverty was not shameful, as it was later to become, but a virtue; and those who preached it recalled the teaching of Christ that 'it is easier for a camel to go through the eye of a needle, than for a rich man to enter the kingdom of God'.

This cult of poverty was seminal to the growth and popularity of pilgrimages. St Francis of Assisi, himself a pilgrim to Santiago de Compostela, practised it to the letter, and under his example a number of communities grew up in the later Middle Ages that were dedicated to poverty.

Edwin Mullins, *The Pilgrimage to Santiago* (1974), p. 53

Also at Constantinople lies Saint Anne, our Lady's mother, whom Saint Helena gert [caused] be brought from Jerusalem. And there lies also the body of John Chrysostom, that was bishop of Constantinople. And there lies Saint Luke, the evangelist; for his bones were brought from Bethany [Bithynia], where he was graven. And many other reliques are there.

Malcolm Letts, trans., *Mandeville's Travels* (1957), p. 11

Also from Acon beforesaid go men three days journey to the city of Palestine, that now is called Gaza, and it is a full fair city and full of riches and of folk. From this city til a hill without bare Samson the forte [strong] the gates of the city, the which were made of brass. And in that city he slew the king in his palace and many others also, about three thousand, and himself with them. For they had taken him and put out both his eyes, and culled off his hair, and put him in prison. And at their feasts they brought him forth before them and made dance before them and make japes. So on a high feast day, when he was weary for that he danced before them, he bad him that led him that he should lead him to the post that bear up all the house; and he took the post in his arms and shook down all the house upon them, and so he slew himself and all that were therein, as it tells in the Bible in sixteenth chapter of *Judicum*.

Malcolm Letts, trans., *Mandeville's Travels* (1957), p. 23

On another inauspicious day we boarded the same ship again...and put ashore at a Greek island, at the city which, like the island, is called Corphu, on the vigil of St James the Apostle. From there we reached an island called Cephallonia, driven there by a great storm, on the first of August. Robert Guiscard died there, and there some of our men died, which caused much grief. After that we sailed on from there and put in at Polipolis. Then we came to the important island of Patras, and went into the city there to pray to blessed Andrew the Apostle: he was martyred and buried there, and later translated to Constantinople. From Patras on the vigil of St Laurence we came to Corinth. Blessed Paul the Apostle preached the word of God there and wrote a letter to his people.

Saewulf, cited in J. Wilkinson, J. Hill, & W. Ryan,
Jerusalem Pilgrimage 1099–1185 (1988), pp. 94–5

Going south to Corinth and standing on the very spot occupied by Paul before the *bema* or tribunal of Galio (Acts 18:12–17) is to have brought home to one the intensity of that love which the apostle was to hymn in his letter to the Christians of that very same city: he was there because 'love bears all things' (1 Corinthians 13:7)...

To follow in the footsteps of St Paul is to be confronted constantly with a creative model, showing experimentally how to be a Christian. There is a newness too about saints: they exemplify what it means to be a disciple in consciously fresh ways, they often therefore on occasion surprise – Paul and his companions were once referred to as those 'who have turned the world upside down' (Acts 17:6). Apart from those among one's contemporaries, each one belongs to a specific bygone age, and so no saint can provide the perfect blue-print to be imitated in every particular, that would be to treat them as if they were ahistorical, so the task of today's pilgrim is to devise an appropriate lifestyle that is inspired by, but does not mimic, what the saints were and did...Christian values, Christian conduct – these are not abstract entities; they have been enfleshed in the saints; they have also to be incarnated in the late twentieth century not always in ways that would have occurred to or even appealed to believers in previous centuries.

John Davies, *Pilgrimage Yesterday and Today* (1988), pp. 197–8

Today the pilgrimage has regained its popularity. Christians of the first postconciliar period, preoccupied by the 'secular city' and the need for solidarity with the world of unbelievers, attached less importance to such manifestations of religiosity. But now we have clearly moved into a new era, for we are less eager to break with the faith of our forefathers and more concerned to give thought to specifically religious values and to renew our ties with the great ecclesial tradition. A country like Poland fascinates the world: there is much evidence that it has never lost the sense of direction which enables it to steer a course between an age-long Christian tradition and the need for the Church's presence in the heart of human realities. A whole people, ranging from young Westerners born of societies ill with boredom and disillusion to the Pope himself, follows the road leading to the sanctuary of the Virgin of Piekary; this scene offers one of the most striking images of today's Church.

At Taizé we feel the consequences of this development. If the young who flocked to our hill ten years ago were mainly concerned to look for a Church 'devoid of all means of power and ready to share with everyone', those of the 80s are stirred by the sources of our faith and thirsting for prayer. The common prayers, the biblical introductions given by the Brothers of our community, the periods of silent meditation, take up much of the day. And with these young people we were recently able to launch a 'world pilgrimage of reconciliation' which aims at large gatherings the first of these will be held in Madras, India, in December 1985, and the second at Taizé during the summer of 1986.

Clearly, many young people are ready to take up the pilgrim's staff and to set out. Some of their elders are delighted, while others are more doubtful about this renewal of the 'pilgrimage' phenomenon. Does it imply a turning away from earthly commitments, an escape to the dream world of the past? These questions prompt us to look at the Bible in an attempt to deepen our reflection on the *meaning* such a practice assumes in the light of faith. Are we beholding a passing fashion, or is something more essential involved here?

Brother John of Taizé, 'Pilgrimage Seen through the Bible',
Lumen Vitae 39 (1984): 380–1

And from Makri to the town of Patara it is 40 versts and here is the birthplace of St Nicholas – Patara is his homeland and family. And from Patara to Myra to Chelidonia 60 versts and from Chelidonia to the great island of Cyprus is 200 versts.

Cyprus is a very large island with many people and it abounds in all good things. It has twenty bishops and one metropolitanate and saints without number lie there. Here lie St Epiphanius, the apostle Barnabas, St Zeno, St Philagrius the Bishop who was baptized by the Apostle Paul.

There is a very high mountain here and on that mountain St Helena erected a great cross of cypress to drive away devils and cure all manner of ills and she placed in the cross one of Christ's sacred nails. And in this place by that cross there occur great signs and miracles even to this day.

Daniel the Abbot, cited in J. Wilkinson, J. Hill, & W. Ryan,
Jerusalem Pilgrimage 1099–1185 (1988), pp. 125–6

The flume Jordan runs into the Dead Sea; and there it ends, for further runs it not. And it is but a mile from a kirk of Saint John the Baptist towards the west, where Saint John baptized our Lord; and there use Christian men to bathe them commonly. And a mile from Jordan is another water that men call Jabbok, which Jacob passed over when he came out of Mesopotamia. The flume Jordan is no great water, but it is right plentifous of fish; and it comes from the Mount Lebanon of two wells that spring up there, of which that one hat [is called] Jor and the tother Dan; and of these two wells takes it the name. And it runs through a country that is called Maran and syne through the sea of Tiberius and under the hills of Gilboa...The flume Jordan departs Galilee and the land of Idumea and the land of Betron; and in some place it runs under the earth until a fair plain that men

call Meldan, and there is Jordan right broad. In that plain is the sepulchre of Job. In this flume was Christ baptized of Saint John; and there
was heard the voice of the Father saying, *Hic est filius meus dilectus, in
quo michi bene compliacui,* that is to say, 'Here is my son that I love, of
who I am well paid. Hear him.'

Malcolm Letts, trans., Mandeville's Travels (1957), p. 73

On the south side there is a door in that church which stands *in cal-
varie loco*, and when one enters, on the right hand side is a chapel
where the blood fell down from the Lord's cross, and one can still see
the blood. East of the chapel is a rock, and on the north side of the
rock there is a winding staircase of nineteen steps for walking up to the
rock. Then it is one fathom east of where the Lord's cross stood when
he was tortured; there is a hole in the rock there, cracked when the
Lord pushed away from himself the wooden cross on which he was
afterwards crucified. South from that, against the wall, there is Saint
Simeon's altar, where the letter written in gold characters came from
above. To the west of the church door is a chapel out in the wall, and
there is the hand of the holy Anastasia, uncorrupted, beside the altar.

Icelandic Guide, cited in J. Wilkinson, J. Hill, & W. Ryan,
Jerusalem Pilgrimage 1099–1185 (1988), p. 220

From the source of the Jordan and these bridges to the Bath of Christ
and the Bath of the Holy Mother of God and the Bath of the Apostles
it is six versts, and from the holy baths to the town of Tiberias it is
one verst. This town of Tiberias was once very great, two versts long
and one verst wide and it is near the Sea of Tiberias. In this town
Christ our God performed many miracles. There is in the town the
place where Christ cleansed the leper; here once stood the house of
the mother-in-law of Peter the Apostle, and Christ entered this house
and cured Peter's mother-in-law of the burning fever, and in this
place a round church has been built and dedicated to Saint Peter.
Here too was the house of Simon the Leper, where the harlot washed
with her tears the most pure feet of Our Lord Jesus Christ and wiped
them with her hair and received remission of her innumerable sins...

Daniel the Abbot, cited in J. Wilkinson, J. Hill, & W. Ryan,
Jerusalem Pilgrimage 1099–1185 (1988), p. 158

Medieval pilgrims to Palestine normally thought of Jesus as the first
pilgrim: they also popularized the legend that his mother spent her

last years making constant pilgrimages to sites' associated with him. Christ's own visit to Emmaus after his Resurrection, during which he appeared as a stranger to two disciples (Luke 24:13–35), was interpreted as a pilgrimage; and throughout the Middle Ages the Emmaus incident served as a liturgical, homiletic, and dramatic focus for commentaries on the meaning of pilgrimage.

> Christian Zacher, *Curiosity and Pilgrimage: The Literature of Discovery in Fourteenth-Century England* (1976), p. 45

The Church of the Nativity was built in AD 326 and is probably the oldest Christian church in the world still used for worship. The Emperor Constantine built it at the wish of his mother, Queen Helena, whose researches had convinced her that this was where Jesus had been born. There was a cave here which Christians had been venerating for at least the previous two centuries as the birthplace of Jesus. Aware of its sanctity for Christians, Hadrian had attempted to defile the site by building a temple to Adonis on top of it. Constantine had this temple pulled down and put in its place the church which is substantially that which still stands there today.

> John Martin, *A Plain Man in the Holy Land* (1978), pp. 9–10

Saint Martha's is still a living church, seating 110 people and holding services every Sunday, but the congregation must be reasonably fit, as the last part must be done on foot, cars only being allowed up to the church for weddings and funerals. And what a place to be buried! The actress Yvonne Arnaud and general Bernard Freyberg VC, who fought at Gallipoli, are among those who rest there.

The name borne by the hill and the church has no association with Saint Martha, though Saint Martha of Bethany, sister of Mary and Lazarus, is patron saint of the church and her day is kept on 29 July. It is in fact a corruption of Martyr's Hill, as it is thought that in about the year AD 600 Christians were martyred there, something often in my mind – after all our destination was a martyr's shrine.

> Shirley du Boulay, *The Road to Canterbury* (1994), p. 109

So about AD 284, [St] Anthony bade his fellow-monks farewell and set off with a caravan bound for the Red Sea travelling east into the Arabian Desert. The courage and dedication of the saint are incredible, for the site he chose for his new hermitage was one of the most desolate in Egypt: specifically, the north face of the mountain called Colzoum, some twenty miles from the Red Sea. There was nothing there but a spring of sweet water.

James Wellard, *Desert Pilgrimage* (1970), p. 78

The crouching village of Northumbrian stone is hardly visible among the windswept trees, but across the further flats on the other side of the island the castle of Beblowe stands high on a mass of basalt, commanding the sea from Berwick to Bamburgh and from Northumbria to the Cheviots. It was built in the sixteenth century with stones from the now ruined monastery destroyed by the Danes. This monastery had contained since the seventh century the cathedral of St Aidan, and above all of St Cuthbert, from which Christianity spread through the north country.

D. Hall, *English Medieval Pilgrimage* (1965), p. 77

The twelfth-century cathedral and the nineteenth-century basilica on its hill top may be good in their way, but they did not inspire me, with my passion to follow in the footsteps of St Augustine. However, the sixth-century church of St Martin d'Ainay rang bells for me for three good reasons. In this church, built on the site of a Roman temple, as Martin and his followers had so often done, Augustine would have been able to share the Eucharist. I once spent a day in meditation at this remarkable place. During this time I looked up at the roof to where my eye was taken by a small quaint figure, near the high altar, of a man being immersed in what looked like a well, just like when King Ethelbert was being baptized in the font of St Martin's Canterbury. I was so thrilled to be there as a modern pilgrim because I was meditating in the Lady Chapel where that remarkable and humble priest Paul Couturier used to say Mass. He, perhaps more than anyone else, has helped to inaugurate the movement for unity of all Christians. It was he who was the architect of the Weeks of Prayer for Christian Unity in the 1930s–1940s which have become world-wide and gone from strength to strength, on the sound basis of Christians of all denominations being asked to meet together, often in silent prayer to pray 'for the unity of all Christians, as Christ wills and by the means He chooses'. For me that church will always be a special place, for later I went up with Père Michalon, his disciple, and prayed at Paul Couturier's tomb. Those days in Lyon must have been most heartwarming times. I gather the Weeks of Prayer still play a large part in the churches' ministry there.

Christopher Donaldson, *The Great English Pilgrimage: From Rome to Canterbury* (1995), pp. 84–5

Chapter Eight

THE JOURNEY WITHIN

A good number of writers have noted that the experience of pilgrimage foreshadowed the development of spiritual disciplines which to some extent replaced the actual act of pilgrimage itself. The monastic life, together with other reflective disciplines of prayer, flows naturally from pilgrimage. To this extent, there has always been a recognition that pilgrimage is more than religious tourism.

But despite the fact that spiritual disciplines can in theory replace the need for an actual physical pilgrimage, it is notable that the connection remains sufficiently strong that those whose interior spiritual life is well developed still engage in the practice of pilgrimage. Embracing the Way and the one who is himself the Way while travelling the pilgrim way connects the two.

The converse is also true. Pilgrimage without an interior journey becomes debased. There is a need to see beyond and within if the experience of pilgrimage is truly to act as a living metaphor for the Christian life. Many set off on pilgrimage with little concept of what the interior journey might mean and meet themselves *en route* in surprising and sometimes disturbing ways. The dark side of our being can be met and dealt with as part of the process of pilgrimage. An awareness of acting so that sin can be confronted and cast off forms an important part of the journey. An experience of being embraced by the love of God stands behind the sometimes unstated hope of every pilgrim.

I pray that out of his glorious riches he may strengthen you with power through his Spirit in your inner being, so that Christ may dwell in your hearts through faith. And I pray that you, being rooted and established in love, may have power, together with all the saints, to grasp how wide and long and high and deep is the love of Christ, and to know this love that surpasses knowledge – that you may be filled to the measure of all the fullness of God.

Now to him who is able to do immeasurably more than all we ask or imagine, according to his power that is at work within us, to him be glory in the church and in Christ Jesus throughout all generations, for ever and ever! Amen.

Ephesians 3:16–21

The first point is: You must ask about the way. He himself says this: *I am the way* (John 14:6). Oh, since he is the way, consider what ways he went – how he worked, and how he burned interiorly with charity and exteriorly in works of the virtues for strangers and for friends. And hear how he commanded men how greatly they should love their God – *with all* their *heart, with all* their *soul, and with all* their *strength* (Matthew 22:37; Luke 10:27); and that they nevermore forget this, sleeping or waking (Deuteronomy 6:6–7). Now consider how he himself did this, although he was himself God – how he gave all, and how he lived exclusively for veritable love of his Father and for charity toward men. He worked with vigilant charity, and he gave to Love all his Heart, and all his soul, and all his strength. This is the way that Jesus teaches, and that he himself is, and that he himself went, and wherein is found eternal life and the fruition of the truth of his Father's glory.

Next ask about the way from the saints, those he has taken to himself, and those who still remain here below, who are following after him in perfect virtues, who have followed him up the mountain of the noble life from the deep valley of humility, and have climbed the high mountain with strong faith and perfect confidence in the contemplation of the Love so sweet to our heart.

And further ask about the way from those that are close to you, and who you see are now going his ways in the manner most like his, and are obedient to him in all works of virtues. Thus follow him who himself is on the way, and those who have gone this way and are now going on it. (Letter 15)

Mother Columba Hart, trans., *Hadewijch: The Complete Works* (1980), p. 78

'What shall I do to be saved?' (*Acts xvi. 30, 31*)…Sir, I perceive, by the book in my hand, that I am condemned to die, and after that to come to judgement; and I find that I am not willing to do the first, nor able to do the second. (*Heb. ix. 27; Job xvi. 21, 22; Ezek. xxii. 14.*)

Then said the Evangelist, Why not willing to die, since this life is attended with so many evils? The man answered, Because I fear that this burden that is upon my back will sink me lower than the grave, and I shall fall into Tophet. (*Isa. xxx. 33.*) And, sir, if I be not fit to go

to prison, I am not fit to go to judgement, and from thence to execu-
tion; and the thoughts of these things make me cry.

Then said Evangelist, If this be thy condition, why standest thou
still? He answered, Because I know not whither to go. Then he gave
him a parchment roll; and there was written within, 'Flee from the
wrath to come!' (*Matt. iii. 7.*) The man, therefore, read it; and looking
upon Evangelist very carefully, said, Wither must I fly? Then said
Evangelist, pointing with his finger over a very wide field, Do you see
yonder Wicket-gate? (*Matt. vii. 13,14*) The man said, No. Then said
the other, Do you see yonder shining light? (*Ps. cxix. 105; 2 Pet. i.
19.*) He said, I think I do. Then said Evangelist, Keep that light in
your eye, and go up directly thereto, so shalt thou see the gate; at
which, when thou knockest, it shall be told thee what thou shalt do.

John Bunyan, *The Pilgrim's Progress* (1678)

I long to know how Jacob saw you fixed above the ladder (cf. Genesis
28:12). That climb, how was it? Tell me, for I long to know. What is
the mode, what is the law joining those steps that the lover has set as
an ascent in his heart (cf. Psalm 83:6). I thirst to know the number of
those steps, and the time required to climb them. He who discovered
Your struggle and Your vision has spoken to us of the guides. But he
would not – perhaps he could not – tell us any more.

This empress, as if coming from heaven, spoke thus in my soul's
hearing: 'My love, you will never be able to know how beautiful I am
unless you get away from the grossness of the flesh. So let this ladder
teach you the spiritual union of the virtues. And I am there on the
summit, for as the great man said, a man who knew me well,
"Remaining now are faith, hope, and love, these three. But love is the
greatest of them all" (1 Corinthians 13:13).'

John Climacus, *The Ladder of Divine Ascent*, trans. Colm Luibheid &
Norman Russell (1982), pp. 289–90

*My reading of St John of the Cross has been particularly blessed by grace.
It has been a real help to me this week. Here is a summary of his
'Nothings':*

To earthly goods
To one's own opinion
To one's own worth
Even to graces received
To oneself

This road leads to the way of the cross and the crucifixion of the ego. You will be buried with Christ, which is a prelude to being resurrected with him for ever.

This spiritual life then, is a journey, so a guide is needed to reveal the Father to us during two fundamental moments in the life of mankind. '*This is my Son, the Beloved; listen to him!*' (at baptism and on Mount Tabor: Mark 9:7).

The guide *is to be found in faith*, as Peter found it, and when it is found Jesus rejoices: 'Blessed are you, Simon...for flesh and blood has not revealed this to you' (Matthew 16:17).

Carlo Carretto, *The Desert Journal* (1992), pp. 82–3

With the drawing of this Love and the voice of this Calling

We shall not cease from exploration
And the end of all our exploring
Will be to arrive where we started
And know the place for the first time.
Through the unknown, remembered gate
When the last of earth left to discover
Is that which was the beginning;
At the source of the longest river
The voice of the hidden waterfall
And the children of the apple-tree
Not known, because not looked for
But heard, half-heard, in the stillness
Between two waves of the sea.
T. S. Eliot, 'Little Gidding', *Poetry 1900 to 1965*, ed. G. Macbeth (1967), p. 101

One Dark Night

We can offer three reasons for calling this journey towards union with God a night.

The first has to do with the point of departure because individuals must deprive themselves of their appetites for worldly possessions. This denial and privation is like a night for all their senses.

The second reason refers to the means or the road along which a person travels to this union. Now this road is faith, and for the intellect faith is also like a dark night.

The third reason pertains to the point of arrival, namely God. And God is also a dark night to the soul in this life. These three nights

pass through a soul, or better, the soul passes through them in order
to reach union with God.

Ⅰ John of the Cross (1540–91), *The Ascent of Mount Carmel, John of the Cross:
Selected Writings*, ed. Kieran Kavanaugh (1987), p. 63

When the soul thinks it is ready, it sets out from Sochoth and camps
at Buthan (Numbers 33:6; Etham). Buthan means 'valley'. Now we
have said that the stages refer to progress in the virtues. And a virtue
is not acquired without training and hard work, nor is it tested as
much in prosperity as in adversity. So the soul comes to a valley. For
in valleys and in low places the struggle against the devil and opposing
powers takes place. Thus, in the valley the battle must be fought.
Then, too, Abraham fought against the barbarian kings in the Valley
of Siddim (Genesis 14:8), and there he gained the victory. Therefore,
this wanderer of ours descends to those who are in deep and low
places, not to linger there, but to gain victory there.

Origen, *An Exhortation to Martyrdom, Prayer and Selected Works*,
trans. Rowan Greer (1979), p. 258

You have received this knowledge and divine love worthily and have
directed it in accordance with the nature given to the soul. You have
assembled zealously, fulfilling together the apostolic ideal in your
actions, and you have requested from us, as a guide and leader for
your life's journey, a discourse which will direct you to the straight
path, indicating accurately what the scope of this life is for those
entering upon it, what 'the good and acceptable and perfect will of
God' is, what kind of road leads to this end, how it is fitting for those
travelling upon it to treat each other, how it is necessary for those in
authority to direct the chorus of philosophy, and what suffering must
be endured by those who are going to ascend to the peak of virtue and
make their own souls worthy of the reception of the spirit.

Gregory of Nyssa, *Fathers of the Church: Gregory of Nyssa: Ascetical Works*,
ed. Virginia Callahan (1967), pp. 127–8

Jerusalem is, as much to say, *a sight of peace*; and betokeneth contemplation in perfect love of God; for contemplation is nothing else but a
sight of God, which is very peace. Then if thou covet to come to this
blessed sight of very peace, and be a true pilgrim towards *Jerusalem*,
though it be so that I was never there, *nevertheless*, as far forth as I
can, I shall set thee in the way towards it.

The beginning of the high way, in which thou shalt go, is reforming in Faith, grounded humbly on the faith and on the laws of the holy Church as I have said before; for trust assuredly, though you have sinned heretofore, if you be now reformed by the Sacrament of Penance, after the law of the holy Church, that thou art in the right way. Now then, since thou art in the safe way, if thou wilt speed in thy going and make a good journey, it behoveth thee to hold these two things often in thy mind: *Humility* and *Love*; and often say to thyself, *I am nothing, I have nothing, I covet nothing, but one...* Humility saith, *I am nothing, I have nothing*, Love saith, *I covet nothing, but one*, and that is Jesus.

Walter Hilton, The Scale of Perfection (1901), p. 188

He transcends all in a manner beyond being, and manifests Himself without disguise and in truth only to those who have passed through ritual consecrations and purifications, and beyond all the ascents of all the holy summits, and have left behind all divine illuminations, and sounds and heavenly words, and entered into the Darkness, where, as the Scriptures say, He who transcends all really is. For not simply is the divine Moses bidden first of all to purify himself and then to separate himself from those not thus purified; but after all purification, he hears the many sounding trumpets and sees many lights which flash forth pure and widely diffused rays. Then he separates himself from the multitude and with the chosen priests he reaches the summit of the divine ascents. But not even here does he hold converse with God Himself, nor does he behold Him (for He is invisible), but only the place where He is. And this, I think, means that the most divine and exalted of the things that are seen with the eye or perceived by the mind are but suggestions that barely hint of the nature of that which transcends any conception whatever, a presence which sets but its feet upon the spiritual pinnacles of its most holy places. And then Moses is cut off from both things seen and those who see and enters into the darkness of unknowing, a truly hidden darkness, according to which he shuts his eyes to all apprehensions that convey knowledge, for he has past into a realm quite beyond any feeling or seeing. Now, belonging wholly to that which is beyond all, and yet to nothing at all, and being neither himself, nor another, and united in his highest part in passivity (*anenergesia*) with Him who is completely unknowable, he knows by not knowing in a manner that transcends understanding.

Pseudo-Dionysius, Mystical Theology, cited in Andrew Louth, The Origins of the
Christian Mystical Tradition (1981), p. 173

Columbanus (*c.* 543–615), the great Celtic monastic founder and wanderer across much of western Europe, employed 'road' and 'journey' as his favourite metaphors for the Christian life. Life itself was a roadway that led to eternity.

> Let us concern ourselves with things divine, and as pilgrims ever sigh for and desire our homeland; for the end of the road is ever the object of the traveller's hopes and desires, and thus, since we are travellers and pilgrims in the world, let us ever ponder on the end of the road, that is of our life, for the end of our roadway is our home. [*Sancti Columbani Opera*]
>
> Philip Sheldrake, *Living Between Worlds* (1995), p. 61

Understand, then, if you can, what the pilgrimages of the soul are in which it laments with groaning and grief that it has been on pilgrimage for so long. We understand these pilgrimages only dully and darkly so long as the pilgrimage still lasts. But when the soul has returned to its rest, that is, to the fatherland in paradise, it will be taught more truly and will understand more truly what the meaning of its pilgrimage was.

Origen, *An Exhortation to Martyrdom, Prayer and Selected Works*,
trans. Rowan Greer (1979), p. 250

In order to achieve some understanding of him, we must first follow the traces which are material, temporal, and external. This means being conducted in the way of God. Then, we must penetrate our own mind, which is an image of God, everlasting, spiritual, and internal. This means walking in the truth of God. We must, finally, pass over to the eternal, the wholly spiritual, which is above us, by looking up to the First Principle. And this means rejoicing in the knowledge of God and in the reverence due to His majesty.

So this is the three-day journey into the wilderness, or the three degrees of light within a single day: dusk, dawn, and noon. It represents the triple existence of things, that is, existence in physical reality, in the mind, and in the Eternal Act, according to what is written: *Let it be; God made it; and it was.* It also represents the presence of Christ, our Ladder, of a triple substance, bodily, rational, and divine.

Bonaventure, *The Works of Bonaventure: Mystical Opuscula*, trans. J. de Vinck
(1960), p. 10

This bridge has walls of stone so that travellers will not be hindered when it rains. Do you know what stones these are? They are the stones of true solid virtue. These stones were not, however, built into walls before my Son's passion. So no one could get to the final destination, even though they walked along the path of virtue. For heaven had not yet been unlocked with the key of my Son's blood, and the rain of justice kept anyone from crossing over...

At the end of the bridge is the gate (which is, in fact, one with the bridge), which is the only way you can enter. This is why he said, 'I am the Way and Truth and Life; whoever walks with me walks not in darkness but in light.'

Catherine of Siena, *The Dialogue*, trans. Suzanne Noffke (1980), p. 66

Now I further saw, that betwixt [the pilgrims] and the gate was a river; but there was no bridge to go over: the river was very deep. At the sight, therefore, of this river, the pilgrims were much stunned; but the men that went with them said, You must go through, or you cannot come at the gate.

The pilgrims then began to inquire if there was no other way to the gate? To which they answered, Yes; but there hath not any, save two — to wit, Enoch and Elijah — been permitted to tread that path since the foundation of the world, nor shall until the last trumpet shall sound. The pilgrims then, especially Christian, began to despond, and looked this way and that; but could find no way by which they might escape the river. Then they asked the men if the waters were all of a depth? They said, No; yet they could not help them in that case; for, said they, you shall find it deeper or shallower, as you believe in the King of the place.

John Bunyan, *The Pilgrim's Progress* (1678)

Three movements of the soul, those of repentance, faith and love, characterize the Godward journey. They are inner attitudes which express themselves in aspiration and action. They are all present and operative throughout the pilgrimage but at different stages one or other will tend to predominate. It is normal in the early stages of the pilgrim's journey for repentance to be of especial importance. Later the deepening and enlarging of faith commonly becomes a major concern. Later still the progress of the spiritual pilgrim is measured chiefly by growth in love for God and one's fellows. But spiritual development is no steady, regular advance, but is punctuated by crises in which growth appears to have come to a stop for a time; old battles have to be refought and old experiences relived at a deeper level.

The movement of repentance involves the determination to make God and his will the guiding principle of life and the struggle to renounce idolatries, the undue attachment to relative goods, such as pleasure, popularity and success, which interfere with the Godward journey. It will mean the battle with selfish inclinations and habits and the endeavour to build up Christlike habits and attitudes. The cardinal virtues of prudence, justice, temperance and fortitude give an outline of the human qualities which are needed to provide a firm foundation for the specifically Christian virtues of faith, hope and love. But Christlike habits and actions will be impossible without a transformation of desires and emotions which no effort can bring about. Only reliance on the cleansing and renewing power of the Holy Spirit can bring about the inner revolution that is necessary. The pilgrim seeks to assist this inner change partly by contemplating the figure of Christ, partly by a self-examination which seeks to uncover the disordered emotions and desires which need to be cleansed and redirected. This area of excessive fear and anxiety, of anger and depression, of disordered sex-desire and morbid guilt, which is the seed-bed of actual sins, needs to be opened up to the healing and renewing of the Holy Spirit.

C. Jones, G. Wainwright & E. Yarnold, eds.,
The Study of Spirituality (1986), p. 566

My Lord God
      I have no idea where I am going.
I do not see the road ahead of me.
I cannot know for certain where it will end.
            Nor do I really know myself,
            and the fact that I think I am following
      your will does not mean
      that I am actually doing so.
But I believe that my desire to please you
      does in fact please you.
            And I hope that I have that desire
            in all that I am doing.
      I hope that I will never do anything
      apart from that desire.
And I know that if I do this
            you will lead me by the right road
            though I may know nothing about it.
Therefore will I trust you always
            though I may seem to be lost
            and in the shadow of death.

I will not fear,
>for you are ever with me,
>and you will never leave me
>to face my perils alone.

Thomas Merton (1915–1968), A Prayer

Trees, trees, millions of trees, massive, immense, running up high; and at their foot, hugging the bank against the stream, crept the little begrimed steamboat, like a sluggish beetle crawling on the floor of a lofty portico. It made you feel very small, very lost, and yet it was not altogether depressing, that feeling...Where the pilgrims imagined it crawled I do not know. To some place where they expected to get something, I bet! For me it crawled towards Kurtz – exclusively; but when the steampipes started leaking we crawled very slow. The reaches opened before us and closed behind, as if the forest had stepped leisurely across the water to bar the way for our return. We penetrated deeper and deeper into the heart of darkness.

Joseph Conrad, Heart of Darkness (1902), p. 50

I ran to a steady jogtrot rhythm, and soon it was so smooth that I forgot I was running, and I was hardly able to know that my legs were lifting and falling and my arms going in and out and my heart stopped that wicked thumping I always get at the beginning of a run. Because you see I never race at all; I just run, and somehow I know that if I forget I'm racing and only jogtrot along until I don't know I'm running I always win the race. For when my eyes recognize that I'm getting near the end of a course – by seeing a stile or cottage corner – I put on a spurt, and such a fast spurt it is because I feel that up till then I haven't been running and that I've used no energy at all. And I've been able to do this because I've been thinking.

Alan Sillitoe, The Loneliness of the Long-Distance Runner (1959), pp. 37–8

The man turned around towards the shore he had just left. Now that shore was obscured by the darkness and the water, vast and savage like the continent of trees stretching beyond it for thousands of kilometres. Between the nearby ocean and this sea of vegetation, the handful of men drifting at that moment on a wild river seemed lost. When the raft bumped the new pier it was as if, having cast off all moorings, they were landing on an island in the darkness after days of frightened sailing.

Albert Camus (1913–60), 'The Growing Stone', *Exile and the Kingdom* trans. Justin O'Brien (1958), p. 120

If but some vengeful god would call to me
From up the sky, and laugh: 'Thou suffering thing,
Know that thy suffering is in my ecstasy,
That thy love's loss is my hate's profiting!'

Then would I bear it, clench myself, and die,
Steeled by the sense of ire unmerited;
Half-eased in that a Powerfuller than I
Had willed and meted me the tears I shed.

But not so. How arrives it joy lies slain,
And why unblooms the best hope ever sown?
– Crass Casualty obstructs the sun and rain,
And dicing Time for gladness casts a moan...
These purblind Doomsters had as readily strown
Blisses about my pilgrimage as pain.

Thomas Hardy (1840–1928), 'Hap', *The Complete Poetical Works of Thomas Hardy*, ed. J. Gibson (1976), p. 9

On the Friday afternoon I was walking on the deck, feeling like 'Pooh' who said somewhere, 'There's nothing I like better than doing nothing.' There is much to be said in favour of doing nothing, withdrawing from all activity for a time and keeping silence, including a silence of the mind, for then we can become aware of deeper levels of our mind and heart. These deeper levels may bring peace, happiness and delight, but they can also be very disturbing and frightening.

I was hanging over the ship's rails thinking of nothing in particular, when suddenly a feeling of despondency hit me like a large wave and submerged me for the next twenty-four hours. I do not know whether the despondency brought to mind the images, or the images the despondency, but whatever the order, the images released thoughts which, as I soon recognized, had been lurking below the surface for a long time.

Gerard Hughes, *Walk to Jerusalem* (1991), p. 214

As I walked slowly back to the abbey through the drab city of Lisieux, stopping in at various bars, a bank and a pharmacy, I thought how central to the lives of so many saints, artists, poets, was the dynamic discovery of their own vast, miserable inadequacy against the pull and summons of their inspiration; some quantum leap has to be made; a leap into the dark. This brave leap forward seems often to fetch a circle back to their own centre. From there, in touch with God, Buddha nature, higher intelligence, various unnamed strengths. Finally the resources necessary are often found to be available, although this does not mean an end to suffering.

Jini Fiennes, *On Pilgrimage: A Time to Seek* (1991), p. 25

The word is a long journey. It leads to the human heart. In my case, the journey led me to Kentucky and Birmingham, to Rome and New York, to Darlington and Pittsburgh. It is a long journey to learn what to say and how to say it so that one speaks in such a manner that he verbalizes the spiritual striving, the intellectual groping, the emotional yearning of his age and brings people the serenity of sharing understanding, mutual faith, common hope, and concrete love. The right word is our act of mercy to one another as well as the most telling theology we can write. It is a long journey and the pilgrim is still far from home.

Gregory Baum, ed., *Journeys: The Impact of Personal Experience*
on Religious Thought (1975), p. 227

The man who does not permit his spirit to be beaten down and upset by dryness and helplessness, but who lets God lead him peacefully through the wilderness, and desires no other support or guidance than that of pure faith and trust in God alone, will be brought to the Promised Land. He will taste the peace and joy of union with God. He will, without 'seeing,' have an habitual, comforting, obscure and mysterious awareness of his God, present and acting in all the events of life...

Just as the light of faith is darkness to the mind, so the supreme supernatural activity of the mind and will in contemplation and infused love at first seems to us like inaction...When you are travelling in a plane close to the ground you realize that you are going somewhere: but in the stratosphere, although you may be going fast, you lose the sense of speed.

Thomas Merton, *Seeds of Contemplation* (1961), pp. 185–6

I have joined myself to a soul who is out of the region of beginnings, and has just entered on the great central wilderness, whose long plains of weary sand join the verdant fields of the beginners with the woody mountains of the long-tired and well-mortified souls. God calls some to himself in their first fervours, others mature in grace on the mountain heights. But more die in the wilderness, some at one point of the pilgrimage, some at another. Of course there is only one good time for each of us to die; and that is the exact hour at which God wills that death should find us. But as the great body of devout men die while they are crossing the central wilderness, it is this wilderness of which I wish to speak: the wilderness of long patient perseverance in the humbling practices of solid virtues...

The soul, then, at this stage of its journey is beset by two opposite temptations. Sometimes it is attacked by one, sometimes by another, according to different moods of mind and diversities of character. These temptations are discouragement and presumption; and our chief business at this point is to be upon our guard against these two things.

Frederick Faber, *Growth in Holiness* (1960), p. 9

As I walked the roads I often thought of [those] Celtic monks, who wandered through Europe, wondering at the glory of God's creation, preaching the Gospel and founding monasteries. At first they were imaginary figures from the distant past, but they are in God, who is eternal, that is, always in the now, in the God who keeps my legs going along these roads, so those Celtic saints are as near to me as the living, in fact nearer. Why shouldn't St Patrick cheer me up on the road, just as the waitress cheered me by lighting the candle at the table? Following this line of thought, I found myself talking with these figures from the past and with my own dead relatives and friends, especially with my sister Marie, who died forty years earlier. These conversations became very natural and they could be very helpful in decision making.

Gerard Hughes, *Walk to Jerusalem* (1991), p. 93

I know how the attraction of possessions pulls against the wish for a more austere lifestyle. Yet now, when shedding clutter had become not only spiritually desirable but a practical necessity, I still wanted things I did not need – the small pleasures of make-up and talcum powder, more than one change of clothes, one or two favourite pieces of jewellery, even my transistor radio. Walter Hilton, the fourteenth-century mystic, would not have considered me a real pilgrim, for he wrote that

A real pilgrim going to Jerusalem...divests himself of all that he possesses, so that he can travel light. Similarly, if you wish to be a spiritual pilgrim, you must strip yourself of all your spiritual possessions; your good deeds as well as your bad deeds must be left behind. You must regard yourself as so spiritually poor that you have no confidence in your own actions; instead you must desire only the presence of Jesus, and his profound love.

I like the idea of stripping oneself of one's deeds, travelling spiritually light, leaving both guilt over the bad and self-righteousness over any good deeds behind. Letting go, something I have never been good at.

Shirley du Boulay, *The Road to Canterbury* (1994), pp. 93–4

The Desert Fathers believe that the wilderness had been created as supremely valuable in the eyes of God precisely because it had no value to men. The wasteland was the land that could never be wasted by men because it offered them nothing. There was nothing to attract them. There was nothing to exploit. The desert was the region in which the Chosen People had wandered for forty years, cared for by God alone. They could have reached the Promised Land in a few months if they had travelled directly to it. God's plan was that they should learn to love Him in the wilderness and that they should always look back upon the time in the desert as the idyllic time of their life with Him alone.

Thomas Merton, *Thoughts in Solitude* (1958), p. 20

Our life is a great pilgrimage away from chaos and death into a fullness of life. John Donne, the dean of St Paul's Cathedral in the seventeenth century, used the Exodus theme in his personal devotions. 'As thou has enlightened and enlarged me to contemplate thy greatness, so, O God, descend and stoop down to see my infirmities and the Egypt in which I live, and (if thy good pleasure be such) hasten mine Exodus and deliverance.'

...John Donne took the image of the Exodus and applied it, through a powerful act of the imagination, to his own life. That image illuminates our own pilgrimage as surely as it enlightened his. It enlarges our hearts to breaking point as it did his. The biblical images have the power to change and catapult us into adventure inasmuch as we allow them to take root in us. The desert is the place where this happens. We have to go to the place of extremity. The adventure really begins here in the desert, 'the last place on earth'.

Alan Jones, *Passion for Pilgrimage* (1995), p. 46

Chapter Nine

WORSHIP ON THE WAY
AND ON ARRIVAL

P recisely because the pilgrim is not merely a religious tourist, the quality of the pilgrim's worship while on pilgrimage is usually taken very seriously. Few would set out on pilgrimage confident that they were experts in worship. The records show that the quality of the devotions of some pilgrims left something to be desired. Popular piety, and indeed popular songs are mixed with the more recognizably liturgical forms to such an extent that pilgrim worship has sometimes contained that inevitable mixture of the sacred and the profane that often accompanies life itself.

But most would want to mark the beginning of pilgrimage with prayer. It is not untypical for the pilgrim to seek the blessing of the local congregation of Christians. That might be in the form of a simple prayer or blessing. It might include the use of holy water or a special ceremony to indicate that a journey of some significance was taking place. Worship continues along the way. Particular shrines might be visited, certain churches entered and prayer to start each day utilized.

The pilgrim bands might also be inclined to sing hymns while travelling, partly to encourage each other and partly to remind themselves of their purpose. But worship is not confined to the journey itself. In many ways the experience of worship is intensified on arrival. Gratitude for safe arrival combined with a sense of the importance of the place itself cause pilgrims to engage in elaborate forms of worship at their destination. To some extent, the pilgrimage sites themselves recognize the need for worship and become dedicated to the cause of assisting pilgrims to engage in meaningful worship. The eucharist in particular seems to become a key component in the devotional life of pilgrims re-enacting as it does the essential elements of the life, death and resurrection of Jesus in the same way that the pilgrimage itself does.

And then, on the return, the grateful pilgrim completes their journey with hymns and prayers in the place where they began. Worship helps to seal all that has taken place and to point the pilgrim to their ultimate destination.

Jacob left Beersheba and set out for Haran. When he reached a certain place, he stopped for the night because the sun had set. Taking one of the stones there, he put it under his head and lay down to sleep. He had a dream in which he saw a stairway resting on the earth, with its top reaching to heaven, and the angels of God were ascending and descending on it. There above it stood the LORD, and he said: 'I am the LORD, the God of your father Abraham and the God of Isaac. I will give you and your descendants the land on which you are lying. Your descendants will be like the dust of the earth, and you will spread out to the west and to the east, to the north and to the south. All peoples on earth will be blessed through you and your offspring. I am with you and will watch over you wherever you go, and I will bring you back to this land. I will not leave you until I have done what I have promised you.'

When Jacob awoke from his sleep, he thought, 'Surely the LORD is in this place, and I was not aware of it.' He was afraid and said, 'How awesome is this place! This is none other than the house of God; this is the gate of heaven.'

Early the next morning Jacob took the stone he had placed under his head and set it up as a pillar and poured oil on top of it.

Genesis 28:10–18

Forth pilgrime! forth best out of thy stalle!
Loke up on hye, and thonke God for alle;
Weyve thy lust, and let thy goste the lede,
And trouthe shal thy delyver, hit is no drede.

Geoffrey Chaucer (c. 1340–1400), 'Good Counseil of Chaucer'

The following is a blessing for a journey. Tenth century or later. Middle Irish.

May this journey be easy, may it be a journey of profit in my
    hands!
Holy Christ against demons, against weapons, against killings!
May Jesus and the Father, may the Holy Spirit sanctify us!
May the mysterious God be not hidden in darkness, may the
    bright King save us!
May the cross of Christ's body and Mary guard us on the road!
May it not be unlucky for us, may it be successful and easy!

Oliver Davies & Fiona Bowie, Celtic Christian Spirituality (1995), p. 38

I then found my way to the Monastery of St Andrew, knocked boldly on the door and asked a young man who answered it if he could find for me an English-speaking monk to whom I could talk. To my delight a leading director of the Benedictine order, a kindly and gracious Italian monk, Father Emanuele Bargellini, spoke English fluently. I told him, without stuttering too much I hope, of my longing for a blessing at this beginning of my pilgrimage to Canterbury. He was more than willing and left me to kneel by Gregory's chair in the gloom. Suddenly the lights came on over the altar, a young man lit the candles, and after a while Father Emanuele came with his white Benedictine habit on and stood by me and we spoke comfortably of what I was planning to do. He then went to the altar, took out the great Mass Book, read out the gospel about Jesus sending out his disciples on their journey, we prayed and then to my joy he sprinkled me with Holy Water and gave me a final blessing. It was all so encouraging and I hope all pilgrims setting off from here to Canterbury will feel so deeply spiritual, happy and at peace with the world.

Christopher Donaldson, *The Great English Pilgrimage:*
From Rome to Canterbury (1995), p. 62

But the pilgrim himself might contribute a good deal to the atmosphere surrounding his expedition according to the extent to which he endeavoured deliberately to impose a Christian character on his travels. It is appropriate to recall at this point Gregory of Nyssa's state carriage, which assumed, according to him, the features of church and monastery, its passengers 'joining in psalms throughout the whole journey, and fasting for the Lord'. Paulinus also vividly imagined the sound of hymns and psalms echoing from the vessel which conveyed bishop Nicetas of Remesiana home from a visit to Nola. Such continuous practice of the Christian liturgy was an obvious and explicit 'label' of the pious nature of the enterprise; there would even be well-to-do lay pilgrims who transported their own clergy among their entourage bishops included. Services of worship, as a matter of rule, always accompanied Egeria's halts at Christian sites; and the central place was given to the reading of the appropriate passage of the Bible.

Edward Hunt, *Holy Land Pilgrimage in the Later Roman Empire* (1982), p. 67

Among these songs, one is outstanding: the great song of the Santiago pilgrims or Spiritual Canticle.

This is a travelling song, a kind of *Vademecum* or tourist guide whose verses relate to various stages of St James's Way (a map set to music), the perils and difficult stretches, the customs, the sanctuaries, the relics, etc. It is the prototype for other wayfaring songs to be found in Europe.

I have researched the entire process of recovery of this 'Great Song' with all the related episodes, and I even know the name of the 80-year-old pilgrim, Mr Moura of the parish of Asson (Lower Pyrenees) who has preserved and transmitted it...

The text of the song was published for the first time in Troyes 1718, but we come across it at a far earlier date at Roncevaux in the thirteenth century. It was presumably brought by a troubadour giving Christian de Boisvert as his name and Troyes as his birthplace. He died and was buried as the Chapel of the Holy Spirit in the European cemetery for pilgrims in the Pyrenees of Navarre. The Prior of Roncevaux recovered the text from the pouch of this pilgrim troubadour.

'The Santiago de Compostela Pilgrim Routes', *Architectural Heritage Reports and Studies* 16 (1989): 85

According to Sherrard 'a pilgrimage is not simply a matter of getting to a particular shrine or holy place. It is a deliberate sundering and surrender of one's habitual conditions of comfort, routine, safety and convenience. Unlike the tourist, whose aim is to see things and to travel around in conditions which are as comfortable, secure, familiar, convenient and unchallenging as possible, the pilgrim breaks with his material servitude, puts his trust in God and sets out on a quest which is inward as much as outward, and which is, in varying degrees, into the unknown. In this sense he becomes the image of the spiritual seeker. He removes himself as far as possible from the artificiality within which he is enclosed by his life in society. Of this spiritual exploration, inward and outward, *walking* is an essential part. His feet tread the earth from which he is made and from which he is usually so cut off, especially in the more or less totally urbanized conditions of modern life. Through his eyes, ears, nose, he renews his sense of natural beauty, the beauty of God's creation. He watches the flight of bird or insect, the ripple of light on leaves, the timeless vistas of the sea; he listens to the song of water, the calls of God's creatures; he breathes in the scent of tree and flower and soil. His feet tire, his body aches, sweat drips from his head and trickles into his eyes and down his neck. He tastes rigour and hardship. But through all this and only through all this, and through his prayer and dedication and confidence slowly an inner change is wrought, a new *rhythm* grows, a deeper harmony. The pilgrimage is at work.'

Rene Gothoni, 'The Progress of Pilgrimage on the Holy Mountain of Athos', *Social Anthropology of Pilgrimage*, ed. Makhan Jha (1991), p. 302

I stood still, gathering my concentration, breathing slowly, relaxing my whole body, and began to walk. I set one foot before another, feeling my feet within my shoes, the texture of the earth beneath my feet, aware of my balance, the movement of my limbs, the easy pace, the ground covered, and the simple joy of walking.

As I walked, paused, turned, walked, I became more aware of the October morning, the slight breeze, the autumn sun, the changing, falling leaves, the clear day, the fields around, the noise of partridges and crows, the cows in the adjoining field.

Still walking...not encouraging or discouraging thoughts, the reality of the season pressed upon me. The dying of the year, the trees and shrubs around my enclosure losing their foliage, the exposed skeleton of bare branches – all the lovely melancholy of late October.

As I walk this linear path I am aware of my own dying, finitude, mortality. My leaves are falling, seasons slip away, I am a pilgrim setting one foot before another on my own mortal journey. One foot before another, one step, another step, keep on walking, mindfully, gently, thankfully. I am tempted to develop my thinking, to 'make a meditation', to construct a homily. But I let it go, establish my concentrated awareness again – and keep on walking...walking...walking. Then I reach the cross once more and stop. I take some deep breaths, feel a quiet sense of gratitude, and return to my hut.

Brother Ramon SSF, *The Heart of Prayer* (1995), pp. 131–2

In the days of the Early Church, 'to go on a pilgrimage' was often rendered by 'to go to a place on account of prayer' – so Egeria, to cite one example, went to the land of Uz to visit the memorial of Job *gratia orationis*. Prayer indeed is the distinctive activity of pilgrimage: not an account has survived that does not refer time and time again to this activity. The Lord's Prayer in particular was constantly on the lips of everyone, including, to take a couple at random, Denis Possot and Charles- Philippe de Champarnoy in the year 1532: when Bethlehem hove in sight, they knelt by the roadside and said together the Pater Noster.

Although intercession for others should certainly be practised, prayer, especially in the context of pilgrimage, is not simply petitionary as if, to use a vivid image employed by Evelyn Underhill, each time one prays one comes to God clutching a supernatural shopping list. Rather, prayer, in its fullest sense, is communion with God, being still in his presence, contemplating him, adoring him, thanking him and frequently praising him.

John Davies, *Pilgrimage Yesterday and Today* (1988), pp. 228–9

SACRED PLACES, PILGRIM PATHS

What most interested Egeria in Jerusalem was the sometimes spectac-
ular liturgy that had already developed around the primary Christian
holy places, and this a scant half-century after Constantine had begun
the conversion of Jerusalem from a Roman city into a Christian city.
The centre of liturgical life was, naturally, the Church of the Anastasis
or the Resurrection:

> Loving sisters, [she writes for those back home, probably in a
> convent somewhere in France] since I know you are eager to
> know about the services they have daily in the holy places, I
> shall tell you about them. All the doors of the Anastasis are
> opened before cock-crow each day, and the monks and virgins,
> monazontes and parthenae, as they call them here, come in, and
> also some lay men and women, at least those who wish to make
> an early vigil. From that hour to daybreak hymns are sung and
> psalms and antiphons sung in response. And after each hymn a
> prayer is offered, since there are two or three presbyters or dea-
> cons each day by turn, who are there with the monazontes, and
> they say prayers after each hymn or antiphon...
> ...At daybreak, because it is the Lord's day, the people
> assemble in the Great Church built by Constantine on Golgo-
> tha behind the Cross. And they do what is everywhere the cus-
> tom on the Lord's Day. But they have this custom, that any
> presbyter who is seated there may preach, if he so wishes, and
> when they have finished, the bishop preaches. The reason why
> they have this preaching every Lord's day is to make sure that
> the people will continually be learning about the Scriptures
> and the love of God. Because of all this preaching it is a long
> time before they are dismissed from the church, which takes
> place not before ten or even eleven o'clock.
>
> F. E. Peters, *Jerusalem* (1985), pp. 148-9

The first church was erected here at the bidding of the Emperor Constantine. The site was chosen at the bidding of Macarius, Bishop of
Jerusalem, who believed that it covered the place of crucifixion and
also the adjacent place of burial. His contemporaries appear to have
been unanimous in their acceptance of his opinion...

In the church itself five different branches of the Christian Church
have rights, centuries old, to which they cling jealously. These are the
Latins, the Greek Orthodox, the Syrians, the Armenians and the Cop-
tics. The whole thing is somewhat confusing and not a little disturbing
to the first-time visitor...

For a few minutes the chapels clear of other pilgrims and we have the place more or less to ourselves. As we read a short extract from the crucifixion story and say a brief prayer, we have the opportunity to reflect that whether or not we can ever be sure of the exact spot where it happened, the important thing is to know that Jesus 'died to save us all'.

Thus Constantine discovered, under the temple of Jupiter Capitolinus on Hadrian's forum in the Upper City, the place of Jesus' burial. The site, it is clear from the account, was known, and indeed it is unlikely that the local Christian community in the city would have forgotten where the Saviour of Mankind had died and been buried, and this despite the fact that the shape and topography of the city had been considerably altered since the days when Pontius Pilate sat in the Roman pretorium in Jerusalem. Jesus had been executed and buried outside the western city wall; that same place was now in the centre of the Upper City, at the commercial and political heart of the Aelia designed by Hadrian's builders. It was a place, Constantine must have thought, for a monumental public statement. Eusebius continues:

> Thereupon the emperor issued sacred edicts and, when he had provided an abundant supply of all the things required for the project, he gave orders that a house of prayer worthy of God should be erected round the Cave of Salvation, and on a scale of rich and imperial costliness...
>
> F. E. Peters, *Jerusalem* (1985), pp. 133-4

Cyril of Jerusalem was building on the foundation laid by Constantine when he devised a series of services, particularly for Holy Week, closely linked with the topography of the city where he presided as bishop. He was well aware of the evidential and didactic value of the sacred sites; thus, speaking in the Martyrium, he told candidates for baptism: 'Christ was truly crucified for our sins. Even supposing you were disposed to contest this, your surroundings rise up before you to refute you, this sacred Golgotha where we now come together because of him who was crucified here.' On another occasion he affirmed that there are many true testimonies to Christ: 'the palm tree of the valley, which provided branches to the children of those days who hailed him. Gethsemane bears witness still, to the imagination all but haunted by the form of Judas. This Golgotha, sacred above all such places, bears witness by its very look. The most holy sepulchre bears witness and the stone lies there to this day.' It was to see these very places and to participate in the celebrations that were arranged at each one of them that pilgrims began to arrive in droves.

John Davies, *Pilgrimage Yesterday and Today* (1988), p. 11

Together with this devotion to stones and wells and the bushes that hang over the spring or take root in the cleft of the rock, the Irish people probably had at a very early period a custom of going on pil-grimage to particular stone circles, stones, wells and so on. The great stone circles are often placed at points which suggest that they were great religious centres to which worshippers could gather: Callanish in Lewis on the island's coast, Stonehenge on the downland ridgeways, Carnac in Brittany, like Callanish related to the sea-ways and the habits of the capable Megalithic sailor. Again, the obvious religious procession at a stone circle would go round it, and if the stone circles were related to sun-worship, to go round in the track of the sun, the right-handed circle or 'round'. However it arose, the chief liturgical act of the pilgrim to well or stone or cairn is this right-handed 'round' circling the object of devotion.

It seems that these pilgrimages took place at special times of the year, marking the changes of the seasons. The wells were supposed to be specially potent at this time: spring water or even the dew on the grass on May day was supposed to have special properties and virtues. There was an associated fire cult with the lighting of fires upon hilltops, which still survives in Ireland in the St John's fires which are lit on Midsummer Eve. The Halloween celebrations are part of the same series of ancient seasonal festivals. Pre-Christian Celtic religion, about which we know very little, seems to have had an intense feeling for this rhythm of the seasons, not unnaturally, for the people's economy was based on crops and cattle and the fertility of both essential to life. It is extraordinary how this idea clings, even when its meaning is forgotten; dour Scots Presbyterians still climb Arthur's Seat in Edinburgh to bathe in the dew on May morning, and of late years, have accompanied the expedition with a religious service.

Catholic liturgy took hold of this idea of seasonal rhythm and transferred it into a new and Christian context. If you follow the Church's liturgy through the year, you still move with the shift and surge of the seasons but in a new way, a way which orientates the whole of life to God.

Daphne Pochin Mould, *Irish Pilgrimage* (1955), pp. 56–7

The priest stood firmly erect, his black robes blowing in the mountain breeze as he recited his prayers. At his feet knelt five young women, some with heads bowed while others stared intently toward a sacred grove nestled into a slight hollow on the hillside. On a rise just beyond the grove, three women knelt with arms outstretched as they prayed aloud. Leading their chorus, a fourth woman knelt beside a patch of muddy earth at the roots of the image-bearing tree. Water seeped from the ground, and among the rivulets and clumps of grass was a stone. Under the stone were soggy slips of paper and soaked pictures left by pilgrims seeking favours or giving thanks. Higher on the heather-clad hillside two women sang. Their voices mingled with the murmur of prayers rising from the grove.

The scene, with its aura of sacred interaction between place and people, could have been set in many different times and locales during the past several thousand years. This particular incident was witnessed on the heights above the village of San Sebastian de Garabandal in northern Spain on July 18, 1981. The kneeling pilgrims were Germans. Judging from their dress and the cars parked in the village, they were reasonably affluent. The singers were French. Prayers included the liturgy of the rosary, although this site of claimed Marian apparitions in the 1960s has not been recognized by the Roman Catholic church as a proper place of pilgrimage.

Garabandal and other new, but ecclesiastically unrecognized, sites of religious pilgrimage in Western Europe represent part of a spectrum that extends from obscure, locally visited chapels and holy wells to world-famous, church-approved shrines such as Rome, Lourdes, and Fatima. At present, Western Europe's more than 6,000 pilgrimage centres generate a conservatively estimated 60 to 70 million religiously motivated visits per year. Total annual visitations at these shrines – including casual tourists, curiosity seekers, and persons referred to as 'art history pilgrims' by West German shrine administrators – almost certainly exceed 100 million.

Sidney & Mary Lee Nolan, Christian Pilgrimage in Modern Western Europe
(1989), pp. 1–2

This complexity which the pilgrim experiences is a phenomena, not of finicky details, although details are of some importance, but one of massing ritual upon ritual. For example, the main church in Catacaos houses some 45 images, many of which are statues, life-sized or even larger and take part in the Easter week ritual. Holy Week simply compacts a pattern of saint's days rituals within one week…Usually the ritual for each saint is not extremely complex but with such a large number being worshipped, decorated, and carried in procession, during Holy Week, the overall picture is impressive. It is especially impressive when one considers that the church in Catacaos is only one of the numerous churches in the Bajo Piura, all with their own special set of saints and ceremonies, although the Catacaos Easter Week is the one attended by the major number of pilgrims. I was also told numerous times that 'Catacaos is a very religious pueblo, probably the most religious in the world.' This general belief and attitude, coupled with the massiveness of the images, length of procession, numbers of pilgrims and locals attending and this specific massing type of complexity represents a general ritual orientation and ritual symbol which is extremely characteristic of and may be unique to this 'Indian' region of the Bajo Piura.

N. Ross Crumrine, 'Intensification Rituals of Revitalization of Sacred Stages in Northwest Mexico and Northwest Peru', *Social Anthropology of Pilgrimage*, ed. Makhan Jha (1991), pp. 356–7

At Canterbury, tears of sorrow and moans of gratitude mingled with the howls and the shrieks of the sick and the newly healed. Crowds pushed forward to investigate as each new miracle was announced, and the clergy had to force their way through to examine the patient for themselves. At the back of the church the less devout pilgrims gathered in their national groups trying to sleep in spite of the noise and the close heat from thousands of candles. Some of them had brought bottles of wine with them, and as they became more inebriated they began to shout abuse at each other or broke into community singing. At Santiago on the eve of St James's day 'all sorts of noises and languages can be heard together, discordant shouts, barbarous singing in German, English, Greek, and every other language under the sun'. The 'worldly songs' which so infuriated the clergy of Santiago were a familiar sound whenever pilgrims gathered in large numbers. At Conques the litany was drowned by 'rustic sing-songs', and a special chapter was summoned at the end of the tenth century to consider this 'absurd and detestable practice'. It concluded, very typically, that pilgrims should be allowed to express their devotion in the only way known to them, even though this might strike cultivated persons as 'inappropriate and rude'. Some sanctuaries, like Durham cathedral, employed muscular stewards to keep order. Others, especially towards the end of the Middle Ages, tried to suppress vigils altogether, or else strove manfully to impose some order on them. But the attempt was a failure, and disorderly vigils remained an inseparable part of the cult of the saints.

Jonathan Sumption, *Pilgrimage – an Image of Medieval Religion* (1975), pp. 212–3

The fourteenth-century Llivre Vermell of Montserrat comes next to
the twelfth-century Codex and thirteenth-century Cantiagas as a source
of pilgrimage songs. According to Mons H. Anglés, Europe has preserved two compendia of medieval music written for pleasure and spiritual diversion during the vigils and days spent in sanctuaries, and
these two collections are part of the Spanish heritage. The first, dating
from the twelfth century, is the one embodied in the miscalled Codex
Calixtinus of Compostela; the second, of a more secular nature, consists
of the songs preserved at Montserrat. This second collection includes a
series of religious dances 'for the pilgrims' pleasure'. *Inter alia*, we have
one of the first dances of death (which others hold to be one of peni-
tence) and also a vernacular song, one of the first known songs in Cata-
lan. This Montserrat codex is the only one in the world to have handed
down to us the folk music of these religious dances for pilgrims...

'The Santiago de Compostela Pilgrim Routes', *Architectural Heritage Reports and
Studies* 16 (1989): 84

With the return of the Crusaders from Palestine a portion of the Virgin's milk found its way to Walsingham, and the popular belief of the
day was that the Virgin herself had come to establish herself in Nor-
folk in consequence of the infidels having invaded the Holy Land. The
result was that a splendid priory stood beside the primitive and original chapel. This priory was founded in 1420 by Godfrey de Faverches,
and given to the Order of St Augustine.

It appears that the pilgrims who arrived here entered the sacred
precincts by a low narrow gate, purposely made difficult to pass as a
precaution against relic-snatchers. On the gate was nailed a copper figure of a knight on horseback, whose miraculous preservation on the
spot by the Virgin formed the subject of one of the numerous legends
with which the shrine abounded. Passing through the gate, the pilgrim
found himself in a small chapel, where, on giving a suitable offering,
he was allowed to kiss a gigantic bone, said to have been the finger-
bone of St Peter. He was then conducted to a building thatched with
reeds and straw, enclosing two wells of water which had attained great
fame for their medicinal properties, but more so, perhaps on account
of the rare virtue they were reputed to have possessed of granting
whatever the pilgrim wished for.

Passing through the outer gateway, an unfinished building in the
time of Erasmus, the devotee found himself before the Chapel of the
Virgin, a small wooden building with a door in each opposite side,
through which the pilgrims made their entrance and exit. Within this
chapel stood the celebrated image of the Virgin, on the right of the

altar. Incense was kept burning perpetually before it, and by the light of the many tapers Erasmus beheld the gold and jewels with which the effigy was adorned. After kneeling awhile in prayer the pilgrim arose and deposited his offering, which was immediately taken up by a priest to prevent the next comer from stealing it when depositing his own coin. At another altar, probably in the outer chapel, was exhibited the far-famed relic of the heavenly milk, enclosed in crystal and set up in the crucifix.

Erasmus saw the sacred relic, which he tells us looked excessively like chalk, mixed with white of egg, and quite solid.

Sidney Heath, *Pilgrim Life in the Middle Ages* (1911), pp. 238–9

'The Pilgrim' is yet another interesting song, a pastourelle. A pilgrim asks a shepherdess if he is on the right road to Santiago. She confirms this and invites him to eat bread and honey and brings him water to bathe his feet. The pilgrim is torn between the stirrings of love and the vow he has made to go to Santiago. He finds the solution:

Agua'dame pastournia	*Wait for me, shepherdess,*
que en llegando tornare...	*for once I arrive at*
	Compostela I shall return...

'The Santiago de Compostela Pilgrim Routes',
Architectural Heritage Reports and Studies 16 (1989): 87

The seven men then pulled ropes, raising the great censer off the floor. At first it moved slowly and it seemed as if it was being pushed by the men from one to the other as in a game, but then it began to gather momentum rhythmically and the men disappeared into the crowd as it mounted higher and higher while flames and trailing clouds of fragrant incense became, as it were, the emanations of the soaring music from the choirs and the organ. It swept exultantly above the galleries to the very roof of the basilica and then rushed vertiginously down like a flaming meteor just above the heads of the watchful multitude. Meanwhile the organ rang out and I heard the choir and the massed pilgrims' voices singing the medieval hymn of Santiago from the Codex of Pope Calixtus and towards the end of the hymn the flights of the monster censer became gradually slower and shorter, as its breath grew fainter, until at last it sank lifeless to earth, whereupon it was seized with amazing skill and rapidity by its custodian dressed in scarlet wool and his assistants, who bore it away to its lair in the library chapter house.

Walter Starkie, *The Road to Santiago* (1957), p. 317

Then the stairs led down again, down, down, deep down into the crypt, to a dim, bare, round-arched, flagstoned space furnished with a single kneeler. Here I knelt before a grille and looked forward. A few feet away through a narrow passage a small chamber was lit with dazzling brilliance. There, encased in solid silver, sat the reliquary which contained the bones of St James.

Logically, I knew it was a fairly slim chance – though far from impossible – that the bones were those of the fisherman that Jesus first called beside the Sea of Galilee, James the son of Zebedee and Salome. But irrespective of their identity, I felt that the bones had been imbued with sanctity and importance through the pain of the tens of millions of pilgrims throughout the ages who had travelled thousands of miles to pray at the kneeler at which I now knelt.

So, despite having long dropped the habit, I did pray there, and the prayers came with a surprising ease. I prayed for the people who had helped me on the journey, the priest who had blessed my stick, and the inn-keeper who had refused payment, the monks who had given me food and the cobbler who had mended my torn shoes. And then I did what I suppose I had come to do: I prayed for Olivia and for the success of my marriage, now barely a week away. Then I got up, climbed the steps, and walked back under the great triple portal and the old rose window. Outside it had begun to rain.

William Dalrymple, 'A Pilgrim's Progress Ends', *The Spectator* 8 June 1991, p. 16

The Eucharist continued slowly and discreetly to unfold. But it was in vain that we tried to raise our voices in order to hear one another give the responses; the voice of the river drowned all other sounds like the accompaniment of great organs. Was it not the mystery of the Voice of the Spirit which fills everything and in which all that is said of God and to God is caught up and given perfect expression? Together we sang the Our Father; we exchanged the kiss of Peace; we divided the bread; together we drank the sacred cup.

The sacrifice was consummated. On the banks of the Ganges, at its very source, the eschatological offering had been celebrated. In the sacrifice of the Lamb everything had finally been brought to completion; every prayer and chant that had been prayed or sung in these places, everything that had been offered symbolically in the temple or near the flowing water, all the trials and tribulations of the pilgrims, all the silence and self-denial of the munis, everything had been finally gathered up.

Murray Rogers, *The Mountain of the Lord: Pilgrimage to Gangotri* (1966), pp. 38–9

The pilgrim lights the candles or *lambadhes* and places them in one of the candelabra before passing behind the row of candelabra and in front of the icon itself. On a very busy day, the attendants may instruct people to do their devotions (*proskinima*) first and then light a candle afterward, in an attempt to keep a more orderly line. It is an attempt that is not usually successful, and when there is a constant stream of pilgrims, a small traffic jam may form in the area around the icon...Eventually, one by one, each pilgrim passes in front of the icon, behind to kiss it and making the sign of the cross three times. The icon itself, resting in an elaborate icon stand, is not visible for it is covered with some of the many jewels that have been given as offerings. All around it other offerings are arranged as well: small replicas of ships hanging from the icon stand, bouquets of fresh flowers, embroidered cloths, pots of basil.

Jill Dubisch, *In a Different Place* (1995), pp. 24–5

On the parvis of the church a peasant woman is trying to extract a franc from her husband for a candle; they argue, and he gives in with a sigh. Clutching her candle, the woman resolutely enters the church. She lights the candle and sticks it in its holder. She's about to go away, but suddenly she stops, as if dumbfounded at the sight of the notice: 'What would my light be without your prayer?' Then she turns towards the Black Virgin of the altar; her lips murmur a prayer and a peaceful look steals over her face.

Jean-Jacques Antier, 'Pilgrimages in France: Religious Tourism or Faith in Action?', *Lumen Vitae* 39 (1984): 377

A warm welcome can be expected from the clergy and cathedral staff. I would suggest that pilgrims make straight for the chapel of Our Lady of the Undercroft, one of those holy, quiet places that has a sense of awe all of its own, and ask for a blessing of thanksgiving and prayer for the unity of all Christians. There pilgrims may light a candle for their family, church, the leaders of people, and for the conversion of all unbelievers. Then they may go on their way cherishing the card of blessing.

Christopher Donaldson, *The Great English Pilgrimage: From Rome to Canterbury* (1995), pp. 102–3

Thou shalt travel thither,
thou shalt travel hither,
Thou shalt travel hill and headland,
Thou shalt travel down,
thou shalt travel up,
Thou shalt travel ocean and narrow.
Christ himself is shepherd over thee,
Enfolding thee on every side;
he will not forsake thee
hand or foot,
Nor let evil come anigh thee.

Avery Brooke, ed., *Celtic Prayers* (1981), pp. 68–9

Chapter Ten

THE DESTINATION

T he moment of arrival produces a torrent of mixed emotions: relief at a safe arrival; wonder at the sights witnessed; disappointment at the extent to which religious trinkets mingle with profound reflection; an awareness that the destination so eagerly anticipated is not really the ultimate destination for the Christian but is itself only one more stage along the way; attempts to assess all that has taken place already; a growing realization that the great adventure is coming to a close and that the homeward journey is all that awaits; a search for appropriate acts of worship to mark the experience of arrival; a reflection on whether or not the pilgrim's original hopes for the pilgrimage have truly been fulfilled.

The strange mixture of all that has been experienced so far: an awareness of the holy, the importance of place, the desire to worship, the encounter with ancient sites, the fellowship of those who are also present, the sense of travelling where others have also trod – all are heightened at the point of arrival.

Destinations are not all that they might seem. Viewed from the beginning of the journey they are indeed a fixed end point. But arrival indicates that the destination may be more transient than it had first appeared. We would all like to arrive somewhere, partly out of our need for certainty – a fixed point. But the destination indicates that contradiction and uncertainty is part of the human and the spiritual experience. We can know ourselves better but not completely. We will always remain strangers on this earth.

And so Jesus also suffered outside the city gate to make the people holy through his own blood. Let us, then, go to him outside the camp, bearing the disgrace he bore. For here we do not have an enduring city, but we are looking for the city that is to come.

Hebrews 13:12–14

O Lord our God and God of our fathers!
Mercifully direct and guide our steps to our destination
and let us arrive there in health, joy and peace!
Keep us from snares and dangers,
and protect us from any enemies that we might meet along the way.
Bless and protect our journey!
Let us win favour in your eyes and in the sight of those around us.
Blessed are you, O Lord,
who hears and grants our prayers!

Mary Batchelor, ed., *The Lion Prayer Collection* (1992), p. 138

Then was Christian glad and lightsome, and said, with a merry heart, He hath given me rest by His sorrow, and life by His death. Then he stood still awhile to look and wonder, for it was very surprising to him that the sight of the Cross should thus ease him of his burden. He looked, therefore, and looked again, even till the springs that were in his head sent the waters down his cheeks. (*Zech. xii. 10.*) Now, as he stood looking and weeping, behold, three Shining Ones came to him and saluted him with 'Peace be to thee.' So the first said to him, 'Thy sins be forgiven thee' (*Mark ii. 5*); the second stripped him of his rags, and clothed him with change of raiment; the third also set a mark on his forehead, and gave him a role with a seal on it (*Zech. iii. 4; Eph. i. 13*), which he bade him look on as he ran, and that he should give it in at the Celestial Gate; so they went their way.

John Bunyan, *The Pilgrim's Progress* (1678)

So they went forth into the Holy Land till they could see Jerusalem. And when this creature saw Jerusalem, riding on an ass, she thanked God with all her heart, praying Him for His mercy that, as He had brought her to see His earthly city of Jerusalem, He would grant her grace to see the blissful city of Jerusalem above, the city of Heaven. Our Lord Jesus Christ, answering her thought, granted her to have her desire.

Then for the joy she had, and the sweetness she felt in the dalliance with Our Lord, she was on the point of falling off her ass, for she could not bear the sweetness and grace that God wrought in her soul.

Margery Kempe (*c.* 1373–1439), *The Book of Margery Kempe*

On the day of the dedication of the new church (November 20, 543) Jerusalem was at the height of its splendour. A Council had been held there in 536. Pilgrims gathered there from all over the world: Licinius, Bishop of Tours; Cerycus, one of Belisarius's generals; monks from Asia Minor, and even a son of a King of Scotland, Berthold, arrived, as well as bishops from Britain...

Hardly a single biblical memory was neglected; the pilgrims visited the tombs of David and Isaiah, below Siloam. In the Kidron Valley they were shown the tomb of the apostle Saint James, as well as many others. This list is far from being an exhaustive one, but further enumeration would be tedious.

Michel Join-Lambert, *Jerusalem*, trans. Charlotte Haldane (1958), pp. 139–40

At last we beheld the prospect of Jerusalem, which was not only a contentment to my weary body, but also being ravished with a kind of unwonted rejoicing, the tears gushed from my eyes for too much joy. In this time the Armenians with whom we had joined began to sing in their own fashion Psalms to praise the Lord: and I also sang the 103rd Psalm all the way, till we arrived near the walls of the city.

William Lithgow, *The Total Discourse of the Rare Adventures of the Paineful Peregrination* (1632), cited in John Davies, *Pilgrimage Yesterday and Today* (1988), p. 123

Before Noon I had sight of the Holy City, and thereupon kneeling down and saying the Lord's Prayer, I gave God most hearty thanks for conducting me to behold with my eyes this Renowned Place...When I and my companions came within a furlong of the Gates, we went all along singing and praising God.

John Bunel, 'Two Journeys', cited in John Davies, *Pilgrimage Yesterday and Today* (1988), p. 126

The Garden Tomb saliently displays the characteristics of the Protestant Holy Land devotion. The tomb, which many Protestants consider the actual site of Christ's burial, is a small enclosed site outside the walls of the Old City within which there is a careful reconstruction of a rich man's garden of the first century AD. Louring over this quiet orchard of olive and carob trees is a rock face which is given the appearance of a skull by the open sockets of two eroded medieval cisterns. The Garden Tomb guides, trained volunteers who are the only persons allowed to guide people while they are within the garden's confines, instruct visitors that the site before them is identical to that described in the biblical texts which present Christ's crucifixion and entombment. They point out that the site is correctly located outside the walls (although they fail to mention that the contemporary walls of the Old City, built in 1542 by Suleiman the Magnificent, are very differently placed from those of the city within which Jesus was condemned and outside which he was crucified). The skull-like hill above it is obviously Golgotha, 'the place of the skull', and the garden itself appears to be the garden of the wealthy land-holder, Joseph of Arimathea. Whether or not they are convinced that the Garden Tomb is the literal site (and there is occasional dissension on this issue), pilgrims assert that 'it is easier to imagine Jesus here than inside that dark pile of stones they call the Holy Sepulchre'.

John Eade & Michael Sallnow, eds., *Contesting the Sacred* (1991), pp. 116–7

All that I can with certainty recall is that when beholding this triumphant sepulchre I could feel nothing but my own weakness; and when my guide cries out with Paul: O death where is your victory? O death where is your sting? I listened as if death would reply that it was vanquished and chained within this monument.

F. de Chateaubriand, *The City of Jerusalem, 120 AD*, Palestine Pilgrim's Text Society VI, 1896, cited in John Davies, *Pilgrimage Yesterday and Today* (1988), p. 133

The Church of the Holy Sepulchre is for many pilgrims, at first sight at least, their biggest disappointment in all the places they visit in the Holy Land.

Calvary, the place where Jesus was crucified to death, is so central to the Gospel story. Few Christians can contemplate actually seeing the very spot without feeling a tug at the heart. When they get there, they find the site of Calvary is covered over by a building which to many seems ugly and to some offensively so.

What they find inside the building usually disappoints them even more. They travel thousands of miles to the place where their Lord was crucified and understandably, even if somewhat unreasonably, they expect to see some kind of 'little green hill' that the centuries have scarcely touched. Instead they find no visible trace of Calvary as it was but everything hidden away beneath the rather unlovely edifice that piety has created.

John Martin, *A Plain Man in the Holy Land* (1978), pp. 19–20

It is really impossible to describe or even remember the impressions of this day. Moving beyond belief; not merely or chiefly because of the

historic scenes of Our Lord's Passion; but because of these events
recalled on such hallowed ground in the midst of clergy and people of
all sorts and all churches, and myself in their midst...I cannot describe
the church. I hardly saw it. I remember the first place I knelt – a stone
on which Our Lord's body was supposed to have rested after being
taken down from the cross. Why can I not recall all of this with exacti-
tude? Because throughout, in a strange way, I became mentally pas-
sive; feeling a kind of victim with Our Lord. From the moment I
entered the church, I was engulfed in a great crowd of Orthodox
monks and Franciscans and others, who surrounded me and, almost
literally, carried me from place to place...At a place I would kneel and
feel Our Lord looking at us in this strange mixture of past and present; then be borne on again, this way and that, and feeling lovingly at
their mercy. And I felt that somehow like this Our Lord was pulled
and hustled and felt at the mercy of his unloving guides. More than
that I cannot recall. At intervals the bells would clang again. The
whole thing was an astonishing outpouring of every kind of excited
motion, all flowing round and over me, not me as a person, but as a
kind of centre point of that triumphal showing forth of Christian fellowship.

W. Purcell, *Fisher of Lambeth: A Portrait of a Life* (1969), cited in John Davies,
Pilgrimage Yesterday and Today (1988), pp. 162–3

Many pilgrims, especially in the past, could only regretfully bring
themselves to leave the place where they had found peace of soul, in
fact, some settled down at the holy site, especially Jerusalem, for
months or even years, devoting themselves to works of mercy, to car-
ing.for the sick in the hospitals, etc. Even into the twentieth century
the faithful who went to the famous Solovetski Island shrine in the
White Sea would often remain for some time in the service of the
monks who were custodians of the shrine. Sources mention pilgrims
who would express the wish that they might die there at the goal of
their pilgrimage lest they fall again into sickness or sin. In exceptional
cases this favour would be granted.

'Pilgrimages', *New Catholic Encyclopedia* (1967)

On the day the armistice came to an end we all had a day off & we
were given the opportunity of visiting Jerusalem. You can bet your life
I was eager to go.

And now I will endeavour to interest you for a little while in what
I saw.

After three hours riding in a lorry up and down the sides of I might say mountains with numerous hairpin bends we made our descent upon Jerusalem.

There was a keen desire to see the Mount of Olives as the lorries took us there, past Gordons Calvary which lies just outside the City Walls, up a winding gradient past the unsightly German Hospice down a slight dip & right onto the Mount where alongside the G.[*sic*] Hospice the Russian Tower stands. Mounting the Tower one gets a most glorious panoramic view of the surrounding country.

Its weird vastness impresses one with a sense of awe to think that here are the scenes and associations of Christ Jesus himself.

> Letter from a British soldier written in 1918 and quoted in 'A Soldier's
> Pilgrimage', *Mediterranean Historical Review* December 1993: 227

Giving what little money [Paula] could afford to the poor who were fellow-servants with her, and going on towards Bethlehem, she paused where Rachel's Tomb stands on the right of the road, the Birthplace of Benjamin...

Then she entered the cave of the Saviour, and saw the Holy Inn of the Virgin, and the Stable, where 'the ox knew his master, and the ass his Lord's manger', to fulfil the words written by the same prophet, 'Blessed is he that casts his seed upon the waters, where the ox and the ass tread'. Then she solemnly declared in my own hearing that, with the eye of faith, she saw a child wrapped in swaddling clothes, weeping in the Lord's manger, the Magi worshipping, the star shining above, the Virgin Mother, the attentive foster-father; and the shepherds coming by night to see this word which had come to pass, already, even then, able to speak the words which open John's Gospel, '*In the beginning was the Word*' and '*The Word was made flesh*'...

> St Jerome (*c.* 347–*c.* 420), Letter 108 to Eustochium, cited in J. Wilkinson,
> *Jerusalem Pilgrims* (1977), pp. 49–50

When we pass through the door which is the entrance nowadays we find ourselves in a cave large enough to accommodate some sixty people standing in reasonable comfort. Beneath the roof blackened by long centuries of human use, I read a few verses of Luke's narrative of the shepherds' involvement in the Christmas story and offer a short prayer. Together in the dim light we sing a verse of

While humble shepherds watched their flock
In Bethlehem's plain by night

before returning to the bright sunlight outside.

John Martin, *A Plain Man in the Holy Land* (1978), p. 9

I leap for joy as I write, and am altogether in the spirit within that holy grotto. I see the cloth which covered our Lord at his birth, the laying of the new-born babe in the manger, and I am thrilled by the thought of the saviour's love for me and his extreme poverty through which he made me worthy for the kingdom of heaven. Yet I think the grotto is a palace, and that the king sat upon the Virgin's bosom as on a throne, and I see choirs of angels encircling the grotto, and the Magi bringing presents to the king. I am filled with all manner of delight, and rejoice to think what grace I have been thought worthy to receive.

Phocas the Cretan, *The Pilgrimage of Johannes Phocas in the Holy Land*, cited in
John Davies, *Pilgrimage Yesterday and Today* (1988), p. 62

The meeting with the good and the beloved, and the memorials of the immense love of the Lord for us men, which are shown in your localities, have been the source to me of the most intense joy and gladness. Doubly indeed have these shone upon divinely festal days; both in beholding and saving tokens of the God who gave us life, and in meeting with souls in whom the tokens of the Lord's grace are to be discerned spiritually in such clearness, that one can believe that Bethlehem, and Golgotha, and Olivet, and the scene of the Resurrection are really in the God-containing heart...When, then, I not only saw with the sense of sight those Sacred Places, but I saw the tokens of places like them, plain in yourselves as well, I was filled with joy so great that the description of its blessing is beyond the power of utterance.

Gregory of Nyssa, 'Letter XVII', cited in H. Wace & P. Schnaff, eds., *A Select Library of Nicene and Post-Nicene Fathers of the Christian Church, Vol. V: Gregory of Nyssa* (1893), p. 542

And the promised splendour
Breaks into the evening of the last stage of the journey,
Which almost exhales the fragrance of regret.

Into the sanctuary, like a vast ship,
Beckoned with glory,
They entered religiously.

The shadows came alive with murmurings,
As if the great ship slowly wakened
From a mysterious dream.

They advanced past column after column,
Altar after altar,
Unthinking and vulnerable,
As their fingers twisted the folds of their pilgrim hats.

Ashamed to find themselves there,
Dirty, destitute, stiff, and poor,
Before the very great Saint, so rich today,
So high up and so very generous.

Their pace slackened; the nave was expanding
To the infinite dimensions of the vault of heaven,
And they walked open-mouthed in awe.

Raymond Oursel, *Les pèlerins du moyen age: les hommes, les chemins, les sanctuaries* (1963),
    cited in Horton & Marie-Helene Davies, *Holy Days and Holidays* (1982), p. 210

To arrive at the planned destination was not to complete a pilgrimage and most reached their climax in what may be best termed a mini-pilgrimage. After entering Rome, for example, there was still the round to be made of the many churches housing relics. To land at Alexandria was first to go to the place where St Mark was believed to have been beheaded, then on to Cairo where the Pyramids were mistakenly identified with the storehouses of Joseph (Genesis 41:56). The stopping places of the Holy Family, fleeing before Herod, were then to be visited before leaving for Sinai in the wake of Moses and the Israelites, and so eventually into Palestine. At Joppa (or Jaffa, now a suburb of modern Tel Aviv), if that was one's port of entry, the entire Holy Land had still to be traversed to see the sites made sacred by mention in the Old and New Testaments. While Jerusalem itself had its own pilgrimage circuit, or rather circuits, with, for example, a day set apart for the sites on the Mount of Olives, another to go to Bethlehem and a protracted series of services and processions in the Church of the Holy Sepulchre.

If this climax was delayed, the arrival itself was an occasion for joy. In fact this experience was such a feature that the place, usually a hill, from which the first glimpse of one's goal could be obtained was called Mountjoy – there was one close to Compostela and another near to Jerusalem. Of the latter John Maundeville (1322) remarked: 'two miles from Jerusalem is Mount Joy ... and it is called Mount Joy because it gives joy to pilgrim's hearts, for from that place men first see Jerusalem'.

Having reached their destinations, the habitual way for pilgrims to express both their delight and their gratitude was to salute the ground with a kiss.

John Davies, Pilgrimage Yesterday and Today (1988), pp. 55–6

At the shrine pilgrims often underwent ritual purification, perhaps involving fasting (though this might have already begun at home) and confession; one of the collectors of miracles who sat at Becket's shrine in the twelfth century claimed – somewhat rhetorically – that the incoming pilgrims were 'rebaptized in the font of confession and their own tears'. Some removed their shoes as they actually approached the tomb, customary from biblical times for those entering on holy ground.

After these preliminary rites they knelt by the shrine and prayed, sometimes aloud, in the midst of bystanders awaiting their turn. At this point the suppliant normally presented his offering, usually a coin or candle. Candles and wax were sometimes on sale at the church, and the income could be considerable; at Hereford cathedral there were years of dispute between the treasurer and the other canons over sharing the wax proceeds. Many pilgrims offered their own home-made candles and on one occasion a woman even came to the church with her personal candle-making kit:

A woman took pity on a poor girl who had nothing to offer at Becket's tomb, and from her pocket took a lump of wax and some thread, which she doubled into a wick, and coated with the wax to make a candle for the girl to offer.

After presenting his offering and uttering a final prayer and request the ordinary pilgrim left the church, but if his visit coincided with a feast-day he would probably also hear a Mass or join in a procession before leaving. For those who had come to the tomb hoping for a cure a different routine followed. They settled down in the church, kneeling, sitting or lying on the cold pavement before the tomb where shadows danced in flickering candlelight. There they remained until impatience conquered hope, or hope was rewarded with a cure, a miracle.

Ronald Finucane, Miracles and Pilgrims (1977), p. 48

While she prayed at the place of the holy relic shrine, she beat against it, not only with the longings of her heart, but with her whole body so that the little grille in front of the relic opened at the impact; and she, taking the Kingdom of Heaven by storm, pushed her head inside and laid it on the holy relics resting there, drenching them with her tears.

'*Miracula Sancti Stephani II*', cited in Peter Brown,
The Cult of the Saints (1981), p. 88

A custom frequently observed at shrines, now as in the past, is the all-night vigil, in which a great number of pilgrims pass the entire night in the shrine itself or nearby in order to saturate themselves with the mysterious power of the saint. This is mentioned as early as the *Miracula* of St Hilary of Poitiers. In the fifteenth century Felix Fabri and his companions spent three nights in the church of the Holy Sepulchre. Even in the twentieth century it used to be a frequent occurrence to see villagers camping out all night singing psalms and canticles during pilgrimages to Uzhgorod in the Ukraine, Russia, or to the Ostra Brama in Vilna, Lithuania. On Tenos, for the vigils of the Annunciation and the Assumption, the church is open for worshippers day and night.

Other pilgrim practices require the pilgrim to circle the tomb or pass under it if the architecture permits. This latter can be observed in Breton 'pardons' (pilgrimages). At some shrines the pilgrims circle the church itself, not unlike the practice in Mecca. Processions made over rocky ground at Fatima are considered especially penitential.

'Pilgrimages', *New Catholic Encyclopedia* (1967)

The pilgrims at times took only too good advantage of the opportunities afforded them. Their devotions paid, they indulged freely in revels and feasting, a characteristic also of an ordinary funeral repast in those days. Many passages from the Fathers have illuminated for us this phase of the complex aspects of the pilgrimages.

When Eustochium, that pious daughter of the pious Paula, sent a present to Jerome on the Feast of St Peter, he replied to her with some serious advice conveyed in a light tone, and remarked:

We must be careful to celebrate the Feast [of St Peter] not so much by abundance of food as by exaltation of spirit: for it is absurd to try to honour by such excess a martyr whom we know to have pleased God by his fasting.

Ethel Ross-Barker, *Rome of the Pilgrims and Martyrs* (1913), p. 26

In medieval times, the pilgrim to Rome came down from the heights of Tuscany to be rewarded with a view of the city's magnificent walls looping over the seven hills. The approach to Jerusalem was an equally suitable climax to so long a journey: the last wonderful stretch of road from Emmaus threading up through the pine trees and oleanders.

In comparison, the first view of Santiago was always unremarkable; even the Romans seemed to have been unimpressed, for the river you cross is named Lavacolla, derived from the Latin 'arse-wipe'. Yet to arrive at any destination which you have longed for has its rewards. I was in a fairly bad way. I was unshaven and none of my clothes had been washed for a week. I stank. More seriously, a blister on the ball of my right foot had gone bad and I had a pronounced Quasimodo limp. Just to arrive, cease walking, seemed enough.

William Dalrymple, 'A Pilgrim's Progress Ends', *The Spectator* 8 June 1991, p. 14

Santiago de Compostela is famed for its wet weather and the natives glory in their damp climate, saying that there are only thirty fine days in the year, and they claim that its medieval buildings and granite-paved streets display their full beauty only in rain and drizzle. This day, however, the sun was shining and the sunbeams and mellow bells roused the colourful crowds of peasants who thronged the narrow streets at an early hour; and some of them had spent the hours before dawn huddled in doorways under the arcades...The chimes reverberated above the clattering of the countless sabots on the granite pavement, and there was a continual dialogue between the booming bells of bronze and the strident clattering bells of brass.

Walter Starkie, *The Road to Santiago* (1957), p. 308

At the foot of the hill I was prepared to enter the city, and lifted up my heart. There was an open space, a tramway: a tram upon it about to be drawn by two lean and tired horses whom in the heat many flies disturbed. There was dust on everything around.

A bridge was immediately in front. It was adorned with statues in soft stone, half-eaten away, but still gesticulating in corruption, after the manner of the seventeenth century. Beneath the bridge there tumbled and swelled and ran fast a great confusion of yellow water: it was the Tiber. Far on the right were white barracks of huge and of hideous appearance; over these the Dome of St Peter's rose and looked like something newly built. It was of a delicate blue, but made a metallic contrast against the sky.

Then...I went on for several hundred yards, having the old wall of Rome before me all this time, till I came right under it at last; and with the hesitation that befits all great actions I entered, putting the right foot first lest I should bring further misfortune upon that capital of all our fortunes.

And so the journey ended.

Hilaire Belloc, *The Path To Rome* (1958), p. 231

The sovereigns of the newly-converted Teutonic peoples were among the most devout of pilgrims.

When Charlemagne and his suite went to spend their Easter in Rome in 774, they performed the last thirty miles on foot, and Charlemagne ascended the steps of St Peter's on his knees, kissing each step as he went up. The pope received him, they embraced, prayed in the church, and then 'descended together to the body of blessed Peter'.

Ethel Ross-Barker, *Rome of the Pilgrims and Martyrs* (1913), p. 23

Here I am at the goal of my journey to Ireland: the Shrine of Our Lady of Knock. Since I first learnt of the Centenary of this Shrine...I have felt a strong desire to come here, the desire to make yet another pilgrimage to the Shrine of the Mother of Christ, the Mother of the Church, the Queen of Peace...Do we not confess with all our brethren, even with those with whom we are not yet linked in full unity, that we are pilgrim people...

I am here then as a pilgrim, a sign of the pilgrim Church throughout the world, participating, through my presence as Peter's successor, in a very special way in the centenary celebration of this shrine.

Pope John Paul II, Homily at Knock Shrine, 30 September 1979

John Paul II arrived at the airport of Tarbes-Ossun on Sunday afternoon, 14 August 1983, the eve of the feast of the Assumption of the Blessed Virgin Mary. He was beginning a pilgrimage to Lourdes – the first by any pope – planned originally for the summer of 1981 when the Eucharistic Congress met there. The 1981 trip had been cancelled after the pope was shot in an assassination attempt on 13 May. At Lourdes, John Paul II followed the traditional pattern of millions of pilgrims, and knelt at the spot where St Bernadette saw eighteen visions of the Madonna in 1858. He drank a glass of water from the spring which Bernadette discovered under instructions given in one of the apparitions, and attributed his own recovery from the attempt on his life to Our Lady of Lourdes.

The pope recalled that the day he was shot was the feast of Our Lady of Fatima, and his assistants vividly remembered the only audible words from the pontiff as he was being sped to Gemelli Hospital in Rome were, 'Madonna, Madonna...' There were 300,000 people in Lourdes for the 24-hour visit – only a fraction of the nearly five million who made the pilgrimage in 1983.

David Sox, *Relics and Shrines* (1985), p. 193

Everywhere throughout the Christian world, as if led by the Spirit, Christians are going back to their roots again...

A notable example of this frame of mind was given when a dignitary of the Roman Catholic Church was describing his arrival in France in 1945:

I have personally and for many years had a great devotion to St Martin. Since the days when I was a student – as a young priest, then as a teacher of patristics at the Lateran – I have always longed to know more of this great saint. I wanted from the first months of my arrival in France as Papal Nuncio, to go to pray at his tomb and to venerate at Candes the places sanctified by his death. In memory of this double visit, I caused to be placed in the crypt of the famous sanctuary at Tours the following inscription:

'Angelus Joseph Roncalli, Bergomas, Apostolic Nunce in Gaul, client of St Martin, the humble man of Tours. Blessed Martin preserve the clergy and people of Gaul. Look after your own everywhere.'

Ten years later the writer was to become Pope John XXIII, and suddenly and quite unexpectedly in the basilica of St Paul in Rome, as if he had been illuminated by a flash of heavenly light, to call into being the Second Vatican Council, from which so much original and creative Christian work in all the churches is still growing.

Christopher Donaldson, *Martin of Tours: Parish Priest,*
Mystic and Exorcist (1980), pp. 152–3

But the pilgrim approaching Tinos sees another sight as well, one that dominates the bustle of the harbour and town and draws the eye and the emotions. On board the ship, the devout cross themselves as this sight comes into view. It is the church of the Madonna of the Annunciation (*Evangelistria*), the sacred home of Panayia (All Holy One) and the object of the pilgrim's journey. The church's white-washed bell tower and ornate façade rise from a hill just above the town, visible from the sea even at night when the church's lighted outline shimmers like a beacon in the dark. As the ship draws closer to the harbour, another sacred place now comes into view. It is the whitewashed monastery of Kehkrovouno, perched high upon the barren slopes above the town. This monastery was the home of Saint Pelayia, the nun whose vision led to the finding of the miraculous icon of the Annunciation, now housed in Tino's famous church. The monastery is also a site of pilgrimage. Thus the two sacred places upon which the approaching pilgrim first lays eyes both gain their sacredness from female holy figures – the Madonna (Panayia) and a now-sainted nun.

Jill Dubisch, *In a Different Place* (1995), p. 20

The most dramatic and fullest expression of the island pilgrimage must be that to the Skellig Rock, which was once much frequented. Here the pilgrims sailed out to make the difficult landing on the rock and then climbed up the steps to the ancient monastery, almost every cleft with its own special name and tradition, and rounds and prayers. From the monastery, they finished with an exposed rock climb to the very summit of the Skellig and, at a height of about 700 feet, leaned out over the sea to kiss a cross cut on the tip of an overhanging rock. Accidents never seem to have happened to the motley crowd, many of whom were probably very sea sick on the voyage out and were certainly not experienced cragsmen. One Protestant however, who went to jeer, fell from the summit, and in the horror of the long drop is said to have cried to the sea to have mercy on him and rise up to meet him.

Daphne Pochin Mould, *Irish Pilgrimage* (1955), p. 113

When people arrive for their week in Taizé they are divided into groups. Each group will have people from several different countries in it, so that they can learn about each other. Life is kept very simple. Most people sleep in tents and eat simple meals together in the open air. Every day the groups meet together to study the Bible and discuss their faith. Three times a day the bells call everyone to the common prayer in the Church of the Reconciliation. For a large part of the year the church is not large enough to hold the thousands of people meeting together, so it is extended on several sides by large tents.

Paul Morris & John Smith, Time Travelling: Pilgrimage for Children
(1995), p. 265

At the door of the sanctuary the pilgrimage receives a resplendent banner. The bells of the basilica scatter their glory on the massed heads. And when they enter the temple of the Virgin, the pilgrims throw themselves on their knees and in this way pass through the church to the very feet of the Virgin. The organ renders even more spiritual the moving scene. And the song surges up anew...*Pues concebida fuiste sin mancha – Ave Maria plena de gracia.* 'Surely thou wert conceived without stain – Holy Mary, full of grace.'

'Fifty Years of Guadalupan Pilgrimage', cited in Victor & Edith Turner,
Image and Pilgrimage in Christian Culture (1978), p. 97

I am constantly humbled when people make Glasshampton a place of pilgrimage. Father William who, from 1913 to 1936 occupied Glasshampton and converted it from stables to a monastery, is buried in the garth, and many people have found salvation, renewal, healing and guidance here, as a place of pilgrimage.

I think of John who cycled from the other side of Birmingham with a light-weight trailer behind his bike, and Ronald whose sense of pilgrimage is clear:

> As a practical step, I left home the day before I was due to arrive at Glasshampton, and stayed the night in Worcester without booking a room in advance. That meant that I was more than usually detached from the normal routine by which I know each day where I shall be sleeping that night. I travelled by public transport – I have no car – and I packed the minimum, and used a rucksack instead of a suitcase so that I could walk from Worcester.

...Last evening Robin and I knelt before the *Vladimir* icon in my hut chapel at the end of his pilgrimage retreat, and he was close to tears as he realized that the Lord had delivered him from a wrong direction in his pilgrimage, and set his feet back on firm ground.

Brother Ramon SSF, The Heart of Prayer (1995), pp. 125–6

I think, I know, now, why God brought us there. All those people living in that village are prepared to take up the challenge and battle
against the elements to make a livelihood. Life is a battle, but it's
worth it, and they care for each other and learn to love the life. There
are many blessings to be had that cannot be found elsewhere.

In the same way Chris and I were facing a battle, not against the
elements, but against Chris's increasing weakness. Seeing Ian believing
in what he was doing, and Linda tired but determined to make a loving home for her children, I was proud to know them both, and they
inspired me to battle on to make Chris's last months full and meaningful. It would be hard, but it would be worth it. I felt toughened up by
the cold and wet, the wind and sun, and the durability of the standing
stones, standing against 4,000 years of wind, rain and snow.

> I shall not fear the battle, if thou art by my side
> Nor wander from the pathway, if thou wilt be my guide

With God, we should win through and find many blessings yet, that
perhaps we could only find by going through the battles ahead. The
Holy Spirit is like the wind, it blew through the room where the disciples were, and the flames sat on each of their heads, blessing each one.
This is Pentecost, frightening, aweful, yet beautiful and loving.

John Key, Journey to Resurrection (1995), pp. 89–90

Toward the end of a pilgrimage, the pilgrim's new-found freedom
from mundane or profane structures is increasingly circumscribed by
symbolic structures: religious buildings, pictorial images, statuary, and
sacralized features of the topography, often described and defined in
sacred tales and legend...

The pilgrim, as he is increasingly hemmed in by such sacred symbols...becomes increasingly capable of entering in imagination and
with sympathy into the culturally defined experiences of the founder
and of those persons depicted as standing in some close relationship to
him, whether it be of love or hate, loyalty or awe. The trials of the
long route will normally have made the pilgrim quite vulnerable to
such impressions. Religious images strike him, in these novel circumstances, as perhaps they have never done before, even though he may
have seen very similar objects in his parish church almost every day of
his life. The innocence of the eye is the whole point here, the 'cleansing of the doors of perception'. Pilgrims have often written of the
'transformative' effect on them of approaching the final altar or the
holy grotto at the end of the way. Purified from structural sins, they
receive the pure imprint of a paradigmatic structure. This paradigm

will give a measure of coherence, direction, and meaning to their action, in proportion to their identification with the symbolic representation of the founder's experiences. For them the founder becomes a saviour, one who saves them from themselves, 'themselves' both as socially defined and as personally experienced.

Victor & Edith Turner, *Image and Pilgrimage in Christian Culture* (1978), pp. 10–11

Life is a pilgrimage. We are on the march, and sooner or later we shall reach our destination. That destination we call heaven. There we shall see God as He is, and that experience will be the cause of a happiness which will be complete and have no end. We are made for that.

While on the road we cannot help wondering about God. What is He like? What does He want for us? What does He expect of us? And sometimes we ask whether He exists at all. So many of our fellow pilgrims have decided that there is no God; others just go through life doubting or not knowing. But the important questions still require answers. What happens after death? Nothing? Has life no meaning? Are we only part of an absurd situation devoid of sense and purpose?

If only we could see God, life would be very different; our uncertainties would go and we should take each step in life, clear about the direction and firm in our tread. There would be no faltering, no confusion. But it is not like that.

...Moreover, there is a great deal of pain and suffering. That can slow the pace. Many simply cannot cope and some, indeed, suffer so much that they cannot believe that there is someone who loves them and wants them to reach the destination, where all things will be well.

When we have acknowledged the existence of that 'Someone' and learned that He has intervened in our affairs, we should begin to respond. We want to find out more about Him, try to be in touch with Him, and then discover that we should obey Him and serve Him. We have to come to recognize that in God are to be found the ultimate meaning and purpose of all things, and especially of ourselves. This response is what we call 'the spiritual life'.

If we do not have a spiritual life, then our living is impoverished. Important questions remain unanswered; life itself will appear to be pointless, and we have no future to which to look forward. But we are made 'to know God, to love Him and serve Him in this world, and to be happy with Him for ever in the next'. This is the point of the pilgrimage.

Basil Hume, *To Be A Pilgrim* (1984), pp. 25–6

The attraction exercised by pilgrimages attests to the anguish of today's men and women, living in a world in which they no longer feel integrated, and in a materialistic civilization which claims that it can do without God, yet remains incapable of finding the slightest answer to life's fundamental questions.

This anguish is clearly visible in an age where motorized pilgrimages are increasingly taking an escapist form, as if the pilgrim were trying to run away from the heaviness of an atheistic society, solely concerned with pleasure and material comfort.

In this sense, the gesture of the pilgrim who *goes* up to Notre-Dame de la Garde under the burning sun of the Midi, or to midnight worship at Montmartre, or who climbs the heights of La Salette, getting away from the hubbub of the sprawling city in order to find at the feet of Jesus, the humble Virgin or a Saint, a transcendent explanation for questions which science admits it cannot answer, is, I feel, a religious and positive step, so true is it that man is called to transcend his ancient animal nature.

That is why, alongside the traditional organized pilgrimage, you will always see 'wild' pilgrimages – those of the gypsies, of fringe groups, and of all the rejected who feel that at last they are being welcomed and loved. For these people as for the usual pilgrims, the successful pilgrimage represents, at one and the same time, the end of a long journey and of their anxious searching, and the beginning of the journey of the *new being* who will now be able to face the real problem – not physical healing, but the fundamental healing, the passing from the egoistic animal being, descended from the mists of time, to the *new man* described by the prophets. In this sense, the pilgrimage is the consequence of waiting for God and a freely made effort to transform oneself by opening one's heart and mind to God.

> Jean-Jacques Antier, 'Pilgrimages in France: Religious Tourism or
> Faith in Action?', *Lumen Vitae* 39 (1984): 374

God of the nomad and the pilgrim, may we find our security in you and not in our possessions. May our homes be open to guests and our hearts to one another so that all our travelling is lighter and together we reach the goal.

> Mary Batchelor, ed., *The Lion Prayer Collection* (1992), p. 139

Chapter Eleven

THE JOURNEY BEYOND

The end of a pilgrimage implies a new beginning. The pilgrim enters on a pilgrimage not as an end in itself, but in the hope of gaining clarity for the continuation of the journey of faith. Some perhaps hope to find God or at least to see him more clearly. Others have in mind a specific preparation for a task, or a new phase of life.

The experience of most suggests that pilgrimage does produce a new point of reference from which to understand life. But this is not so for all. Those who come without understanding the need for an internal journey to mirror the physical journey may end up more bereft than before. Simply hoping against hope to find faith in an ill-defined experience occasioned by the physical act of pilgrimage is rarely sufficient. Even so, some who travel without a well-defined faith can be surprised by the discovery of a dimension which is unsought and even unimagined. But even in these cases, there is a need to place that new experience in the context of an ongoing community of the faithful if it is not to be lost entirely – remembered only as just one more interesting but essentially meaningless experience amongst many others.

It is at this point that the rhythm of the Christian community – the festivals, the sacraments, the liturgy and personal prayer – enable the benefits of pilgrimage to be further enriched and developed as the journey home begins. Just as the pilgrimage itself needs to be prepared for, so pilgrimage itself is merely preparation for that greater journey which has as its end the imitation of Christ, a life lived for him, in him and ultimately with him.

Dear friends, now we are children of God, and what we will be has not yet been made known. But we know that when he appears, we shall be like him, for we shall see him as he is. Everyone who has this hope in him purifies himself, just as he is pure.

1 John 3:2–3

PRAYER AT THE END OF A PILGRIMAGE

Father, we have walked in the land where Jesus walked.
We have touched the soil and rocks where the seed falls.
We have seen the lilies of the field and heard the birds of the air.
We have been warmed by the sun that warmed him and
    cooled by the breezes that touched his face.
We have been to the sea where he walked,
and to the river where he was baptized.
We have felt the presence of the Holy Spirit where he first sent it,
and anguished at the spot where he gave himself for us.
We have rejoiced at the emptiness of the tomb
and the fullness of his love in our hearts.
Be with us, as we continue our earthly pilgrimage to the new
    Jerusalem
where every tear will be wiped away,
and we will be with you, your Son and the Holy Spirit forever.

Stephen Doyle OFM, cited in Margaret Pawley,
Prayers for Pilgrims (1991), p. 132

I beg of you, beloved pilgrim, leave not this place, any more than any other, without previous meditation. See and reflect upon the importance of what was done here. The Son of God, mighty by reason of his eternal Godhead, and mighty with the beauty of the mind of the Father, he who laid the foundations of the world, and made it pleasant to sight, he to whom the heavens and all the stars in their courses do homage, he who, as Job says, shakes the earth out of her place, and the pillars thereof do tremble, did so bow down and abase his divine majesty in this place as with his own hands to wash the foul, filthy, muddy feet of his disciples, low-born fishermen, sinners, and traitors as they were, that he might thereby give us a most wholesome example of humanity.

Felix Fabri, *The Wanderings of Felix Fabri*, cited in John Davies,
Pilgrimage Yesterday and Today (1988), p. 226

With a zeal and courage unbelievable in a woman [Paula] forgot her sex and her physical weakness, and longed to make there, amongst those thousands of monks, a dwelling for herself and her daughters. All were welcoming her, and she might have done so, if she had not been summoned away by a still greater longing for the holy places. The heat was excessive, and she therefore took a ship from Pelsium, and arrived at Maiuma as swiftly as a bird. It was not long before she was back in Bethlehem for good, living for three years in a tiny lodging till she had finished building her cells and monasteries, and different places beside the road where pilgrims would be able to stay, at the place where Mary and Joseph had been unable to find hospitality.

St Jerome (*c.* 347–*c.* 420), Letter 108 to Eustochium, cited in J. Wilkinson,
Jerusalem Pilgrims (1977), pp. 49–50

Charles de Foucauld rediscovered God in the sacraments of confession and the Eucharist, the sacraments of Jesus Christ, in October 1886.

Then he made a pilgrimage to the Holy Land, the land of Jesus Christ, at Christmas 1888:

Bethlehem first, then a few days later Jerusalem, the Upper Room, the Mount of Olives, Calvary; and, in January 1889, Nazareth...

This was how he saw Jesus of Nazareth from that January day in 1889, when for the first time he set foot in Nazareth. On 24 June 1896 he wrote to Mme de Bondy:

I'm longing to start on that life I've been looking for seven years, the life...I glimpsed, felt, as I walked through the streets of Nazareth where our Lord had trod, a poor workman lost in self-effacement and obscurity.

Jeremy Moiser, trans., *Silent Pilgrimage to God:*
The Spirituality of Charles de Foucauld (1974), p. 28

A young pilgrim:

'It means going to Chartres and returning home again with a greater sense of brotherhood...It means adding one step to another, one action to another. Building hope stone by stone, step by step.'

...A pilgrim at Rocamadour:

'We recently lost our child and we were angry with God. Mary helped us to understand that we couldn't go on like that.'

A pilgrim at La Salette:

'I came here as a tourist, and I'm returning as a pilgrim. In the silence of the heights, I heard the call of the Weeping Virgin. That call wounded me, and my wound will never heal. For that's what the Church is: a profound community life, brotherly groups, people loving one another.'

Jean-Jacques Antier, 'Pilgrimages in France: Religious Tourism or Faith in
Action?', *Lumen Vitae* 39 (1984): 376–7

To what extent Jerusalem was regarded in the twelfth century as a spiritual symbol of eternal bliss is evident in poetry of the time. Among the authors of such poems is the Cluniac monk Bernard of Morlass, whose *Urbs Sion aurea* is still found in many hymnals ('Jerusalem the golden, with milk and honey blest...'). This yearning for the heavenly city also existed outside monastic circles, for example, in the hymn for the sabbath written by the controversial philosopher and theologian Peter Abelard (d. 1141), remarkable for its sonorous first line: *O Quanta Qualia Sunt Illa Sabbata.*

> How mighty are the Sabbaths,
> How mighty and how deep,
> That the high courts of Heaven
> To everlasting keep.
> What peace unto the weary,
> What pride unto the strong,
> When God in Whom are all things
> Shall be all things to men.
>
> Jerusalem is the city
> of everlasting Peace,
> A peace that is surpassing
> And utter blessedness;
> Where finds the dreamer waking
> Truth beyond dreaming far,
> Nor is the heart's possessing
> Less than the heart's desire...
>
> But ours, with minds uplifted
> Unto the heights of God,
> With our whole heart's desiring,
> To take the homeward road,
> And the long exile over,
> Captive in Babylon,
> Again unto Jerusalem
> to win at last return.

Adriaan Bredero, *Christendom and Christianity in the Middle Ages* (1994), pp. 102–3

According to Turner, 'the return road is, psychologically, different from the approach road.' While approaching the sacred goal, the pilgrim is burdened by stress, uneasiness, anxiety and lagging feelings of guilt piled up in the course of time. On the road back, the pilgrim wants to come home as swiftly as possible. The sins have been forgiven, and the pilgrim can, due to the transformative and curative effect of the pilgrimage, relax and enjoy himself, while looking forward to a warm and admiring welcome at home.'

To some extent, my own field material from Athos supports Turner's interpretation of the return from pilgrimage. The travellers indeed experience a feeling of relief after having returned to the world. But, the picture of a black and white process, *i.e.* a sinful phase and a sinless phase, is more idealistic than real. Many of the visitors felt their days on Athos to be somewhat strenuous and were therefore relieved not to have to live there for ever. After the visit to Athos the world was, in fact, seen with newly opened eyes.

Rene Gothoni, 'The Progress of Pilgrimage on the Holy Mountain of Athos', *Social Anthropology of Pilgrimage*, ed. Makhan Jha (1991), p. 305

I left the fountain and walked into St Peter's, entering by the door which is opened only for the Holy Year, a sign of God's continuous indulgence to us all...

I thought of my own family, living and dead, of my relations, friends, acquaintances who have given me so much and I thanked God for them.

'I don't think you know who you are,' Laura had said this to me eight years before, a comment which had disturbed and distressed me. Now at the end of the pilgrimage I could see the truth of it and thank God for it. It no longer distressed: it gave me hope and encouragement. I don't know who I am. None of us know who we are, because God created us for himself and we shall never know who we are until we are at one with him.

Gerard Hughes, *In Search of a Way: Two Journeys of Spiritual Discovery* (1984), pp. 173–4

Now I exhort you in the name of God's holy Love that you make your pilgrimage with beauty and purity, without sadness or any hindrance from wilfulness, in a sweet spirit of peace and joy. Pass through this place of exile so upright and so pure and so ardent that you may find God your Love at the end. In this may your help be God himself and his holy Love! (*Letter 15*)

Mother Columba Hart, trans., *Hadewijch, the Complete Works* (1980), pp. 79–80

A principal role for places held to be sacred is to encourage the pilgrim to move on and indeed to seek God in people, especially people 'back home'. God is there as much as he is here, and if the purpose is to know him more deeply, then the pilgrim should return home to make use of his or her greater understanding there. The conversation between Jesus and the Samaritan woman in the fourth chapter of John's Gospel makes the point that worship is neither to be in Samaritan nor in Jewish holy places, for 'the hour is coming, and now is, when the true worshippers will worship the Father in spirit and truth' (John 4:23). God is to be worshipped anywhere and if he is to be met, the meeting is first and foremost in those in need and in the sacraments, not in places of any particular kind.

Christopher Lewis, 'On Going to Sacred Places', *Theology* September 1989: 393

Behold, a clear light appeared in high, and raising my eyes towards it, I see the window above me full of brightness, and from out of that brightness there appeared One, in aspect, indeed, similar to a man, but in His splendour truly God. His countenance shone exceedingly, yet could human eyes gaze at it, for it caused not terror; rather had it a loveliness such as I had never seen in the world. He then – kindness itself, friendliness itself – addressed me in these words: 'Welcome, welcome, my son and dear brother.' And having said these words, He embraced me, and kissed me kindly.

John Amos Komensky, *The Labyrinth of the World and the Paradise of the Heart* (1905), cited in Anne Freemantle, ed., *The Protestant Mystics* (1965), p. 49

The centre of the town is called Manger Square – at one end of which is the Church of the Nativity, built over the traditional birthplace of Jesus. Some people are a little disappointed that there should be a building at all standing on the spot where Jesus was born. But here – as everywhere in the Holy Land – the Christian pilgrim should be prepared to look for the holy thing beyond the holy place. It is always there to be found.

John Martin, *A Plain Man in the Holy Land* (1978), p. 9

I had been disappointed at first at this noisy ending to the pilgrimage, but as I sat, I became glad that it was this way. We need temples, churches and shrines, we need solitude and silence, but we need all these things to make us more aware of the mystery in which we are all living all the time...

...We are all called to that inner knowing which recognizes God at work in all things, heart of the universe, the life-giving power, which bonds our tiny fragmented selves to the heart of God in whom all things exist. Anything, no matter how ridiculous and meaningless it seems, which can deepen that inner knowing, whether it is a walk to Jerusalem on foot, or a visit to a church, or just a moment's silence to worship him in spirit and in truth, is more precious and life-giving than anything else we can do. I had walked to Jerusalem knowing that his peace is offered to us in every place and at every time. For its dwelling place is in our hearts.

Gerard Hughes, *Walk to Jerusalem* (1991), p. 239

A pilgrim wanders through life, often limping, sometimes bewildered, at times quite lost; and the pilgrim is searching, often quite unconsciously, for something or someone to make sense of life, and certainly to make sense of death. He or she may discover that God has spoken in many ways but most emphatically through a Son, whom to see is to have seen the Father Himself. I need to dwell on certain experiences which can lead me to catch just a glimpse of God (in a manner of speaking). These experiences are foretastes of something that will be mine one day, hints of realities that cannot be known through my senses but are nonetheless true.

Basil Hume, *To Be A Pilgrim* (1984), p. 38

The early history of God's people thus provides the basic structure of the 'pilgrim faith'. In its simplicity, the story of Abraham sums up the essence of the relationship between God and the human being, and this gives it an amazing explanatory power. If we use it as a frame of reference for the reading of another text, such as Genesis 2:24 for instance, astonishing correlations begin to emerge. 'That is why a man leaves his father and mother and joins himself to his wife, and they become one flesh.' The Creator incorporates into the very structure of the human person, 'created male and female' (Genesis 1:27), a preparation for faith, a same call to leave everything in order to set out for; but in this text, taken up again by Jesus (Matthew 19:5), the goal of the pilgrimage is already present, 'to become one flesh'. So here we have in germ a whole theology of marriage the communion of the human couple sends us, beyond itself, to communion with God. The marriage partners remain pilgrims, on the way to communion with

God, but God already gives them a foretaste of that communion, the image of the Promised Land.

Brother John of Taizé, 'Pilgrimage Seen through the Bible',
Lumen Vitae 39 (1984): 385

Historically, pilgrimage has involved physical movement to a numinous location: the due performance there of certain acts and attitudes of piety, perhaps focusing an intrinsic aspect of the professed faith of the pilgrim: and a return in a fulfilled state of mind. Not as much attention has been devoted to what might be termed pilgrimage-in-imagination: where soul, as it were alone, moves out and away in pursuit of that-which-beckons. Some hints may be sufficient.

In daily prayer soul may travel imaginatively into any of the regions where the-one-who-gracious-listens is encountered: indeed there is no true pilgrimage that lacks this imaginal under pinning...

Many biblical stories can be imaginatively rather than 'exegetically' engaged: with results that may perhaps not be utterly 'orthodox', yet may be suggestive for the pilgrim-work of the soul. A mention of the garden story of Genesis: the movement or 'transgression' of Mother Eve, in crossing over decreed limits, and initiating a tendentious interaction with the tree-of-total-experience: conceivably this may give heart to women or men who perceive themselves to be webbed by unilateral strictures: pilgrim-Eve must surely enkindle a deep wondering in many, as they listen to our contemporary soul. In different ways, perhaps nearer to 'orthodoxy', the Ruth-story and the Gethsemane-story reflect back to us the pilgrim-pattern: the 'locus' as place-or-struggle: place of refuge, rest, refurbishment, affirmation.

Tom Hamill, 'Pilgrimage', *The Furrow* 16 (1990): 228–9

And by the happy blissful way
More peaceful pilgrims I shall see,
That have shook off their gowns of clay
And go apparelled fresh like me.
I'll bring them first
To slake their thirst,
And then to taste those nectar suckets
At the clear wells
Where sweetness dwells,
Drawn up by saints in crystal buckets.

Sir Walter Ralegh (*c.* 1552–1618), 'The Passionate Man's Pilgrimage',
The Faber Book of Religious Verse (1972), p. 76

Just as at Rocamadour and Vézelay, it was sad to be in Santiago for the last time. It is easy to try too hard to see and feel. To be filled with excitement and longing, and miss the point completely.

I wondered what I had been looking for. Certainly the adventure with cancer had been an impetus. There had been some sense of urgency after that, urgency towards a deeper understanding of oneself; the nature and opportunity of one's being. Obviously quality of life depends on the kind of trigger you choose.

Carl Jung once said, 'To my mind it is more important that an idea exists, than that it is true.'

...Then gradually it dawned on me, that some sort of intellectual pride had held me back from the only possible conclusion.

It is not enough to seek and care; to pay lip service to all manner of ideals. Real witness is what counts. Why is it so difficult?

It is something to do with leaps in the dark. Recognizing that truth is hidden. But transformation towards truth is something else. It is practice and diligence, as Lama Jigme said.

Referring to belief and faith Thomas Merton wrote, 'We do not see first and then act; we act, then see.'

Jini Fiennes, *On Pilgrimage: A Time to Seek* (1991), pp. 225–6

...our mind has finally reached a point where, within the First and Supreme Principle, Jesus Christ, *the Mediator between God and men*, it considers those things whose likeness is never found in creatures, and which far exceed the power of penetration of the human intellect. It now remains for the soul, by considering such things, to transcend and go beyond not only this sensible world, but even its own self. In this going beyond, Christ is the way and the door, Christ is the conveyance, the propitiatory, as it were, placed over the Ark of God, and *the mystery which has been hidden from eternity*.

Bonaventure, *The Works of Bonaventure: Mystical Opuscula*, trans. J. de Vinck (1960), pp. 55–6

As we settle back in our seats, many of my fellow pilgrims are saying to themselves, 'Well, that's it.' There is still the journey home to enjoy. There are still entrancing views to be caught of the Mediterranean, dazzling blue in the sun, of Crete, of the Greek Islands, of the Italian coast, of the Alps, of Mont Blanc, of the French countryside, of the English Channel – and many things besides. But, they muse sadly, the pilgrimage is over.

During these two weeks, the experience was so marvellous that it often seemed as if it could never come to an end. Now it has and the realization plucks at the heartstrings.

For my part I am hoping that they will soon recall what I said to them, as leader, at our final group meeting last night. Our time together in the Holy Land has come to a close as we all knew it must. But the pilgrimage we have shared will never end. The Bible, our faith, life itself, have all been given a new dimension which we can never lose.

John Martin, *A Plain Man in the Holy Land* (1978), pp. 99–100

Lastly when the twenty-four hours are expired, for now we are come to the last Act, they are revisited by the overseer of the pilgrims, by whom they are brought to the waterside where they duck themselves overhead in that water by which expiation being purged as new soldiers of Christ and by the bath of repentance being born again, they go into the Church, according to the custom being thereby renewed to go forward boldly in their Christian warfare and courageously to carry the Cross of Christ. And thus is the great work finished.

Shane Leslie, *Saint Patrick's Purgatory* (1932), p. 102

Eventually we left and drove back to Oxford. For much of the early part of the journey the road runs parallel with the Pilgrims' Way. It felt odd, speeding in the opposite direction, past the places that we had known so recently and explored at such a leisurely pace. The journey that had taken us nearly fourteen days to walk was over in less than three hours. Then home to a pile of post and messages and a broken washing machine. Life must now return to normal, but would it ever be the same again?

Shirley du Boulay, *The Road to Canterbury* (1994), pp. 228–9

Just as the three apostles had to descend from the Mount of Transfiguration and return to the workaday world, despite Peter's desire to remain there permanently in booths (Mark 9:5), so today's pilgrims have to take their leave and make the journey back home. Many, before departure, obtain souvenirs which correspond to the medieval tokens providing evidence of a task completed.

The return journey differs in character from the outward one, in the same way that going up to the altar at the Lord's Supper differs from the reverse movement after communion. To approach the Lord's table is to advance with anticipation, to leave it is to be full of gratitude.

In like manner to travel homeward from the Holy Land or Rome or
wherever should be an act of thanksgiving for the fulfilment of what
ideally had been a spiritual exercise leading to a closer union with
God...

...Little more needs to be said, but one suggestion may be acceptable; on the Sunday following arrival home, should not the pilgrims
attend their local church, give a brief account of their experience and
ask their fellow members in the congregation to join with them in an
act of thanksgiving?

John Davies, *Pilgrimage Yesterday and Today* (1988), pp. 238–40

Many pilgrims in the Middle Ages were anxious to prove themselves
bona fide returning pilgrims and so to distinguish themselves from the
swarms of pseudo pilgrims, such as those Chaucer so mordantly
depicted on the Canterbury roads. Their proof was the emblem
(*signum*) they prominently displayed while returning home. The most
renowned insignia were Holy Land palm branches broken off at Jericho (hence the term 'palmer' to designate the pilgrim) and the St
James's shell gathered on the beaches of Galicia when at Compostela.
Insignia from Rome, which began to appear only about the fourteenth
century, were more likely to be a Veil of Veronica with a reproduction
of the Holy Face than an emblem picturing the heads of the Apostles.
The periodic exposition of Veronica's Veil at St Peter's was enriched
by popular indulgences. Other insignia included the picture of
Thomas Becket on Canterbury phials, the Sinai torture wheel recalling
the martyrdom of St Catherine, the head of John the Baptist for
Amiens, leaden statues of Our Lady of Walsingham, of Rocamadour,
and the other Marian sanctuaries, such as the statuettes that King
Louis XI was fond of carrying.

Pilgrims generally wanted to repeat their pilgrimages. The case of
Duke William V of Acquitaine (*c.* 1000) is famous: each year he went
to Rome or else to Compostela...There were perpetual pilgrims in the
West during most of the Middle Ages and in Russia until modern
times (called *peregrinantes* as opposed to *peregrini*; in Russia *startsy*).
They went from shrine to shrine throughout most of their life, with
no other aim than to proclaim Christ by their lonely wandering.

'Pilgrimages', *New Catholic Encyclopedia* (1967)

Apparelled as a pagan, in pilgrim's guise
He bare him a staff, with broad strip bound,
That round it was twined like a woodbine's twist;

A bowl and a bag he bare by his side;
A hundred of vials was set on his hat,
Signs from Sinai, Gallacian shells;
With crosses on his cloak, and the keys of Rome,
And the Vernicle before, for that men should discern
And see by his signs what shrines he had sought.
Then fain would this folk know from whence he had come.
'From Sinai,' he said, 'and the Sepulchre Holy,
Bethlehem and Babylon, I've been in them both,
Armenia, Alexandria, and other places.
Ye may see by the signs that sit here on my hat
I have walked full widely, in wet and in dry,
And sought out good saints for the health of my soul.'

William Langland (*c.* 1300–*c.* 1387), *The Vision of Piers the Plowman*

They passed through all the countries and strange lands, and arrived in the good city of Paris, where they went to Saint-Denis and entered the church. Charlemagne the brave prostrated himself in prayer and, when he had prayed to God, he rose, placed the nail and the crown upon the altar, and distributed the other relics throughout the kingdom. The queen, who was there, fell at his feet. The King abandoned his resentment against her because of the sepulchre which he had adored.

Glyn Burgess, ed. & trans., *The Pilgrimage of Charlemagne* (1988) p. 71

O happy band of pilgrims
If onward ye will tread
With Jesus as your fellow
To Jesus as your Head!

...The Cross that Jesus carried
He carried as your due:
The Crown that Jesus weareth
He weareth it for you.

O happy band of pilgrims,
Look upward to the skies,
Where such a light affliction
Shall win so great a prize.

John Mason Neale, cited in Margaret Pawley,
Prayers for Pilgrims (1991), p. 39

I had been changed by this pilgrimage, but I do not expect to know how for a long time. Though on this Sunday morning I knew the pilgrimage had reached some sort of completion, it had not ended. This symbolic microcosm of the inner journey had to find its resonances with the longer, day-to-day, pilgrimage. Perhaps my inability to know when it ended was a precise reflection of its inner parallel. We were resuming our day-to-day lives, our journeys of perpetual pilgrimage. This pilgrimage from Winchester to Canterbury had not ended on arrival any more than life ends with death. But I did feel that I understood better where the sacred place is to be found.

Shirley du Boulay, *The Road to Canterbury* (1994), p. 232

As he walks on from the sixties towards the mid-seventies, this Canterbury pilgrim begins to find himself in a different scene and a different climate. The apathy about God and Christianity remains, morals are even more chaotic, and the world is even more cruel. Nor is the dislike of 'institutions' any less. But amongst the faithful there is a lively faith, worship has a greater 'boldness of access', and the loss of nerve seems to belong to yesterday. The pilgrim sees more often not the spectre of atheism within the Church but powerful movements of spirituality of one kind and another, some without and some within the Churches, and his problem is what to do and to say about these.

'Death of God' belongs to the past. I sense that in the realm of theology it is Christology which is returning to the centre. This may be partly because Jesus Movements, both popular and academic, are making themselves felt. But I think it is partly also because for theism itself the question of the Christlikeness of God has come to the fore, as well as the exploration of how far the death and resurrection of Jesus Christ is the clue to the sovereignty of God and to Man's hope for himself and the world. Christ, Hope, Resurrection are increasingly the themes of theology today.

Michael Ramsey, *Canterbury Pilgrim* (1974), p. 7

So there is meaning in our journey. We in search of God, and God in search of us. God, in Jesus Christ, spoke indeed of things I could not see or touch, and with words which dispelled the darkness of my mind and brought warmth to the coldness of my heart. I saw clearly that the Stranger who had become my friend was himself God who had become man. The Son of God had become the Son of man. My mind could hardly receive the truth, so great and so wondrous was it. In his presence I was overcome. I knelt and could but say: 'Depart from me for I am a sinful man'. What once did seem absurd to me now dawned upon my mind as real and true. I knew, but my senses had not told me. Other voices spoke, but they were speaking and commanding in ways that were strange and unknown. It was the voice of him who knows and loves, and came in search of us. It was a light that pierced the darkness of my mind and gave me strength to see.

Basil Hume, *To Be A Pilgrim* (1984), p. 22

Who would true valour see,
    Let him come hither;
One here will constant be,
    Come wind, come weather;
There's no discouragement
Shall make him once relent
His first avow'd intent
    To be a pilgrim.

Whoso beset him round
    With dismal stories,
Do but themselves confound;
    His strength the more is.
No lion can him fright,
He'll with a giant fight,
But he will have a right
    To be a pilgrim.

Hobgoblin nor foul fiend
    Can daunt his spirit;
He knows he at the end
    Shall life inherit.
Then fancies fly away,
He'll fear not what men say;
He'll labour night and day
    To be a pilgrim.

John Bunyan, *The Pilgrim's Progress* (1678)

BIBLIOGRAPHY

Anonymous, 'A Soldier's Pilgrimage', *The Mediterranean Historical Review* December 1993

Antier, Jean-Jacques, 'Pilgrimages in France: Religious Tourism or Faith in Action?', *Lumen Vitae* 39 (1984)

Armstrong, Karen, 'A Passion for Holy Places', *The Sunday Times Magazine* 15 April 1990

Batchelor, Mary, ed., *The Lion Prayer Collection* (Lion, 1992)

Baum, Gregory, ed., *Journeys: The Impact of Personal Experience on Religious Thought* (Paulist Press, 1975)

Bede, The Venerable, *Ecclesiastical History of the English Church and People*, ed. G. Radice (Penguin, 1955)

Belloc, Hilaire, *The Path to Rome* (Penguin, 1958)

Blunt, Wilfred, *Pietro's Pilgrimage* (James Barrie, 1953)

Bonaventure, *The Works of Bonaventure: Mystical Opuscula*, trans. J. de Vinck (St Anthony Guild Press, 1960)

Bourdeau, Francis, 'Pilgrimage, Eucharist, Reconciliation', *Lumen Vitae* 39 (1984)

Boyd, Robin, *Ireland: Christianity Discredited or Pilgrim's Progress?* (World Council of Churches, 1988)

Bredero, Adriaan, *Christendom and Christianity in the Middle Ages* (Eerdmans, 1994)

Brennan, J. P., *Jerusalem – A Christian Perspective* (John Day, 1974)

Brooke, Avery, ed., *Celtic Prayers* (Seabury Press, 1981)

Brooke, Daphne, *Wild Men and Holy Places* (Canongate Press, 1994)

Brown, Peter, *The Cult of the Saints* (SCM Press, 1981)

Bunyan, John, *The Pilgrim's Progress* (Fount, 1979)

Burgess, Glyn, ed. & trans., *The Pilgrimage of Charlemagne* (Garland Publishing, 1988)

Campbell, Joseph, ed., *Spirit and Nature: Papers from the Eranos Yearbooks* (Routledge and Kegan Paul, 1955)

Campion, Thomas, *The Works of Thomas Campion*, ed. W. Davies (Faber & Faber, 1969)

Camus, Albert, *Exile and the Kingdom*, trans. Justin O'Brien (Penguin, 1958)

Carretto, Carlo, *The Desert Journal* (Fount, 1992)

Catherine of Siena, *The Dialogue*, trans. Suzanne Noffke (SPCK, 1980)

Chaucer, Geoffrey, *The General Prologue to the Canterbury Tales*, ed. James Winney (Cambridge University Press, 1965)

—, *The Poetical Works of Geoffrey Chaucer*, vol.6 (Bell and Daldy, 1866)

Conrad, Joseph, *Heart of Darkness* (Penguin, 1973)

Council of Europe Congress, 'The Santiago de Compostela Pilgrim Routes', *Architectural Heritage Reports & Studies* 16 (1989)

Dalrymple, William, 'A Pilgrim's Progress Ends', *The Spectator* 8 June 1991

Davies, John, *Pilgrimage Yesterday and Today* (SCM Press, 1988)

Davies, Horton & Marie-Helene, *Holy Days and Holidays* (Bucknell University Press, 1982)

Davies, Oliver, & Bowie, Fiona, *Celtic Christian Spirituality* (SPCK, 1995)

Dobson, A. Mary, *Mount Sinai* (Methuen, 1925)

Donaldson, Christopher, *The Great English Pilgrimage: From Rome to Canterbury* (The Canterbury Press, 1995)

—, *Martin of Tours: Parish Priest, Mystic and Exorcist* (Routledge & Kegan Paul, 1980)

Du Boulay, Shirley, *The Road to Canterbury: A Modern Pilgrimage* (HarperCollins, 1994)

Dubisch, Jill, *A Different Place* (Princeton University Press, 1995)

Dumoulin, Anne, 'Towards a Psychological Understanding of the Pilgrim', *Lumen Vitae* 32 (1977)

Dunne, John, *The Reasons of the Heart* (SCM Press, 1978)

Eade, John, & Sallnow, Michael, eds., *Contesting the Sacred* (Routledge, 1991)

Eliot, T. S., *The Complete Poems and Plays of T. S. Eliot* (Faber & Faber, 1969)

Ellis, Christopher, *Together on the Way: A Theology of Ecumenism* (British Council of Churches, 1990)

Erasmus, Desiderius, *Pilgrimages to St Mary of Walsingham and St Thomas of Canterbury* (John Bowyer Nichols & Son, 1849)

Evans, G. R., & Wright, J. R., *The Anglican Tradition: A Handbook of Sources* (SPCK, 1991)

Faber, Frederick, *Growth in Holiness* (Burns & Oates, 1960)

Falkenburg, R., *Joachim Patrini: Landscape as an Image of the Pilgrimage of Life* (John Benjamins, 1988)

Fiennes, Jini, *On Pilgrimage: A Time to Seek* (Sinclair-Stevenson, 1991)

Finucane, Ronald, *Miracles and Pilgrims* (J. M. Dent, 1977)

Freemantle, Anne, *The Protestant Mystics* (Mentor Books, 1965)

Gardner, Helen, ed., *The Faber Book of Religious Verse* (Faber & Faber, 1972)

George, K., *The Silent Roots: Orthodox Perspectives on Christian Spirituality* (World Council of Churches, 1994)

Gregory of Nyssa, *Fathers of the Church: Gregory of Nyssa: Ascetical Works*, ed. Virginia Callahan (Catholic University of America Press, 1967)

Guimaraes, Therezinha Stella, 'On the Road to Juazerio', *Lumen Vitae* 32 (1977)

Habig, Marion, ed., *St. Francis of Assisi: Omnibus of Sources* (SPCK, 1964)

Hall, D., *English Medieval Pilgrimage* (Routledge & Kegan Paul, 1965)

Hadrill, D. S. W., *Eusebius of Caescrea* (Mowbray, 1960)

Hamill, Tom, 'Pilgrimage', *The Furrow* 16 (1990)

Hardy, Thomas, *The Complete Poetical Works of Thomas Hardy*, ed. J. Gibson (Macmillan, 1976)

Hart, Mother Columba, trans., *Hadewijch: The Complete Works* (SPCK, 1980)

Heath, Sidney, *Pilgrim Life in the Middle Ages* (Fisher Unwin, 1911)

Hilton, Walter, *The Scale of Perfection* (The Art and Book Company, 1901)

Hughes, Gerard, *In Search of a Way: Two Journeys of Spiritual Discovery* (DLT, 1994)

—, *Walk to Jerusalem*, (DLT, 1991)

Hume, Basil, *To Be A Pilgrim* (St Paul's Publications, 1984)

Hunt, Edward, *Holy Land Pilgrimage in the Later Roman Empire* (Clarendon, 1982)

Jha, Makhan, ed., *Social Anthropology of Pilgrimage* (Inter-India Publications, 1991)

John, of Taizé, Brother, 'Pilgrimage Seen through the Bible', *Lumen Vitae* 39 (1984)

John Climacus, *The Ladder of Divine Ascent*, trans. Colm Luibheid & Norman Russell (SPCK, 1982)

John of the Cross, *John of the Cross, Selected Writings*, trans. Kieran Kavanaugh (SPCK, 1987)

Join-Lambert, Michel, *Jerusalem*, trans. Charlotte Haldane (Elek Books, 1958)

Jones, Alan, *Passion for Pilgrimage* (HarperSanFrancisco, 1995)

Jones, C., Wainwright, G., & Yarnold, E., eds., *The Study of Spirituality* (SPCK, 1986)

Kempe, Margery, *The Book of Margery Kempe*, trans. W. Butler-Bowden (Jonathan Cape, 1936)

Key, John, *Journey to Resurrection* (United Reformed Church, 1995)

Kierkegaard, Søren, *Søren Kierkegaard's Pilgrimage to Jutland*, trans. T. Croxall (Danish Tourist Association, 1948)

Koyama, Kosuke, *Pilgrim or Tourist?* (Christians Conference of Asia, 1974)

Langland, William, *The Vision of Piers the Plowman* (Oxford University Press, 1922)

Larkin, Dennis, *A Walk to Rome* (Trinity Communications, 1987)

Leslie, Shane, *St Patrick's Purgatory* (Burns Oates & Washbourne, 1932)

Letts, Malcolm, trans., *Mandeville's Travels* (The Hakluyt Society, 1953)

Lewis, Christopher, 'On Going to Sacred Places', *Theology* September 1989

Lietzmann, Hans, *From Constantine to Julian: A History of the Early Church Volume III* (Lutterworth, 1950)

Louth, Andrew, *The Origins of the Christian Mystical Tradition* (Clarendon, 1981)

Macbeth, G., ed., *Poetry 1900–1965* (Longman, 1967)

Macquarrie, John, *Paths in Spirituality* (SCM Press, 1972)

Martin, John, *A Plain Man in the Holy Land* (The Saint Andrew Press, 1978)

Meissner, William, *Ignatius of Loyola: The Psychology of a Saint* (Yale University Press, 1992)

Merton, Thomas, *Asian Journal* (Sheldon Press, 1973)

—, *Seeds of Contemplation* (Anthony Clarke Books, 1961)

—, *Thoughts in Solitude* (Burns & Oates, 1958)

Mitchell, Walter, *Early Christian Prayers* (Longman's Green, 1951)

Moiser, Jeremy, trans., *Silent Pilgrimage to God: The Spirituality of Charles de Foucauld* (DLT, 1974)

Morris, Paul, & Smith, John, *Time Travelling: Pilgrimage for Children* (Diocese of Southwell, 1995)

Mullins, Edwin, *The Pilgrimage to Santiago* (Secker & Warburg, 1974)

New Catholic Encyclopedia (The Catholic University of America, 1967)

Nibley, Hugh, *Jerusalem* (Keter Publishing House, 1973)

Nolan, Sidney & Mary Lee, *Christian Pilgrimage in Modern Western Europe* (University of North Carolina Press, 1989)

Origen, *Origen: An Exhortation to Martyrdom, Prayer and Selected Works,* trans. Rowan Greer (Paulist Press, 1979)

Orsenigo, Cesare, *The Life of St Charles of Borromeo* (B. Herder Book Company, 1945)

Pawley, Margaret, *Prayers for Pilgrims* (Triangle, 1991)

Peace Pilgrim, Her Life and Works in Her Own Words (Ocean Tree Books, 1993)

Peters, F. E., *Jerusalem* (Princeton University Press, 1985)

Petrarch, *Petrarch: Sonnets and Songs*, trans. A. Armi (Grosset & Dunlap, 1968)

Pochin Mould, Daphne, *Irish Pilgrimage* (M. H. Gill & Son, 1955)

Preston, J., ed, *Mother Worship* (University of North Carolina Press, 1982)

Raitt, Jill, ed., *Christian Spirituality: High Middle Ages and Reformation* (Routledge and Kegan Paul, 1987)

Ramon, Brother, SSF, *The Heart of Prayer* (Marshall Pickering, 1995)

Ramsey, Michael, *Canterbury Pilgrim* (SPCK, 1974)

Ranson, C. W., *A Missionary Pilgrimage* (Eerdmans, 1988)

Reith, Martin, *God in Our Midst: Prayers and Devotions from the Celtic Tradition* (Triangle, 1975)

Riley-Smith, Jonathan, *The First Crusade and the Idea of Crusading* (1993)

Rogers, Murray, *The Mountain of the Lord: Pilgrimage to Gangotri* (Christian Institute for the Study of Religion and Society, 1966)

Rose, Martial, ed., *The Wakefield Mystery Plays* (Evans Brothers, 1961)

Ross-Barker, Ethel, *Rome of the Pilgrims and Martyrs* (Methuen, 1913)

Rossetti, Christina, *Goblin Market, The Prince's Progress and Other Poems* (Macmillan, 1884)

Salinger, J. D., *Franny and Zooey* (Penguin, 1964)

Sheldrake, Philip, *Living Between Worlds* (DLT, 1995)

—, *Spirituality and History* (SPCK, 1991)

Sillitoe, Alan, *The Loneliness of the Long-Distance Runner and Other Stories* (Pan Books, 1959)

Soerfgel, Phillip, *Wondrous In His Saints: Counter Reformation Propaganda in Bavaria* (University of California Press, 1993)

Sox, David, *Relics and Shrines* (George Allen and Unwin, 1985)

Starkie, Walter, *The Road to Santiago* (John Murray, 1957)

Sumption, Jonathan, *Pilgrimage – An Image of Medieval Religion* (Faber & Faber, 1975)

Tate, Robert, *Pilgrimages to St James of Compostella from the British Isles during the Middle Ages* (Liverpool University Press, 1990)

Toulson, Shirley, *Celtic Journeys in Scotland and the North of England* (Fount, 1995)

Turner, Victor & Edith, *Image and Pilgrimage in Christian Culture* (Basil Blackwell, 1978)

Von Campenausen, Hans, *Tradition and Life in the Church: Essays and Lectures on Church History* (Collins, 1986)

Wace, H. & Schnaff, P., eds., *A Select Library of Nicene and*

Post-Nicene Fathers of the Christian Church, Vol. V: Gregory of Nyssa (Parker and Company, 1893)

Wellard, James, *Desert Pilgrimage* (Hutchinson of London, 1970)

Wicham-Legg, J., ed., *The Sarum Missal Edited from Three Early Manuscripts* (Clarendon Press, 1916)

Wilkinson, John, *Jerusalem Pilgrims* (Aris and Phillips, 1977)

Wilkinson, J., Hill, J., & Ryan, W., *Jerusalem Pilgrimage 1099–1185* (The Hakluyt Society, 1988)

Wyon, Olive, *The Way of the Pilgrim: Some Reflections on the Christian Life* (SCM Press, 1958)

Yeats, W. B., *The Collected Poems of W. B. Yeats* (Macmillan, 1965)

Zacher, Christian, *Curiosity and Pilgrimage: The Literature of Discovery in Fourteenth-Century England* (John Hopkins University Press, 1976)

ACKNOWLEDGEMENTS

The compiler and publishers would like to thank all the authors, publishers and literary representatives who have given permission to reprint copyright material included in this anthology.

JEAN-JACQUES ANTIER: to *Lumen Vitae* for 'Pilgrimages in France: Religious Tourism or Faith in Action?' (1984); KAREN ARMSTRONG: to *The Sunday Times Magazine* for 'A Passion for Holy Places' (15 April 1990), copyright © Times Newspapers Ltd 1996; HILLAIRE BELLOC: *The Path to Rome*, reprinted by permission of the Peters Fraser & Dunlop Group Ltd (Penguin, 1958); FRANCIS BOURDEAU: to *Lumen Vitae* for 'Pilgrimage, Eucharist, Reconciliation' (1984); ADRIAAN H. BREDERO: *Christendom and Christianity in the Middle Ages*, © Wm. B. Eerdmans Publishing Co. 1994, used by permission; PETER BROWN: to SCM Press Ltd for *The Cult of the Saints* (1981); W. BUTLER-BOWDEN: to Jonathan Cape for *The Book of Margery Kempe* (1936); GLYN BURGESS: to Garland Publishing Inc. for *The Pilgrimage of Charlemagne* (1988); VIRGINIA CALLAHAN: to The Catholic University of America Press for *The Fathers of the Church: Gregory of Nyssa: Ascetical Works* (1967); CARLO CARRETTO: to HarperCollins*Publishers* for *The Desert Journal* (Fount, 1992); THE CATHOLIC UNIVERSITY OF AMERICA PRESS for *New Catholic Encyclopedia*, vol. XI (1967); MARY CLARK: to Paulist Press for *Augustine of Hippo* (SPCK, 1984), © 1984 by Mary T. Clark, used by permission of Paulist Press; WILLIAM DALRYMPLE: to *The Spectator* for 'A Pilgrim's Progress Ends' (1991); OLIVER DAVIES & FIONA BROWN: to SPCK for *Celtic Christian Spirituality* (1995), used by permission of the publishers; HORTON & MARIE-HELENE DAVIES: to the Associated University Presses for *Holy Days and Holidays* (Bucknell University Press, 1982); JOHN DAVIES: to SCM Press Ltd for *Pilgrimage Yesterday and Today* (1988); A. MARY DOBSON: to Methuen & Co. for *Mount Sinai* (1925); CHRISTOPHER DONALDSON: to Routledge for *Martin of Tours* (Routledge and Kegan Paul, 1980); SHIRLEY DU BOULAY: to HarperCollins*Publishers* for *The Road to Canterbury* (1994); JILL DUBISCH: *A Different Place*, copyright © 1995 by Princeton University

NORMAN: to Paulist Press for *John Climacus: The Ladder of Divine Ascent* (SPCK, 1982), © 1982 by The Missionary Society of St Paul the Apostle in the State of New York, used by permission of Paulist Press; G. MACBETH: to Addison Wesley Longman for *Poetry 1900–1965* (Longman, 1967); JOHN MACQUARRIE: to SCM Press Ltd for *Paths in Spirituality* (1972); WILLIAM MEISSNER: to Yale University Press for *Ignatius of Loyola: The Psychology of a Saint* (1992), copyright © Yale University Press, 1992; THOMAS MERTON: to SPCK for *Asian Journal* (Sheldon Press, 1973), used by permission of the publishers; WALTER MITCHELL: to Addison Wesley Longman for *Early Christian Prayers* (Longman's Green, 1951); EDWIN MULLINS: to Secker and Warburg Ltd for *The Pilgrimage to Santiago*, copyright © Edwin Mullins 1974; SUZANNE NOFFKE: to Paulist Press for *Catherine of Siena: The Dialogue* (SPCK, 1980), © 1980 by The Missionary Society of St Paul the Apostle in the State of New York, used by permission of Paulist Press; SIDNEY & MARY LEE NOLAN: *Christian Pilgrimage in Modern Western Europe*, copyright © 1989 by the University of North Carolina Press, used by permission of the publishers; MARGARET PAWLEY: to SPCK for *Prayers for Pilgrims* (Triangle, 1991), used by permission of the publishers; PEACE PILGRIM: to Ocean Tree Books at 1325 Cerro Gordo Road, Post Office Box 1295, Santa Fe, New Mexico 87504, USA for *Peace Pilgrim: Her Life and Work in Her Own Words* (1993); F. E. PETERS: *Jerusalem*, copyright © 1985 by Princeton University Press, reprinted by permission of Princeton University Press; DAPHNE POCHIN MOULD: to the author for *Irish Pilgrimage* (Gill & Macmillan, 1955); BROTHER RAMON SSF: to HarperCollins*Publishers* for *The Heart of Prayer* (Marshall Pickering, 1995); MICHAEL RAMSEY: to SPCK for *Canterbury Pilgrim* (1974), used by permission of the publishers; CHARLES W. RANSON: *A Missionary Pilgrimage*, Wm. B. Eerdmans Publishing Co., © 1988, used by permission; MARTIN REITH: to SPCK for *God in Our Midst* (Triangle, 1975); used by permission of the publishers; JONATHAN RILEY-SMITH: to The Athlone Press for *The First Crusade and the Idea of Crusading* (1993); MARTIAL ROSE: to the author for *The Wakefield Mystery Plays* (Evans Brothers Ltd, 1961); ETHEL ROSS-BARKER: to Methuen & Co. for *Rome of the Pilgrims and Martyrs* (1913); PHILIP SHELDRAKE: to SPCK for *Spirituality and History* (1991), used by permission of the publishers and to Darton Longman & Todd for *Living Between Worlds* (1995); PHILIP SOERFGEL: to the University of California Press for *Wondrous In His Saints: Counter Reformation Propaganda in Bavaria* (1993), copyright © The Regents of the University of California 1993; DAVID SOX: to the author for *Relics and Shrines* (George Allen & Unwin, 1985); WALTER STARKIE: to John Murray (Publishers) Ltd for *The Road to Santiago* (1957); JONATHAN

SUMPTION: to Faber and Faber Ltd for *Pilgrimage – An Image of Medieval Religion* (1975) ROBERT TATE: to Liverpool University Press for *Pilgrimages to St James of Compostella* (1990); VICTOR & EDITH TURNER: to Blackwell Publishers for *Image and Pilgrimage in Christian Culture* (1978); JAMES WELLARD: to Curtis Brown Group Ltd for *Desert Pilgrimage* (Hutchinson, 1970) copyright © James Wellard, 1970; JOHN WILKINSON: to Aris and Phillips Ltd for *Jerusalem Pilgrims* (1977); J. WILKINSON, J. HILL & W. RYAN: to David Higham Associates for *Jerusalem Pilgrimage 1099–1185* (The Hakluyt Society, 1988); JAMES WINNEY: to Cambridge University Press for *The General Prologue to the Canterbury Tales* (1965); OLIVE WYON: TO SCM Press Ltd for *The Way of the Pilgrim* (1958); CHRISTIAN ZACHER: to the John Hopkins University Press for *Curiosity and Pilgrimage: The Literature of Discovery in Fourteenth-Century England* (1976).

Every effort has been made to contact all copyright holders. The publishers will be glad to make good any errors or omissions brought to our attention in future editions.

INDEX OF AUTHORS AND SOURCES

WELLARD, JAMES
Desert Pilgrimage 14, 92–3, 125–6

WESLEY, JOHN
'The Heart of Wesley's Journal' 89

WICHAM-LEGG, J., ED.
The Sarum Missal 52

WILKINSON, JOHN
Jerusalem Pilgrims 161

WILKINSON, J., HILL, J., & RYAN, W.
Jerusalem Pilgrimage 1099–1185 113, 113–14, 114, 121, 123, 124

WYON, OLIVE
The Way of the Pilgrim 28–9, 95, 175–6

YEATS, W. B.
'The Pilgrim' 99

ZACHER, CHRISTIAN
Curiosity and Pilgrimage: The Literature of Discovery in Fourteenth-Century England 68–9, 108–9, 109–10, 113, 124–5

LIKE WATER IN A DRY LAND

A JOURNEY INTO MODERN ISRAEL

Bettina Selby

In December 1994, at a time of intense political initiative for peace in the Middle East, Bettina Selby set off on a journey from Cyprus to the Holy Land. Riding her bicycle wherever possible, she travelled through Lebanon, Syria and Jordan to Jerusalem. Her final destination was a city she knew and loved, so much so that the political turmoil of recent years had made her unwilling to return.

Now, spurred on by the Jordan/Israel peace treaty and an audience with King Hussein, Bettina felt that at last perhaps a new perspective on Israel could be achieved. Over the next two months, she travelled widely, from the ruins of Byblos in Lebanon to the Armenian Cathedral Church in Jerusalem, to the refugee camps of Gaza. In every place she was offered the hand of friendship by people of diverse race and culture.

What begins as an enjoyable and quirky travelogue fast becomes a compelling critique of Middle Eastern politics, and its historical and religious foundations. In clear and lyrical prose, Bettina Selby has produced a fascinating account of her travels and a valuable contribution to our understanding of the modern Holy Land.

Bettina Selby is one of Britain's best-loved travel writers, with a string of books to her credit. Her mode of transport is usually bicycle. Her books include *Riding to Jerusalem*, *The Fragile Islands*, *Riding North One Summer*, *Riding the Desert Trail*, *Beyond Ararat*, and, most recently, *Pilgrim's Road: A Journey to Santiago de Compostela*.

CELTIC JOURNEYS

Shirley Toulson

As interest grows in Britain's Celtic heritage, Shirley Toulson's book provides an easy guide to the places associated with its remarkable teachers and missionaries – the Celtic Saints.

Celtic Journeys contains eight tours in Scotland and the North of England, each based upon the movements of specific individuals and their followers. They include Ninian, Kentigern, Columba, Kenneth, Adomnan, Cuthbert, Aidan and Hilda.

With informative maps to accompany the tours, this beautiful book will help the traveller to understand the way in which the Celtic Saints turned their backs on the dark centuries that preceded their emergence, bringing the light of learning and of faith to the barbarous tribes of England and Scotland.

THE ROAD TO CANTERBURY

A MODERN PILGRIMAGE

Shirley du Boulay

The Road to Canterbury is Shirley du Boulay's walk along the 130-mile Pilgrims' Way. Beginning at Winchester, the ancient capital of Wessex, she follows in the footsteps of the millions of medieval pilgrims who journeyed to Canterbury Cathedral and its shrine to the martyr St Thomas Becket.

Along the way she finds much to remind her of the countryside and monuments that witnessed the great age of pilgrimage, and yet she also observes how much has changed. As she walks through car-ridden Home Counties suburbia, she is led to reflect upon the relevance of pilgrimage today.

Both a travelogue and a series of fascinating meditations upon spirituality in the contemporary world, *The Road to Canterbury* is a worthy successor to Hilaire Belloc's legendary *The Old Road*.

'...the charm of her book is most apparent...It makes you feel that, once we have got winter out of the way, there can be few better things to do, next spring, than to set out on a pilgrimage.'

SUE GAISFORD, *THE INDEPENDENT*

'Chaucer would not have been disappointed to find du Boulay an addition to his 29 companions, and would no doubt have found a tale for her somewhere between those of the Prioress and the Wife of Bath.'

LAURENCE FREEMAN, *THE TABLET*

'Cuts across time and place to discover a landscape as seemingly eternal as the attraction of the Pilgrims' Way itself.'

JOE KELLY, *THE UNIVERSE*

PILGRIMS

THE ARCHBISHOP OF CANTERBURY'S LENT BOOK 1997

Stephen Platten

Foreword by the Archbishop of Canterbury

The Christian life compels us to move on, to break new ground, to
take the Gospel message to fresh people and places. We are all
pilgrims journeying towards God and carrying each other along.
Indeed, the history of Christian literature is littered with imagery of
such restlessness and journeying, from Chaucer's *Canterbury Tales* to
Bunyan's *Pilgrim's Progress*.

This journey is not one undertaken without guidance. There are
signposts from the earliest days of Christianity. St Augustine of
Canterbury arrived a missionary pilgrim in Britain exactly 1400 years
ago, the same year that Columba, the great Celtic saint, died on Iona.
In this fascinating and expertly researched book, Stephen Platten
traces the lasting significance of these and other pioneering people of
God down the centuries.

But the journey is more than historical. It takes us beyond ancient
sites and shrines of the saints to the towns and cities of modern life,
where the Christian mission is lived out at the end of the twentieth
century. Here, the legacy of Augustine, Columba and their fellow
pilgrims finds a relevance for all Christians today and for the coming
years.